RONALD
REAGAN

RONALD REAGAN

His Life and Rise
to the Presidency

BILL BOYARSKY

Random House
New York

Library of Congress Cataloging in Publication Data
Boyarsky, Bill.
Ronald Reagan, his life and rise to the Presidency.
Includes index.
1. Reagan, Ronald. 2. Presidents—United States—
Biography. I. Title.
E877.B69 1981   973.927′092′4 [B]   80-54499
ISBN 0-394-51598-6   AACR2
Manufactured in the United States of America
24689753
First Edition

For My Mother and Father

ACKNOWLEDGMENTS

I would like to acknowledge the invaluable assistance of Trish Beall, who did the research for this book. My gratitude also goes to Nancy Boyarsky, my wife, who edited the chapters before they were sent to the publisher; Robert D. Loomis, executive editor and vice president at Random House, who encouraged me and edited the book; and Kathy Varie, who typed the manuscript. Thanks also to Robert Scheer, who prodded me to write the book, and to Molly Sturges Tuthill, curator of the Reagan archives at the Hoover Institution on War, Revolution and Peace of Stanford University, who guided Ms. Beall through the huge number of papers in the archives. Edwin Meese III arranged for us to have access to the archives and provided other assistance. The staff of the Los Angeles *Times* library was a big help. Norman Livermore had much information on Reagan and the environment, and Norman Emerson also assisted in this area. Lyn Nofziger, Richard Wirthlin, Stuart Spencer, Nancy Clark Reynolds, Donald Livingston and George Steffes were among several past and present members of the Reagan team who shared their recollections, as did former legislators William T. Bagley and Robert Monagan. I. A. Lewis, director of the Los Angeles *Times* poll, had valuable advice on political trends. Michael Levett provided important information for the chapter on Reagan and the law.

B. B.

CONTENTS

RONALD REAGAN

1

REAGAN'S CALIFORNIA: A CHANGE OF DIRECTION

Not many in the California capitol on January 31, 1967, understood they were watching the beginning of something new in American political life, a change that would carry Ronald Reagan, the new governor, to the presidency thirteen years later. America was still a rich, victorious nation living in the bounty of the Great Society, far from defeat in Vietnam, painful inflation and oil shortages that would slow its auto-bound population.

But even in 1967, the estrangement from liberal government that would help elect him President could be seen in the white middle-class suburbs of California, the heart of the Reagan constituency. There, in the tract ranch houses and pleasant backyards, homeowners began to feel betrayed by a government they believed was much too generous to the poor. Time after time in the next eight years, Reagan would rally these suburbanites behind his conservative ideas, articulating their resentment, creating the climate for the 1970s tax revolt and Proposition 13, the California property-tax-limit initiative. By 1980 the resentment had spread around the country as a declining economic picture deprived millions of their chance to share the American dream. When that happened, Reagan became their spokesman and their President.

In the capitol that January day in 1967, most of the politicians were unaware of the implications of Reagan's election as governor. They watched him go through a ceremony which, by its unchanging nature, assured them there would be no change. For almost a hundred years the governors of California had stepped up to the rostrum of the assembly chamber in Sacramento and announced their plans for governing the state. Now that it was Ronald Reagan's turn, he did not discard that tradition. He walked from his wood-paneled office in a corner of the capitol and down the hallways crowded with visiting schoolchildren, took an elevator to the second floor and entered the room where legislators have watched over California since it was a rural state grown rich on gold. Not even when Reagan started to speak did the legislators, government officials and reporters who made up the insular capitol society realize the state would never be the same.

In Reagan's hand was an important document, his first budget message for the people who had elected him by almost a million votes three months before. The message, fresh from the state printing plant, would tell in seven and a half pages how the governor intended to make good on his campaign promise and put California on the conservative path. The message—which few believed at the time— described how Reagan would change the course of one of the union's most liberal state governments, which not only had welcomed the largest domestic immigration in American history but readily supplied the newcomers with free schools, parks and highways—and with generous welfare aid if they lost their jobs.

Reagan was accompanied upstairs by a committee of three senators and five assemblymen, whose job it was to escort the governor into the legislative sanctuary. In the ritual of government, they were symbols of a strong-minded legislative branch, still controlled by Democrats who, along with many Republican legislators, had voted for the expensive programs Reagan wanted to cut. In many ways, California's legislature was one of the nation's best, its consultants and lawmakers producing new and creative programs in every field. But it was also dominated by lobbyists for banks, race tracks, manufacturers, real estate developers, the beer and liquor business, big agriculture and all of the other interests of a commercially diverse state. Years before, Carey McWilliams had written: "California's legislature is really a corporate state in which commodities, not people, are represented." The same could be said when Reagan took office.

Reagan and his assistants, new to Sacramento, had contempt for the legislature. "They were campaign ideologues who believed anyone in Sacramento was automatically characterized as a political hack," Assemblyman William T. Bagley remembered. But when something came up that was of personal importance to him, Reagan turned out to be a great help to the powerful industry that employed the capitol's most cynical, effective and generous lobbyists, the horse-racing industry. For years the thoroughbred tracks, which had political power in the state senate, and the harness and quarter-horse tracks, which influenced the assembly, had been trying to increase the amount of horse racing in the state. They could not agree, and the man who was governor at the time, Edmund G. Brown Sr., opposed any more racing. Reagan, however, loves horses. As a young man he was an officer in the National Guard cavalry. Later he bred thoroughbreds. He had sold his breeding horses when elected governor, but Reagan was now an honorary member of the California Thoroughbred Breeders Association. As governor he threatened to veto bills hostile to the thoroughbred breeders, and a compromise was eventually worked out that greatly increased revenue for the entire racing industry and gave a tax break to the breeders.

On that day at the outset of his administration, Reagan was something new to the legislators' experience, new in a way that made it difficult for them to take him seriously. He looked like a governor —but of course he would. Twenty-nine years as an actor, the legislators assumed, had taught him to look like any part he was playing.

Reagan's face was even-featured and heavily tanned, and although it was deeply wrinkled with lines reaching out from each eye and lines stretching across his forehead and neck, he looked almost young. Part of the impression of youth was due to his hair, brown and thick, a fortunate inheritance from his father. Most of it, however, was due to the way Reagan carried himself. He walked briskly with the controlled grace that a motion picture and television star learns. He always seemed on camera. His former bodyguard took thousands of candid photographs of Reagan over the years; not one showed him with an ugly scowl, a hint of a potbelly, a slouch or any of the unrehearsed defects that ruin most people's candid shots. From his first film to his last, he had a touch of magnetism that helped him stand out from long-forgotten co-stars and later from the politicians who ran against him. He was in some big movies—*Kings Row* and *Brother Rat*—and some small ones—*International Squadron* and *Cattle Queen of Montana*. He was never, by his own admission, a "whole actor." But on the screen and later on television, Reagan projected something of a star quality, a warm, sympathetic and friendly manner.

Seldom has a more inexperienced person stepped into a more difficult job—but it worried neither him nor a majority of the voters. "Once in a while," he said, "when you come to a tough problem, you choose someone who doesn't know anything about it because he doesn't know what you can't do."

The fifty-six-year-old governor was a willing student. Early in his administration, when George Steffes, his chief lobbyist, arranged for Reagan to be photographed with six or eight legislators, one after the other, Reagan protested by throwing his glasses on the desk. "Goddamn it," he complained, "why do I have to do that kind of stuff?" Steffes replied, "Listen, you forget you have the luxury in this political world that none of these guys have. It is that when you need publicity or coverage you don't even have to think about it; you can get it in spite of yourself. In fact, you do. But for most of these guys, the biggest thing in their lives is trying to find a way to get in the paper next week. And one of the best ways they can do it is with you in the picture." Reagan told Steffes, "I never thought of it. OK, great." He posed for the pictures.

An example of how quickly he learned came a year after he became governor. Reagan, after some difficulties with the legislature, walked across the street from the capitol to the Sutter Club one evening for a big annual event, the Frank Belotti Crab Feed, named for an assemblyman from the North Coast. Reagan, who usually has just one drink, nervously had three martinis before dinner. At dinner, Steffes recalled, "He was fantastic. It was the first time he loosened up with legislators. He was the MC, and he wowed them with one-liners." Afterward Assemblyman Bagley, one of Reagan's most persistent Republican critics, shouted over to Reagan and Steffes, "George Steffes is really a great guy," which was a joking attempt to discredit Steffes with Reagan by suggesting the lobbyist was too friendly with the legislature. Reagan played along, pausing theatrically in mid-sentence and, in a scolding manner, said, "George, come out to the car, I want to talk to you." Everyone laughed. Later, driving home, Reagan told Steffes, "All Bill Bagley wants is for me to give him a little attention, and we'll have him on our side."

An important part of the Reagan team from the beginning was his wife, Nancy, a wide-eyed, attractive woman who had graduated from Smith College, worked as a movie actress and then quit to be a mother and completely devoted wife. Like her husband, Nancy Reagan was deeply conservative. In public, she smiled often and talked blandly. But in private, she was a powerful force in Reagan's career. A reporter, Warren Olney, was in the governor's office on a confusing day early in his administration: Reagan had made a statement in Sacramento and his finance director contradicted it in Los Angeles. The phone rang. Reagan picked it up and apologized to the reporter, explaining, "It's my wife."

"Yes, dear," he said several times. Finally he said of the finance director, "No, dear, I don't think he was being insubordinate. It's just when I say something in Sacramento and he says something in Los Angeles, we'll have to get together." The reporter carried away the impression that Mrs. Reagan had considerable influence. The influence continued over the years. Mrs. Reagan tried to settle the early 1980 presidential-campaign dispute which resulted in the firing of Reagan's campaign manager, John Sears. "I was just trying to be helpful," she told writer Lally Weymouth. "Being helpful and being influential are different things. I was not trying to pull strings or make decisions as to who stayed or went." Later, when Reagan hurt his presidential campaign with misstatements, it was Mrs. Reagan who telephoned an old Reagan adviser, Stuart Spencer, and persuaded him to join the campaign plane, where he remained at Reagan's side until Election Day, cautioning him to be careful with his words.

The budget message Reagan presented to the legislature on that January day in 1967 was the financial blueprint for the biggest retrenchment of California government since the Depression. The reception was not enthusiastic. Never adept at unpracticed reading of a script, Reagan stumbled often. A Democratic senator shifted his pipe to the other side of his mouth and shook his head in disagreement and disbelief. The audience was silent and unresponsive. But finally the governor roused the legislators with a quip. "You know, one of the economies we won't effect is in regard to the state printing plant. I propose they use darker ink." Then he put on his reading glasses and said, "I was hoping I wouldn't have to do that. The next time they make the Rockne movie, I'll play Rockne." He had played the young football hero George Gipp when the movie was made in the late 1930s.

The reaction to the budget message was hostile because Reagan proposed that every department of state government share the burden of the unaccustomed economies, even the University of California and the state universities, the traditional recipients of special consideration by previous governors. "We have fallen heir," he said, "to the most serious fiscal dilemma that has faced the state of California for more than a decade."

It was a new message for Californians. For the past quarter of a century the government had lived up to a standard set by another Republican, Earl Warren, a moderate who believed the state should step in and assist social progress. In 1953 President Eisenhower appointed him Chief Justice of the United States, but his policies influenced the two administrations that followed him. For years Governor Warren had stood on the assembly rostrum, presenting his plans in a high-pitched, slow-moving delivery, a typical pre-television politician. He talked of a state moving forward, always expanding services to help a growing population. The administrations of Warren and the men who followed him, Goodwin J. Knight and Edmund Brown, tended to melt into one long moderate reign.

California had been a warm and friendly land, growing in a way that was beyond control. If you considered California a nation, its gross national product would be seventh among the countries of the world. The promise and the booming economy made it an optimistic place. The state government had surpassed the visions of the New Deal in many ways. While Eastern states suffered from drought, California, with little federal help, built a storage dam that dwarfed the pyramids and an aqueduct that stretched almost the length of the state. Easterners paid tolls on their highways. Californians did not; their gasoline taxes were set aside to pay for freeways. The range of state services was dazzling—parks, generous welfare, liberal medical aid to the poor, tuition-free universities—and the governors Warren, Knight and Brown believed California was rich enough to pay for it all, and more. "In Washington," Brown once boasted, "they call it the Great Society. We just call it California."

But the period of optimistic growth was ending. The problems

Governor Reagan would face during his two terms were more complex than those that had confronted his predecessors. Students who
had once placidly accepted the state's generosity now began demonstrating on the campuses, first against the chilly university bureaucracy that operated the schools, and then against the Vietnam war and
in favor of causes such as creation of black-studies departments. In
the cities the permanent layer of black unemployed was increasing
in the ghettos, bringing with it more despair, alcoholism, drugs and
violent crime. The class difference grew between the affluent, who
were able to enjoy California's good life, and those who could ob-
serve but not participate. Cesar Chavez's drive to unionize farm
workers was becoming an important social issue. A great immigration from Mexico and Asia had already begun, changing the ethnic
composition of the cities. Activists were stepping forward with other
demands for the preservation of scenic resources, prison reform and
other causes.

Employment was relatively high but so were the property taxes
paid by homeowners, for the most part those in the middle class and
above. They were beginning to find it irksome that those property
taxes paid for welfare services to the poor and to support schools that
increasingly reflected the social turmoil of society.

Reagan's message of economy was directed more at these Californians than at the legislators in the assembly chamber. From his
experience in the recent governorship campaign, he knew Californians were beginning to feel liberal government had gone too far.
Aware that the legislators and the interest groups that influenced
them would oppose him, he took his case to the people. "There is
no doubt," he said, "that tremendous pressure will be applied by
many special-interest groups to force a relaxation of economy measures. The legislature, of course, must consider these concerns, but
pressure should not overrule sound judgment."

Later, when Democratic legislators refused to support his proposed cutbacks in welfare, Reagan went on television, equipped with
charts and a convincing speech. His aides made sure the response
was mobilized into grassroots support by organizing anti-welfare
groups in each county, each engaging in a letter writing campaign.
The methods were sufficiently effective to prompt legislators to tell
Reagan to stop. They had received enough postcards from unhappy
constituents. Reagan's White House counselor and his chief aide as

governor, Edwin Meese III, said Reagan will do the same as President "when he thinks it is important on a particular issue or perhaps to make periodic reports to them [the people]."

Reagan began his governorship as a naïve novice who considered inexperience a virtue. In eight years of dealing with social and economic issues he became an experienced politician backed by a team well able to put many of his conservative policies into practice. Despite the persistent myth that there was a more moderate side to Reagan, the most important characteristic of his governorship was his unchanging conservative political philosophy. It is true that he often had to compromise with a legislature controlled most of the years by Democrats. In fact, he had to abandon some of his toughest welfare cutbacks. In long negotiating sessions with Democrats, Reagan agreed to tax increases that brought in far more revenue than was needed—an arrangement that would shock most conservatives. And even though he insisted on returning some of the money to taxpayers, the size of the state budget increased. But that was because Reagan was pragmatic enough to see that continued resistance to the Democrats would produce a fruitless stalemate that would damage him politically. His goal was always to be an effective conservative, not an ideologue.

What is most important in judging his administration are those items over which he had complete control—the original proposals he submitted to the legislature, the ones often rejected by Democrats, and the nature of the Democratic bills he chose to veto. That is when the real Reagan becomes visible. For example, in 1973 his select committee on law enforcement problems proposed legalizing what were then illegal search and seizures; requiring prison sentences for marijuana pushers; and allowing defendants to be prosecuted for perjury after they have been convicted of a crime. A year later Reagan vetoed a bill that would have decriminalized possession of a small amount of marijuana, saying: "I cannot approve any measure which weakens the social sanction against the illicit use of marijuana or which could be interpreted as a move by the state to condone its use." That year he also vetoed bills that would have financed bilingual education in the schools, sealed job applicants' arrest records from prospective government employers and financed low- and moderate-income housing.

He went about this in a manner much different from John F. Kennedy's activism, Lyndon B. Johnson's detailed knowledge and drive, Richard Nixon's vindictiveness and intensity or Jimmy Carter's nitpicking workaholism.

Reagan was not a tough boss. He was more the relaxed chairman of the board, placing complete faith in subordinates to whom he delegated authority. Proposals usually came from below instead of originating with Reagan. "The great strength of Ronald Reagan is that when he sees a need, or is presented with a need or duty or requirement, he takes care of it and he does it without bitching," said a veteran of those days. "His weakness is that he doesn't go looking for the needs or the duties. He would never come into my office and say, 'Should I stay tonight because they're bringing up the budget?' He would wait for me to come up and say, 'You should stay tonight because the budget may come up.' He's a reactor, not an initiator."

In the first year, his administration was chaotic. His inexperience and dislike of government were shared by assistants more at home in the disciplined atmosphere of a corporation or a large law office. "A bunch of young guys trying to scratch their way over other guys" is how one of them described it. But later, especially after Reagan was re-elected in 1970, work settled into a structured routine.

His governorship was a time of learning. The simplistic speeches of his campaigns were slowly translated into policies that turned the California state government in a more conservative direction. The innate political instincts he first showed as a candidate were sharpened and used in the much more difficult job of being a chief executive. The intense pressures, the constant visibility and the great war, peace and economic decisions of the presidency cannot be compared with the problems of governing a state, even one as large and complex as California. But in his eight years in Sacramento, Reagan encountered many of the issues he now faces and he felt he mastered them. He developed his style of governing. He learned how to deal with opposing political forces. It was his training ground for the presidency, and after his election Reagan made it clear that those eight years in Sacramento would have a great influence over his conduct in the White House.

2

THE MAN

In the photographic collection of Arthur Van Court are hundreds of pictures of a Ronald Reagan that few people ever see. As Reagan's bodyguard in the late sixties and as a prolific amateur photographer, Van Court had an opportunity to capture on film scenes from a private life that the Reagans guard from public view. There they are, enjoying an elegant picnic in the Southern California hills with their friends the William Wilsons, the Earle Jorgensens, the Alfred Bloomingdales, the William French Smiths, and others. Reagan looks moved when Nancy's birthday is toasted. In another picture he and Smith, who years later would become his attorney general, stand side by side holding drinks, Smith smiling in the relaxed atmosphere of the countryside. There is a picture of the Reagans on another day, both dressed in red and white and holding ice cream cones, every bit the cutest couple. Reagan at Palm Springs, sharing a golf cart with President Eisenhower, listening intently to Ike's advice and later talking to him and Bob Hope over cocktails. And best of all, Reagan on a horse—at his ranch, on back-country trails, on an outing with a socially elite men's group—looking so perfect that one understands Reagan's anger at never being starred in a first-class Western.

These are photographs of good times in the California sunshine, a way of living that has shaped Reagan's outlook. It is not the sort of life that gave the state a reputation for unconventional living. Although Reagan and his wife acted in films, they had not recently been part of the entertainment business or the flashy society which shapes the culture of Southern California through films, records and fashions. The Reagans have no connection with the California of hot tubs, encounter groups, health foods and Zen. And while Reagan has been a successful politician since 1966, he does not spend his off-hours in the boozy, gossipy evenings so beloved by many who take politics seriously.

The Reagans are part of another California—conventional, conservative, wealthy, devoted to a private world of family and close friends. It is the post–World War II California, represented by a home and a fenced backyard where a family could retreat from the dirt and noise of the city. Most who achieved that dream did so modestly, in tract homes built in flat, unstylish suburbs. The Reagans and their friends were more successful. Their backyards were bigger, their vacation retreats more exclusive, their friends more powerful. But in his view of the world, and in his choice of pastimes, Reagan is the ultimate suburbanite, happiest when he has a fence to build or a tree to plant.

That was evident soon after the Reagans arrived in Sacramento. It had been a tradition for the governors to give an annual party for the press. The exclusively male press corps would come to the executive mansion with their wives. An open bar before dinner always helped get them in the mood to reminisce, a process stimulated by wine with the meal and brandy afterward. By midnight, reporters and gubernatorial staff members would be refighting ancient campaigns and feuds while their wives sat quiet, bored, waiting for the evening to end.

The Reagans drastically changed the style of this event. Their press party was held in the backyard on a Sunday afternoon. Children were invited, and everyone went swimming in the pool. There was no hard liquor, just beer and soft drinks and barbecued beef. The Reagans, usually reserved and cautious around reporters, were warm and friendly in this family atmosphere. Unlike the governor, Mrs. Reagan would sometimes be cold and hostile to a reporter whose story had displeased her. But at this event she would soften when she met the reporter's family. She would be charming, talking to children in the way people do when they truly enjoy them.

His retreat was Rancho del Cielo, or Ranch in the Sky, 688 acres of rugged land in the Santa Ynez Mountains east of Santa Barbara which he purchased in 1974 for $527,000. There he built fences and remodeled the hundred-year-old two-bedroom adobe house. Often Reagan and his friend Willard (Barney) Barnett, his former California Highway Patrol driver, would go to the ranch alone and spend the day doing strenuous construction projects or clearing brush. He loves that kind of work. The Reagans' friend Betty Wilson told Jody Jacobs of the Los Angeles *Times* how Reagan trimmed the trees on the Wilsons' Mexican ranch.

Wherever they were, the Reagans always insisted on privacy. In the early seventies the press did a series of exposés about the financial holdings of public officials. Someone—possibly a temporary worker in the income-tax office—looked up Reagan's 1970 state income-tax returns and discovered that he had paid none. The information was leaked to a reporter at Sacramento State College's student-operated radio station, and it was soon picked up by the state's major news organizations. An aide confirmed the story, saying Reagan had suffered business losses but refusing to give details. The next day Reagan told reporters, "Frankly, I think the capitol press corps yesterday demeaned itself a little by engaging in invasion of privacy. They know someone illegally provided the information from the franchise tax board." But as the furor grew, Reagan explained what had happened. "Last year, a rather trying year for a number of people, investment losses in relation to earnings were such that while I still owed and paid federal income tax, I did not have a state tax liability. Frankly, I hope that does not happen again. Not that I enjoy paying taxes, but because I do not enjoy losing money."

The same need for privacy extended to the lives of their children, Patti and Ronald. They were shielded from public view while growing up. And from the way Reagan publicly denounced the new moral standards and protest that had affected almost everyone else's children, it was assumed the Reagans had somehow escaped the conflicts of a difficult decade. But they had not. In fact, both children were rebels. Eventually Patti became an actress, singer and composer, and was for a time estranged from her parents, who objected to her relationship with a musician from the Eagles rock group. Their son, Ronald, dropped out of Yale and joined the Joffrey Ballet, where he began a promising career as a dancer. He and his woman friend lived together before they were married. What made their life styles worthy of note was not the conduct, but the Reagans' harsh criticism of that same behavior in other young people.

This insistence on privacy is not used to hide another, more complex Reagan. He does not have one personality in public and another in private. He is not like Richard Nixon, who carefully constructed an outward façade of calm and dignity to hide an overly ambitious and vindictive private self, or like Jimmy Carter, a gentle Sunday-school teacher in public who displays, in private, a most un-Christian cold anger against erring assistants or anyone who opposes him. The genial Reagan you see on television is exactly the same in his dealings with the people close to him.

Reagan is intelligent but not brilliant; quick-witted but without deep intellectual curiosity. Although he says he reads a lot, he is, on occasion, vague about it. When he was governor, he was asked by reporters what books he had been reading. There was a pause, and then he said he had been reading a book during his vacation at the beach, one Nancy had given him. But he could not remember the title.

He talks in long, rambling sentences, and once he has found an answer to a question he will use it over and over again, clinging to familiar words as if they were part of a movie script. The same phrases, and even the same paragraphs, appear in speech after speech. A visitor once mentioned that three of Reagan's old movies had been on television the day before. One of them—a favorite of Reagan's—was the life story of Grover Cleveland Alexander, the baseball pitcher. Reagan was immediately reminded of an anecdote. He told about the studio bosses' trying to disguise Alexander's epileptic seizures by portraying them as fainting spells; but that had only served to anger the public and the critics, who thought the studio had another motive in mind: using the fainting spells to cover up a well-known Alexander affliction—alcoholism.

The story was interesting but it had been told before, and in exactly the same words, in Reagan's autobiography. The visitor felt he had pushed a button marked "Grover Cleveland Alexander," and the story had come out, just as questions about taxes, welfare and other issues drew identical answers day after day. Reagan was annoyed by those who said his fondness for the familiar prompted him to always give the same speeches. Sometimes he would use the beginning of one, the middle of another and the climax of a third. By alternating them, he actually could give a variety of speeches.

He is a pleasant companion, an amusing storyteller full of anecdotes about his fellow actors in the great days of Warner Bros. and the other old Hollywood studios. Although he likes to be on schedule, he can be patient when things go wrong. One day he and two or three others were flying from San Diego to Orange County, where he was to meet Nancy for dinner. He did not want to be late. But he and his companions did not arrive at the airport until late in the afternoon, and commercial flights were lined up waiting for permission to take off. Reagan's plane was ordered to the back of the line. "We've got the governor of California on board," his pilot protested. The official in the tower replied, "I don't care what he's governor of, you wait in line." Reagan shrugged, smiled and went back to his reading.

He is an unpretentious, commonplace man, unembarrassed by what many would consider simple notions. In one of his less sophisticated moments Reagan confided that he did not discount the possibility of flying saucers. It was early in his political career, in the weeks before he became a candidate for governor, during a tour of the Central Valley farm country of California. With him were a campaign aide, a friend and a reporter. It was late at night; everyone in the car was tired from a long evening, and the drowsy conversation turned to the surrounding countryside and finally to the stars shining clearly above. Someone mentioned flying saucers. Reagan said he thought unidentified flying objects existed; so did the friend. Reagan said he had an acquaintance, a Navy reserve pilot, who had seen UFOs while on a flight through the Midwest.

His habit of reading the astrology column resulted in one of the more farcical disputes at the beginning of his governorship. He had decided to be sworn in as governor at 12:10 A.M., his term beginning officially at 12:01 A.M. on January 2. His reason: "The law prescribes that at midnight it is the end of the present administration. I hate to be a pessimist but accidents may happen. I don't want anything to interfere." He also noted there were several football bowl games on television on January 2, too, and didn't want to interfere with those.

Former Governor Edmund Brown thought the hour peculiar. "My only guess is that it's because he believes in astrology. I understand he does," said Brown. Two astrologers agreed with Brown's surmise. In San Francisco a local character, Gavin Chester Arthur, a newsboy astrologer who was a grandson of Chester Arthur, the Twenty-first President of the United States, noted that Jupiter, the sign of kings and the symbol of prosperity and fame, would be high in the sky at the moment of the inauguration. "I truly suspect that Reagan was advised by an astrologer because no better time could be picked," said Arthur. "It's not just a coincidence," said Louise Huebner, an astrologist in Los Angeles.

All this speculation made Reagan angry. "He does not believe in astrology," said Philip Battaglia, his first executive secretary. "He is not guided by the stars, nor do we intend to have stargazers in the administration." The inauguration was held at 12:01 A.M., a time with less astrological significance.

Reagan believes in the simple virtues of a less complex time. That was apparent one afternoon during his governorship when he visited Loara High School in Orange County. The school was as conservative as the county. This was in 1970, but at Loara High the coaches and football players shaved their heads through the season for discipline's sake and, in the words of the coach, to separate them from the campus longhairs. The bald players and coaches listened while Reagan described how he had taken his son, then eleven, to the Los Angeles Rams dressing room the previous year, after a loss to Minnesota, and how, amid the sweat and misery of the athletes, he had encountered a spiritually uplifting event.

"Coach [George] Allen came in and said 'OK, let's give thanks,' " Reagan said. "He [his son] watched his heroes, those great big monsters, drop to their knees and repeat the Lord's Prayer, reverently and quietly, and I'll tell you, for the father of a small boy it was an experience that renewed my faith in the men who follow sports." Reagan found a lesson in the experience, something of value in the larger game of life or even the conduct of national affairs. "There are people around who try to tell us that winning is kind of bad for us," Reagan said, "that we should have group calisthenics. There isn't anything wrong with winning as long as you don't do it at any cost. This is the last frontier, the last place where you can go out and hate the next guy because he's got a different jersey on and throw yourself at him until after the last gun and then you discover you kind of like the fellow."

Simple and maudlin though they may be, the sentiments are the essence of the Reagan message: that competition is good and that success or victory is possible only if people work or fight hard enough. In the beginning, however, it was not the message that drew the crowds. Before he had made a single political speech, the public knew Reagan as a friendly, sincere, hard-working sort of fellow, one who had no major vices. The producers had picked Reagan as Shirley Temple's first grown-up boyfriend in *That Hagen Girl,* confident that his forthright honesty wouldn't damage her virginal charm. In *Voice of the Turtle* he was the puritanical soldier who insisted that Eleanor Parker sleep in another room when a rainstorm forced him to spend a night in her apartment. In *Bedtime for Bonzo* he played a well-meaning and good-natured scientist who was raising a chimpanzee to prove to his prospective father-in-law that environment is more important than heredity—and that his own father's criminal background was not important. Even when Reagan portrayed a playboy, the script and Reagan's own clean-cut manner would sanitize the character. In his films, whiskey bottles and pool cues were taken from the hands of Grover Cleveland Alexander and George Gipp, the old Notre Dame football hero.

As for his ideas, Reagan is a man who did not refine his conservative philosophy until late in life. The change came when he was in his thirties and forties, and it came slowly. Before that, he had few well-defined beliefs. Even when he was forty-five, he apparently had not arrived at a clearly defined political philosophy. At that age he began making speeches for General Electric, and the company's president, Ralph Cordiner, became concerned over his difficulties in answering audiences' questions. "I told him," Cordiner recalled, "You'd better get yourself a philosophy, something you can stand for and something you think this country stands for.' I think this is when he really started to change."

Those who find a philosophy in middle age, after years of wandering, often develop a stubborn faith, and that is what happened to Reagan. Once he arrived at his philosophy, Reagan clung to it with a determination that is sometimes found among late converts to a religious faith. There is a fervor in him when he talks about the philosophy, and he conveys it to the audience whether he is on television or in a meeting hall. Reagan is a true believer, and when Californians became more conservative, he was the best qualified spokesman for their new cause.

Without this deep commitment to conservatism, Reagan would have been just another celebrity in the parade of actors and actresses who appear each election year to help their favorite candidates and then return to private life. He was committed, however, and ready to accept when his party summoned him.

The image Hollywood gave him and the conservative philosophy were only part of the reason for Reagan's instant success in politics. Just as important—and maybe more important—is his skill on television, his ability to handle himself in front of the camera. It is a perfect marriage of the man and the medium, a medium he knows and believes in. He has a rather naïve view that because he is convincing on television, it proves he believes what he says. "When you go on that TV tube and you're in a close-up—that happens to be my business. I came from the camera business and I know one rule we had in Hollywood and you can't break it—that camera knows when you're lying. That camera knows when an actor really doesn't feel the line he is saying."

Reagan approached political appearances on television the way he approached the movies: as a business that requires dedication and hard work. In 1968 he was going to make a television appearance with Senator Robert F. Kennedy. Kennedy was at the height of his popularity and power, heading for his presidential candidacy, whereas Reagan was thought of nationally as a lightweight, an actor who happened to get elected governor of California. This is the kind of situation in which Reagan does well—as the underdog who must prove himself in a single appearance before the camera. Before the event he sat tense and silent, not hearing the chatter of his assistants. But once the show began, Reagan was calm and agile as he briskly answered questions from hostile college students, handling himself more impressively than Kennedy.

As governor Reagan used television the way Franklin D. Roosevelt had used radio three decades before. Roosevelt talked directly to the people in his "fireside chats," appealing to them over the heads of recalcitrant congressmen. The warm, rich voice evoked confidence and friendship, and when he died, millions felt the sharp pain that accompanies the death of a friend or relative. Radio took Roosevelt out of the impersonality of the printed page and into the home. Reagan modernized the fireside chat: in his first few months in office he filmed fifteen-minute and two-minute films and handed them out to television stations around the state. The aim was to present Reagan without the editorial comment of newspapers who were critical of his reductions in state programs. By all standards of Reagan's show-business background, the reports were a success. The ratings were high, and public opinion polls showed that a majority of Californians approved of the way Reagan was doing his job, even after he saddled the state with record tax increases and budgets.

He also showed his mastery of television in his 1980 debate with President Carter. Reagan, who was slow to get started, took command in the second half of the debate, and there was one particularly memorable moment when Carter accused Reagan of being against national health insurance. Smiling, shaking his head in mock disappointment, Reagan turned to Carter and said, "There you go again," then went on to say that he had opposed one medical-aid bill but supported another plan. However, what he said was less important than the grin and good humor displayed in handling the attack. It was a combination of levity and a nimble parry, showing that he was in command of the situation. With his performance during the debate he proved to the viewers that he was at least Carter's equal, destroying Carter's argument that Reagan was incompetent.

Earlier in the 1980 campaign there was an even more clear-cut triumph. It was during a debate in the New Hampshire Republican primary, and although the event was not televised live, the dramatic moments were shown repeatedly the following day. Reagan, who had lost to George Bush in Iowa, was trying to catch up in New Hampshire and agreed to meet him in a debate sponsored by the Nashua *Telegraph*. Bush and Reagan were leading the New Hampshire public opinion polls, and the newspaper wanted the drama of a one-on-one debate. But the other Republican presidential candidates insisted on taking part, and the Republican national chairman, William Brock, supported them. The newspaper refused. Reagan stated publicly that all candidates should be allowed to appear and he arranged to pay for the high school auditorium with his own campaign funds.

The audience was filled with Nashua residents who had come to see the big show, and the crowd was beginning to clamor for the candidates. But backstage the candidates and their aides were still arguing over who would be on the platform. A newspaper official insisted that only Reagan and Bush should be allowed to speak. Bush agreed with the newspaper, but Reagan still sided with the other candidates. Suddenly Bush forced the issue by striding on stage. "We're here to debate," said his press secretary, Peter Teeley. The crowd chanted "We want Reagan." Now the next move was Reagan's, and he walked onstage, followed by the other candidates. None of the reporters present had ever seen him so angry. He gave Bush a look of utter dislike. Bush sat down at the debating table, but Reagan walked over to the candidates standing on the other side of the stage. There was a pause, and then, in one of those brief, inexplicable moments when one person gains power over another, Reagan motioned to the seated Bush. As if Bush were a boy, Reagan said, "George, stand up." Bush stood, and at that moment Reagan won a tremendous psychological victory.

But the climax was yet to come. John Breen, the editor of the newspaper, repeated that only Reagan and Bush would be allowed to debate, and that the others would be limited to brief statements at the end. The hall exploded in boos. Reagan grabbed the microphone to protest while Breen shouted, "Will the sound man please turn off the microphone!" Then, with full use of his superlative sense of timing, Reagan spoke one of the great lines of the 1980 campaign, his voice slightly hoarse with tension and anger: "I am paying for this microphone, Mr. Breen." The audience cheered. "The paper could not finance the debate," Reagan went on. "I then volunteered to pick up the tab with our campaign funds and pay for the debate . . . I was technically the sponsor, and sponsors have certain rights." By then he was in charge. Chairs were brought in for the other candidates so that they could all participate. As in the presidential debate later in the year, what was said during the discussion was not as important as the commanding impression Reagan made, an impression that was spread across the country the following day with replays of the dramatic scene.

Such presence is the product of years of training. As an actor Reagan learned to control his voice and body movements to create the desired effect. "It has taken me many years to get used to seeing myself as others see me," Reagan wrote in his autobiography. "Very few of us ever see ourselves except as we look directly at ourselves in a mirror. Thus we don't know how we look from behind, from the sides, talking, standing, moving normally through a room. It's quite a jolt."

Professional training gives him an advantage over politicians whose knowledge is limited to government. On the stage at Nashua the other candidates either slumped or sat stiffly. Reagan, his body always under control, played the part of the outraged citizen to perfection. And during the presidential debate when he told Carter,

"There you go again," it was more than a chance remark; it was a superb bit of scene stealing.

His training was especially helpful when he started in politics in the mid-sixties, especially since politicians of that era were barely aware of the potential of television. Most were terrible at it: their clothes were all wrong, and most rejected the idea of hiring a speech coach. When most politicians read a speech from the Teleprompter, their eyes darted back and forth. In contrast, Reagan followed it with ease and was even able to audaciously look away without losing his place. That was important, for it allowed him to look directly at the audience and establish direct communication, or he could look downward to grimace in disgust at his opponents, another characteristic gesture that brought him closer to the folks at home.

He has ease, superb timing and "empathy with an audience," explained Nancy Reynolds, who served as a Reagan press secretary for years in Sacramento and is still close to the family. "He started in a profession where he memorized scripts. He had a retentive memory, and I'm sure that comes from reading scripts."

Reagan was not the first to use television effectively. Eisenhower's advisers were aware of the possibilities of the medium and hired television producer Robert Montgomery to prepare Ike for the screen. And John F. Kennedy, with his youth, good looks and vigorous manner, dominated the small screen as effectively as Reagan does. But Reagan was the first politician to ignore the traditional pageantry of the political campaign—the long rallies, handshaking tours, dawn-to-midnight schedules—and rely so heavily on television. Two years after Reagan's 1966 campaign, Nixon used the same technique nationally in a coast-to-coast campaign completely aimed at and scheduled for television. In 1976 Reagan, after losing five straight primaries to Gerald Ford, came back with a single television speech on the eve of the North Carolina primary. He won the primary, brought in $1.4 million to his dwindling campaign treasury, and began the comeback that nearly won the national convention. That same year Carter, just an ex-governor of Georgia, used television to build a victorious Democratic constituency in a party structure that had nearly been shattered by party reforms. But Reagan was the first, and as he proved in the 1980 campaign, is still the best.

Has the nation reached the long-prophesied era of the manufactured candidate—a product carefully picked and nurtured by public relations specialists and then sold to the voters on television? Despite the importance of television, as Carter's presidency proved, the electronic medium alone can't sell a politician. Carter thought he could continue the tactics of the campaign in the White House, building his image as a well-loved President on television. He walked, instead of riding, in his inaugural parade. He wore a cardigan sweater during a televised speech on energy. But as it turned out, the public was more concerned with job performance than image when it came to the presidency. And Reagan, as Carter learned, was more than a manufactured candidate. True, his techniques changed American politics, making them more visual and teaching strategists to think of simple issues that could be discussed in short telecasts. His success, however, was due as much to his message as to the medium he used to spread it. He deeply believed in what he was saying, and in a sense, he was correct in his impression that his delivery had a sincerity that reached out of the screen and into the living room.

3

A HUMBLE BEGINNING

There is in American literature a portrait of the Midwest of the 1920s
—conservative, materialistic, admiring of the businessman, intoler-
ant of social service, foreigners and dissenters. It is the Midwest
described by Sinclair Lewis, and its typical community was Zenith,
"the Zip City, Zeal, Zest and Zowie—1 million in 1935." Zenith's
typical citizen was George F. Babbitt, who said of politics: "I'll tell
you—and my stand on this is just the same as it was four years ago
and eight years ago and it'll be my stand four years from now. What
I tell everybody, and it can't be too generally understood, is that what
we need first, last and all the time is a good, sound business administration." It was, in the words of Lewis' biographer, Mark Schorer,
"the world of the little businessman. . . . He boasts and boosts with
all his fellows, sings and cheers and prays with the throng, derides
all difference, denounces all dissent—and all to climb with the
crowd. With the supremacy of public relations, he abolishes human
relations."

Ronald Reagan grew up in this era and in one of these communities. He was a boy of nine in 1920. But unlike Lewis, he loves the
small towns, admires the conservative men who run them and looks
back on his youth with fond memories. Reagan was shaped by the

small towns of the Midwest, and that explains in large part the simple moral and conservative approach he brought to public life. Where Lewis satirized the Midwest communities, Reagan glorifies them. He enthusiastically accepts the values that Lewis criticized. As a result, he is deeply respectful of business; determinedly conservative; mistrusting of change; unintellectual and slightly suspicious of higher education; firmly wedded to the Protestant religion of his boyhood; convinced that, as his father said, "all men were created equal and [that] man's own ambition determines what happens to him the rest of his life." As he has done with all the values of his boyhood, Reagan applies this to public life and opposes state intervention in the problems of minorities. He likes neither open-housing laws nor big welfare programs. He has clung to these values all his life. In 1947, when he was a Democrat, his ideas didn't sound much different from his pronouncements as a conservative Republican twenty years later.

He has remained, through his life, a small-town boy from the Midwest, boosting its values, doubting the worth of other backgrounds, certain that the simple answers of his youth were still valid in his adulthood. He believes strongly that any individual, if determined enough, can succeed without the help of big government. "For two hundred years," he once said, "American business and industry have fought the greatest war on poverty the world has ever known. At the height of the Great Depression, it was employing ninety percent of the nation's workers." Yet Reagan's own father was unemployed by the Depression and didn't find work until he got a government job administering relief, a reward for campaigning for Franklin D. Roosevelt in 1932. Later, his father was in charge of the local Works Progress Administration.

Reagan was born in Tampico, Illinois, on February 11, 1911, in a five-room flat above the H. C. Pitney General Store, where his father sold shoes. His father, John Edward Reagan, once commented that his son looked "like a fat Dutchman." The name stuck, and Reagan was "Dutch" to his friends ever since. His brother Neil, then two years old, was brought into the bedroom to see the new baby, but he wouldn't look at him. His parents had promised him a sister, and he was disappointed.

There was only one block of paved street in Tampico, and the main communication with the outside world was through the two passenger trains that stopped each day at the small station near the grain elevator; they were local trains connecting the villages of the area.

Reagan loved this village of 1,200 people and wrote of it in his autobiography: "There were woods, and mysteries, life and death among the small creatures, hunting and fishing; these were the days when I learned the real riches of rags." It was a vigorous dissent against the view of the Midwest taken by Sinclair Lewis, who fled the area and became a socialist. In *Main Street* Lewis described a similar town, picturing it through the eyes of his heroine, Carol Kennicott. She wanted to run away from the village because "oozing out of every drab wall she felt a forbidding spirit she could not conquer." Even the drab town jewelry store depressed her. But in Reagan's memories, the Tampico jewelry store was a wonderful place, owned by a kindly childless couple, Aunt Emma and Uncle Jim, who gave him an allowance of ten cents a week, hot chocolate and permission to spend hours "hidden in a corner downstairs in Uncle Jim's jewelry store, with its curious relics, faint lights from the gold and silver and bronze, lulled by the erratic ticking of a dozen clocks and the drone of customers who came in."

Soon after Dutch was born, the family moved out of the flat to a house. The general store was across the railroad tracks from the house, and a park with a Civil War cannon was nearby. On the porch, Reagan's father hung a swing, and children would swing on it sideways instead of back and forth, shattering the Midwestern evening quiet with the squeaking and thumping. Downstairs was a living room, a kitchen, a parlor and a service porch. Upstairs was the luxury of three bedrooms.

They were a close family. The father distressed his religious wife (she was Protestant of Scottish-English descent, and he was an Irish Catholic) by periodic drinking binges, but even in their most distressing moments together, she would say, "The Lord will provide." Most of the time he was sober and hard-working, always watching for better-paying jobs. There were many light moments in their lives. He and his wife were in the Parent-Teacher Association, and one night he put on a crepe-paper hula skirt, smeared make-up on his face, put on a wig and appeared with his wife in the PTA talent show. Other nights the Reagans—devoted to amateur theatricals—would bring the drama group over to their home to rehearse for a play at the Tampico Opera House, located in an upstairs room in the town with space for about a hundred folding chairs. The boys would sneak behind a corner and watch the rehearsals. Afterward there was a big pot of oyster stew for everybody.

Within the close-knit family there was a strong bond between the brothers that continued through their lives. Later, when they were young men, Neil passed up college to work in a cement plant. Reagan went to college equipped with his proudest possession, a new, shiny black steamer trunk. When he came home at the end of his junior year, he told Neil he had made arrangements for him to also go to college, having lined up an athletic scholarship and a part-time job. Neil refused. When the new semester began, Neil came home from the cement plant one night and found his brother gone, but the steamer trunk remained in the middle of his bedroom.

"Nelle," he said to his mother, "I thought Dutch was leaving." The boys always called their parents by their first names.

"He has," replied his mother, "but your brother left that in case you changed your mind about going to college. He packed up all his things in cardboard boxes and shipped them down to school."

Neil considered the generous gift and his mother's unspoken rebuke for a moment and then said, "If that's the case, I'll go to college. I'll pack and go tomorrow."

During Reagan's early childhood, his father had constantly been searching for advancement, a quest that kept the family moving throughout Illinois. A job at Marshall Field's Department Store brought the Reagans to the South Side of Chicago when Dutch was two. But instead of improving the family fortunes, the move turned out to be a disaster. Jack Reagan's salary was so low that the family had to live in a flat lighted by a gas jet which provided light only if someone put a quarter in the meter down the hall—"If we had a quarter," Neil Reagan recalled later. On Saturdays, Neil was sent to the butcher shop with a dime for a soup bone. He'd also beg some liver for a nonexistent cat—and then bring it home for the main course for Sunday dinner. His mother would make a big pot of soup with the bone and keep it on the stove the rest of the week, adding carrots and potatoes. "That was the entrée," said Neil. For breakfast she would buy a carton of rolled Quaker Oats and serve it each day with condensed milk. When there were football games at the nearby University of Chicago stadium, Mrs. Reagan would make popcorn, put it in bags and send the boys out to try, without much success, to sell it. She made all the clothes for the boys.

The family lived in the flat on Cottage Way for almost two years, and finally Jack Reagan found a job that returned them to rural Illinois, this time Galesburg. He bought a bike to ride to work at the

O. T. Johnson Department Store, and the family rose to new economic heights by moving into a rented two-story frame house, their first with hardwood floors. Big lawns were in front and back, just right for the football games the boys enjoyed. In three years his father found a better job in Monmouth, a city of between 35,000 and 40,000 people with three colleges nearby. In another two years, his old employer from Tampico, H. C. Pitney, asked him back for a year. Wearing the bibbed overalls of the era, eight-year-old Reagan would trudge off to the two-story country school each day. In the summer Ronald and Neil sometimes spent a week on the farm of their parents' friends, the Lutyens, where they hauled water to the men thrashing grain in the fields and stuffed themselves with fried chicken, pie and cold watermelon when the women brought the heavy noonday meals out to the fields. Of that period of his childhood, Reagan wrote: "Those were the happiest times of my life."

It was a picture-book boyhood, something out of an old Norman Rockwell cover for the *Saturday Evening Post* or a Booth Tarkington novel. It was *Tom Sawyer* and *Huckleberry Finn* without the tragedy of Nigger Jim's slavery. There were, of course, some bleak times. Sometimes children would drown in the deep canal outside of town where everyone swam. And once, when Reagan and his friend Monkey Winchell were playing with a gun, Monkey fired it and blew a hole in the ceiling. Another time Jack Reagan bought a carload of potatoes for speculation and made his two sons sit in the car for days, sorting them. But mostly there were good times. Football and other sports occupied most of Reagan's time. Undersized and near-sighted, he was introduced to football in games in the park, with a lopsided ball. He would enthusiastically charge down the field with the other boys and jump into the battling pile of youngsters scrambling for the ball.

When Reagan was nine the family moved again. H. C. Pitney, the general-store owner, agreed to become a partner with Reagan's father in a high-quality shoe store in Dixon, Illinois. Jack Reagan would do the work while Pitney put up the capital. Reagan lived there from the age of nine until he was twenty-one. Here, in the schools, on the playing field and at home, Reagan's character was shaped. "All of us have to have a place to go back to," he said. "Dixon is that place for me."

In 1920 Dixon was a town of 10,000 located on the Rock River about a hundred miles west of Chicago. Driving into town on the

Lincoln Highway from the rolling hills surrounding Dixon, you headed into the business district. The streets were lined with trees, many of which were later felled by disease and road projects. Now there are petunias instead of trees on the streets, and every July the city, grown to 20,000, has a petunia festival. The main street—then, as now—was Galena Avenue. Over it was the rustic memorial arch, built of wood, to honor the dead of World War I. Near the arch was the post office and the leading hotel, the Nachusa House, where Abraham Lincoln once slept, and the Nachusa Tavern, where, according to local legend, he had debated Stephen A. Douglas. Boynton-Richards and the Daile Clothing Company were the big retail stores downtown. On the other side of town was Lowell Park, a 320-acre, city-owned area rich in historic tradition. The land was given to Dixon by the family of James Russell Lowell, who liked to spend time watching the Rock River. Today the river is too polluted for swimming.

The town's schools were also along the river. The elementary school was built during the Civil War. Next to it was Northside High, a sturdy red-brick building with big bay windows of the post–Civil War period, which Reagan entered a few years later. He was five feet three inches tall, weighed one hundred and eight pounds and wore thick, black-rimmed glasses. With his friends, he walked through the main door and up the big stairway. At the top of the stairs was a study hall. To the right was the principal's office. Classrooms were on the left and upstairs on the third floor. The building was dark, solid, dignified and almost pretty, with trees in front and a yard of grass and pavement. About one hundred and fifty students, equally divided between boys and girls, attended the school.

Reagan's greatest challenge was not in the classroom but on the nearby football field. He couldn't see the ball well enough to catch it, and he was too small at first to play in the line. But the game, he remembered as an adult, "was a matter of life and death. Every year at the beginning of the football season you were kind of ready for summer to end. You'd begin to think about the smell of burning leaves. The new high school uniforms would be put on display in a store downtown. Your heroes were the high school stars. They seemed like grown men." To make the high school team was "your goal and aim in life. Everything is a game except football," he said. "It is the last thing in our civilized life where a man can physically throw himself, his full body, into combat with another man."

It took Reagan two years to make the high school varsity, but in his junior year, when he weighed one hundred and twenty pounds and was "still a string bean," he made the team. His bad eyes prevented him from playing where he wanted, at end or in the backfield. Instead he was a guard. But that didn't reduce the satisfaction the game gave him, and he retained his love for football as an adult. No role was more enjoyable to him than that of George Gipp in the Knute Rockne movie. In public life he liked to put his problems in the context of a football game. Handed a defeat in the legislature, he assured Republicans that it was only half time and that "there are still two quarters left to play." As governor he gave a staff job to Jack Kemp, then the quarterback of the Buffalo Bills and now a congressman. Kemp, an articulate and intelligent man, used to complain that in their private conversations he wanted to talk politics while Reagan insisted on talking football. When a photographer took pictures of Reagan and Kemp, they tossed a ball back and forth for him in the governor's office. After the photographer finished, the two engaged in a forty-five-minute game of catch.

Football was the main interest in his life, but he had others. For a time young Reagan and his brother had a museum and zoo in the loft of the carriage house in back of their home. Their father gave them an old display case and they filled it with a collection of birds' eggs and butterflies. In the summer they had to pick tomato worms and potato bugs from their father's vegetable gardens. One year he gave them each a set of prize pigeons, which multiplied quickly. They also raised rabbits and persuaded a friend who had goats to join them in putting on circuses in a tent along the side of the house. But when the friend and Neil Reagan decided to go out of the circus business and into the meat and poultry business with the pigeons and rabbits, Dutch withdrew. "He couldn't go for killing," said Neil.

There were also overnight hikes with the YMCA youth group—Reagan was too poor for a boy scout uniform—and swimming lessons at the YMCA pool. And he shared the interest of his parents and brother in acting. The man who first taught Reagan about acting was B. J. Fraser, a slender, tweedy drama and English teacher. When Reagan was governor, Fraser was still living in Dixon, retired from the school but alert, busy with an insurance business and willing to talk at length about his former student. Fraser thought the young Reagan "had possibilities" as an actor, but it was almost unheard of in the Midwest in those days for anyone to choose the theater as a career.

Reagan remembered himself as an indifferent student, concerned only with making the grades needed to remain eligible for football and other activities. But Fraser said, "He was quite interested in literature and English. He was an above-average student. He was curious. He was original and creative, and he had a quality that not too many high school kids had. He did what he started." Brother Neil recalled that Reagan was "never one to crack a book"; instead he had "a truly photographic mind," an ability to read a large amount of material and retain it. Those around him have always commented on his memory. As an actor he learned scripts easily and remembered them. Later on, he could read summaries of complex government documents quickly and absorb them well enough to discuss them in public.

Reagan also wrote for the high school yearbook, enthusiastically took part in student government and clubs and was one of the few youngsters in town who planned to go to college. But he did not know what he wanted to do after that.

The happy boyhood produced the optimistic adult. Except for the two years on the South Side of Chicago, his growing up was a catalog of pleasant memories. When he reminisces about his childhood, it becomes clear that it was then that he learned the lessons that govern his life. He was asked once if he had a happy childhood. "Oh, yes," said Reagan. "Not a blissful, idyllic thing, but as you look back through the rosy glow of time, yes. I realize now, looking back on it, that we were poor, but I didn't know it at the time." Growing philosophical, he went on, "I think this is one thing that might be wrong today. The government seems intent on telling people they are poor. One of the reasons we didn't know it was that my mother was always finding someone who needed help."

The life of rural Illinois provided him with the material with which he justified the conservative opinions of his adulthood. There were, for example, the part-time and summer jobs that furnished him with spending money and helped him through college. For seven summers he was the lifeguard at Lowell Park, and during that time he pulled seventy-seven people from the water. In the mornings he would pick up hamburgers and other supplies for the park and then go on duty at the beach until swimming ended at night. "It was great," he said.

"There was no place to spend money. I could save twenty dollars a week and, of course, they fed me, and if it was too crowded, they brought food down to me." The hours were so long that he didn't have time for girls, although they remembered him years later as the handsome lifeguard at the beach.

Many young men have such jobs and are enriched only with a little spending money. Reagan carried away something more; he left his lifeguard's post on the Rock River with a philosophy about independence and working. Looking back, he liked to say he had advantages the government now denies children. "This whole thing about teen-agers and summer jobs" annoyed him. "We have taken jobs away from them. We have taken them away in some instances by way of unions, but more by way of our own social legislation, and I think we've got to make some exceptions." As a teen-ager he once worked for a company that remodeled old houses. At the end of every week, Reagan recalled, "The boss paid you out of his pocket in cash. He didn't have to sit down and do a lot of paperwork for Social Security and all those things. Now, don't get me wrong. I'm not criticizing it for the legitimate work force, but for the kids who have to go through school, it seems to me, we could make some exceptions; the employer today is resisting hiring the teen-ager part-time because of these fringes and these excessive things and the paperwork, and I would think Social Security could wait until a fellow becomes a legitimate member of the working force instead of being a kid in school with a summer job."

The values of the Midwest were also a great influence on his views about the problems of poverty and bigotry. As governor he opposed laws to stop bigotry in housing, although he was raised to respect minorities and personally was not a bigot. But such laws represented collective action through the state, something alien to the lessons of his youth. He much preferred individual action, the kind his father took when he refused to permit his sons to see *Birth of a Nation* because "it deals with the Ku Klux Klan against the colored folks and I'm damned if anyone in this family will go see it." Once when Jack Reagan was traveling during the Depression, a hotel clerk assured him, "We don't permit a Jew in the place." Jack Reagan walked out after telling the clerk, "I'm a Catholic, and if it's come to a point where you won't take Jews, you won't take Catholics." He spent the night in his car and became so ill that he later suffered a heart attack.

Government efforts to help the poor, such as the War on Poverty in the 1960s, were considered unnecessary by Reagan, and he was irritated by the way the Kennedy brother-in-law, Sargent Shriver, led the federal anti-poverty program. "I was born in a small town back in the Midwest, and I was in poverty before the rich folks got hold of it," he said. Reagan believed that the poor should work hard and pull themselves up by their bootstraps, as he and his brother did. Welfare rolls, in his view, were full of the lazy. "Because most people believe in reward for productive labor, they voted against giving that reward to those who are able but unwilling to work," he said of his election as governor. His thoughts on assisting the poor and distressed came from his mother, who taught him that 10 percent of what he earned was the Lord's share. After receiving permission from a minister, Reagan sent $10 a month from his first job to his brother in college. Then, "just to gild the lily," he gave ten cents each day to the first man on the street who asked him for coffee.

That sort of generosity was part of Reagan's family's life. Years later in Southern California, his brother found a poor family, gave them food and clothing and a Christmas tree and then wrote a poem to Reagan saying the good deed was Neil's Christmas present to him.

As a political candidate and later as governor, Reagan tried vainly to translate that sort of private generosity to public life. As a candidate he proposed a unique, neighbor-to-neighbor solution to one of California's greatest problems, floods. In one of the worst flood years, 1964, it took a Navy aircraft carrier, helicopters, planes, and twelve hundred airmen, marines and soldiers—all at federal expense—for the rescue operation. Afterward, millions of dollars in low-interest government loans helped rebuild the area. Reagan questioned the federal help. He said he had a better way, taking advantage of the good will of concerned citizens who wanted to help their neighbors. "Suppose," he asked, "it happened next year? What do you think would happen if a governor of California, instead of calling Washington, would get on the radio and television and say to the people of California: 'These are our neighbors, our fellow Californians, this is what they need. I am appointing a citizens committee and shortly you will be told what it is that you can do to help your neighbors.' " In this way, Reagan said, "we could solve the problem and we wouldn't have to set foot across the borders of California and I think everyone in the state would like it better that way." This simple philosophy was also at the heart of Reagan's solutions to the complicated urban problems of the 1960s.

His opponents mocked such ideas. They said government was so big, complex and expensive that it had to be left to experts. "This is your citizen pilot," said Governor Edmund Brown, in a campaign speech parodying Reagan's "citizen politician" slogan. "I've never flown a plane before, but don't worry. I've always had a deep interest in aviation." But once again Reagan's opponents were wrong. Nobody, of course, would entrust his life to an untrained pilot. But Californians did not feel that way about their government. They agreed with Reagan that the professionals had been in charge too long. He came along at a time when people were looking for simpler answers, when they were tired of big government. He assured them that easy answers were available. "We have been told," he said, "that the problems are too complex for simple answers, until gradually we have accepted government by mystery; there seems to have evolved a special kind of government language, incomprehensible to simple citizens like ourselves." Reagan's complaints of rule "by an intellectual elite in a distant capital"—what he called "the puzzle palaces on the Potomac"—rang true to people who were as suspicious as he was of the intellectuals and progressives promising peace and prosperity that never seemed to come. Hoping for simpler answers from an earlier time, they turned to Reagan. He looked and acted like— in fact, he was—the homespun, small-town American boy whom politicians always pretended to be. Although he had lived in Hollywood since 1937, he still talked like the boy from Dixon, Illinois. Told of the complexities of the state's big water project, he said, "It's a little more complicated than laying down by a crick bank and getting a bellyful." He often shook his head in sorrow that his youngest son wasn't being raised in the country.

God, Home and Country—that's what Reagan believes in, and that is what he sells so well on television and before live audiences. To critics, Reagan's philosophy is Babbittry, thoughtless boasting and dangerous oversimplification of problems that can be solved only by cooperation of every talented and expert element of society, including government. But this was an era when the experts had seemingly failed. Thus, when Reagan came along with his message of the virtues of the old values, the voters began to think that maybe folks had the right idea back then in Dixon, Illinois.

4

COLLEGE HERO

Eureka, Illinois, is even smaller than Dixon. Today, as in Reagan's youth, it is a town of less than 3,000 people built around Eureka College, a Disciples of Christ school. Its slogan is "City on the Go —with Young Men on the Go." Old homes, some of them built more than a century ago, are shaded by maple trees. Only five men are on the police force, and there hasn't been a robbery in town for almost a decade. No bars are allowed and no liquor is sold within city limits. It was in this small college community that Dutch Reagan, fulfilling an ambition he had had since he was a teen-ager, enrolled as a freshman in September 1928. Puritan rules governed Eureka, giving a highly moral tone to the school. The young man who grew up to run for public office on a morality platform could not have found a more suitable alma mater.

But in 1928 there was an undercurrent of unrest and rebelliousness against authority at Eureka, and surprisingly Reagan found himself in the middle of it. At seventeen, Reagan did not look like a candidate for student rebel. By now he was approaching one hundred and seventy-five pounds, a handsome, smiling, self-assured young man with horn-rimmed glasses and thick auburn hair parted in the middle. He was neatly dressed and obedient to authority the day he arrived at Eureka, his clothes packed in his new steamer trunk, $400 in lifeguard wages in his savings. There was a scholarship for half of his tuition awaiting him, awarded because of athletic ability, not good grades. His main goal was to make the football team. He had already been pledged to a fraternity, Tau Kappa Epsilon, and he was expecting the same pleasant experience in college that he had had in high school. But he arrived to find morale low on the campus. Signs of unhappiness against the strict rules were evident. Backsliders ignored the no-smoking rule and went across the street between classes for cigarettes, sending up a thick blue haze of smoke into the air. The administration said that girls must be in Lyda's Wood, the women's dormitory, at 9:30 P.M. on weekdays and at midnight on Saturdays, but some girls slipped out for after-hours dates, sticking a pin in the front-door lock so they could get back in, a staggering offense on that disciplined campus.

Elsewhere, it was the Jazz Age, the Roaring Twenties, the time of flaming youth. Movies, novels and lurid newspaper stories told of college students drinking home-made gin, of immorality, of rejection of traditional American standards. But at Eureka, in the ivy-covered brick buildings and at chapel, where attendance was required each day, President Bert Wilson fought the tide. Eureka students who were caught drinking were dismissed. The year before Reagan enrolled, there had been an ugly scene when students defied the ban on dancing at the annual get-acquainted party. One of the rebels was the daughter of the chairman of the board of trustees; another was the chairman's nephew. They were among a group of about eight students who persuaded the orchestra leader to put aside his regular chamber music and play dance music. When the orchestra started, the rebels began to dance. Furious, President Wilson ordered the band to stop playing, led the violators up to the platform, made them sit down as a sign of disgrace and publicly chastised them. Even respectable places off campus were not free from the rules. The president penalized students caught attending the twice-a-week family-night dances at the American Legion Hall, even those who were there with their parents. He took away grade points needed for graduation from some of the students and required others to remain on campus.

Now a spirit of rebellion was on the campus, even though the ban on dancing had been relaxed. An underground movement to force out President Wilson had been started, and some of the faculty had joined it, for the declining economy of the Midwest had forced the already unpopular administration to propose some budget cuts that affected staff as well as students. As Reagan remembered it, the economies were the reason for the strike. Others, however, recalled it differently and said that the real motive was a rebelliousness against the unreasonably strict administration. In a 1967 article for *West* magazine about Reagan's college days, Thomas Driscoll concluded: "No doubt the students seized upon the cutback as the issue they could use to get rid of Wilson and his puritan restrictions. Faculty members were upset by it because it called for combining several departments and eliminating a few others, with the eventual dismissal of six or seven professors and the downgrading of several more. Later, it became clear that a number of professors were actively stirring up the students, working with equal fervor for Wilson's removal."

The tradition at Eureka was that freshmen were supposed to remain silent, and the leadership of the dissenting students was in the hands of the upperclassmen. But as a boy, and as a young man, Dutch Reagan was never one to remain silent. He was audacious, a quality that was not softened with the passing of the years. As a legacy from his Irish shoe salesman father, he inherited brashness and the love of making a speech for a cause. Sometimes the speech was more important than the cause—as in the months following World War II, when Reagan spoke enthusiastically before veterans and labor groups and later found to his amazement that their views were far to the left of his. In Eureka's student rebellion Reagan found his first cause, and he joined with an eagerness that surprised some of his fellow students.

Quick of tongue and eager to help, Reagan was made a freshman representative on the student committee, and when the trustees accepted Wilson's economies, he was among the one hundred and forty-three students who signed a petition asking for the president's resignation. When the trustees refused to act on the petition, the students disobeyed the campus rules and prepared to strike. A strike was contrary to all of the traditions of the little school, but powerful forces were at work. The night the trustees turned down the students, the college bell announced a meeting in the chapel. Faculty and students, some of them roused from bed and wearing coats over their pajamas, crowded into the chapel, which was big enough for only two hundred and fifty people. Eureka graduates from around the town were also there, unhappy with Wilson because of a statement in which he indicated he thought the town was too small to support the college. They also wanted the trustees to demand his resignation.

Speeches were made by student leaders criticizing the administration. Then it was time for Reagan, the freshman representative, to speak. He did not call for a return to law and order or ask the students to protest to the trustees through established channels. Nor did he—as he did as governor—criticize the faculty for supporting the students. Instead he offered a resolution calling for a student strike. He had been asked to introduce the strike motion because the upperclassmen did not want to be accused of having a vested interest in preventing cutbacks they felt might affect their chance to graduate. His motion was adopted unanimously, and when classes resumed, all but a few students stayed away. Professors joined the protest, taking roll and reporting none of the missing students absent. It was complete defiance of the rules. As an adult Reagan liked to give the strike more respectability by recalling how students meticulously continued to study. But as others remembered, the strikers sat on the steps of homes across from the school, smoked cigarettes and engaged in a week-long bull session. "If any studying was done, it was a pretext," said one graduate. Pressure on Wilson grew. Even some of the trustees privately were sympathetic to the students. Finally Wilson submitted his resignation, on December 7. "Other avenues of service are open to me, and a burden will be lifted from my shoulders if tonight I know that I am freed from any further connection with this unfortunate situation," he said. The students met again and accepted their complete victory. With Wilson gone, they graciously said that in view of the "fine spirited statement made last evening by President Wilson . . . we instruct our leaders to withdraw our petition." Now, the students said, they recognized they were dealing with matters that concerned the trustees and did not "presume to dictate what their action shall be in any matters affecting the policy and the program of the school. . . . We love Eureka College." That abruptly put an end to the student unrest.

So out of tune was the revolt with the traditions and thinking at Eureka College that it took two or three years for it to dwindle as a topic of conversation. But life did settle back into a routine, and the strike assumed its place as just another memory of college—a momentary display of youthful spirit. Surprisingly, neither Reagan nor the other participants were to find any resemblance between it and a student rebellion of another day, the 1964 free-speech revolt at the University of California at Berkeley. Reagan drew a distinction between the two student movements. He said that the Eureka strike had the backing of nearly all the faculty, and that made it different from the protest at Berkeley. But when University of California faculty members and students protested his own budget cuts, Reagan said, "It is disturbing to see supposedly mature members of the academic community inciting students to intemperate acts with inflammatory charges." For despite his three-week fling as a student rebel, Reagan learned no lessons from Eureka that would prepare him for his later confrontation with the big and complex system of university and college campuses, a system which drew students from every level of society—some of them questioning, searching rebels and others just as conventional as Reagan was in college. Eureka's puritanical atmosphere did not prepare him for the intellectual ferment, the hippies, the coffeehouses, the interracial couples, the long-haired beardies, the undisciplined demonstrations of the University of California at Berkeley.

Except for those few weeks, the rest of his college life was so typical of a student of that time and place that it could have been used as a plot for a Hollywood college movie of the thirties and forties. The happy college of his youth, in fact, didn't seem too different from the fictitious college Reagan taught at in the fanciful movie of the forties, *Working Her Way Through College.*

Home was the Tau Kappa Epsilon fraternity house. His friends from the fraternity were among his friends later in life. Long after graduation he still corresponded with some of them. When Reagan moved into the Teke house, the kitchen, dining room and living room were crowded into a very small area on the first floor. But once again his eagerness came to the surface, and he and two friends, Enos (Bud) Cole and Elmer Fisher, decided that the house needed a new dining area. They ripped out the old basement so it could be remodeled into a dining room and kitchen. "We mainly tore things down and someone who had the skill put things back," said Cole.

Reagan was an average student, and there are no intellectual triumphs among his memories of college. By his own account, there was not the fierce commitment to scholarly excellence at Eureka that was found at Harvard, Columbia, the University of California, the University of Chicago or others. "The student who was going into pre-law was going to have to work harder for a good grade than I was because the professor knew that all I wanted was a diploma, that there wasn't a chance in the world that the actual subject matter was going to be vital to me, that I would have to remember it, so he wouldn't be as strict with me." He majored in economics, and as in high school, his photographic memory got him through examinations. His extracurricular activities were so extensive that they left little time for studying. Reagan was on the football team. He was also cheerleader during basketball season, president of the student council, active on the yearbook and the student newspaper, the school's best swimmer, and a member of the debate team and the dramatic club. He was elected president of the boosters club three years in a row. As he said later, "I was so busy with these other things that I apportioned only a certain amount of time to study. A C average was required for eligibility for outside activities. I set my goals at maintaining eligibility. I know that wasn't right, but it also made room and time for other things that I think were valuable."

Most important was the football field, flanked by wooden stands where Eureka's team ran out every Saturday for its weekly battles in the "Little 19," a conference of small colleges. "I remember him best as the freshman who stuck with the football squad all fall, although he never even got a first-class jersey. . . . It was difficult not to get one at Eureka," said Howard Short, the manager of the football team. Reagan sulked on the bench through his first year, believing that coach Ralph McKenzie didn't appreciate him. But in the second year, friends commented on his "payday pepper," as he attracted McKenzie's attention in some bruising practices. Early in the year he was elevated to first-string guard next to Pebe Leitch, the right tackle, the team captain and his roommate in the fraternity house. "Dutch was not an outstanding football player, but he was a good plugger, dedicated, put out a lot, had a lot of spirit and desire," said Coach McKenzie.

On fall evenings Reagan, Pebe Leitch, Bud Cole and later Neil Reagan would walk back to the Teke house from football practice, college heroes in an era when life from September through November revolved around the football team. There was the homecoming show every year, when each of the fraternities and sororities put on "stunts" or skits. Reagan was forever ready to give a speech, act in a play, somersault through the air in the acrobatics of a basketball cheerleader or do an imitation of a radio sportscaster in a fraternity skit.

In the winter, now that the restrictions against dancing were lifted, students had a Christmas dance. By Reagan's second year the Depression had hit the parents of most of the Eureka students, and that simplified the campus social life. Reagan would often visit his girl friend, Margaret Cleaver, daughter of a Eureka minister. At night, young men and women without any money would go on dates to the drugstore for a ten-cent cherry phosphate. Sometimes they would dance in the living room of a fraternity house or walk through the walnut orchard in back of the campus. Few had cars, so the lover's lane was a graveyard within walking distance of the campus. At the fraternity house the boys would play pinochle, with the loser required to walk eight or ten blocks downtown to bring back hamburgers and malted milks.

In this idyllic setting Reagan used his activities to develop what was later to become his profession. He became seriously interested in acting. Miss Ellen Marie Johnston taught drama, and under her guidance he became as convincing on the stage as he was when giving a strike speech in the chapel. With others in the small college's drama group, he traveled to Northwestern University for an annual one-act play contest. The Eureka players made the finals in the competition with their performance of *Aria da Campo,* Edna St. Vincent Millay's play about the foolishness of war. They didn't win first prize, but there was a bit of unexpected glory for Reagan, something he would remember when he wondered what to do with his life. He received an individual acting award and bounded out of his seat with a big smile as he hurried toward the stage to receive it. "The fact was, I suppose, that I just liked showing off," he said.

At home, Jack Reagan's Fashion Boot Shop staggered under the Depression and finally went out of business. Reagan had to provide for himself, and in addition to washing dishes at the fraternity, he was the school's swimming coach and teacher and worked in the kitchen of the girls' dormitory. Every Saturday when there wasn't a football game, he and the other hashers would scour the cupboard doors, working their way around the kitchen, giving each door a quick wipe. The housemother followed them, holding a pencil and writing "Brush here" on each of the doors. Inevitably the boys would do them over again.

This was his life at Eureka—content and centered. For the most part he was untouched by the powerful political currents sweeping the nation. Here there was none of the tumult of the big-city campuses. No radicals on soapboxes called for the overthrow of the government. At Eureka the Depression was an economic inconvenience and not a sign of a sick social system. In 1932 Reagan graduated, taking part in the symbolic cutting of the ivy vines—a tradition for Eureka graduates. He left college without prospects of a job, but he was not bitter. Forever the optimist, he was confident that something would turn up.

He was, by the standards of the great universities of today, undereducated. By his own admission he had not taken advantage of even the limited opportunities at Eureka. But even with his minimum college education, Reagan left college with no regrets. He believed then, as now, that he had chosen the correct course in dedicating his energies to activities outside the classroom. There is more to college, he believes, than books. He makes a distinction between knowledge and wisdom. Knowledge is acquaintance with facts. It means expensive and often obscure research conducted in equally expensive facilities. But more than knowledge is needed. "What good is it," he said, "to teach someone all the facts if they don't know how to live and if they don't know the use of them for the solutions of the problems they are going to meet as life goes on?" Young people need wisdom, a virtue that in his view is something else altogether. It is an ability to deal with the world; it is based on experience, good judgment and discretion rather than knowledge of facts. Wisdom comes with growing up. He believes that Eureka gave him wisdom—an ability to continue to learn and grow—even though his academic record was spotty.

Perhaps of everything he learned at Eureka, his ideas on education would most significantly affect his political philosophy. He values folk wisdom, an awareness of the hard-headed practical ways of the world. And the small college of his youth gave better individual care than does the well-equipped big state university. He drew from his own college years a concept of education that made him hostile to big universities, especially to the University of California—committed as it is to intellectual perfection and academic freedom. He was uniquely unsuited to sit on the board of regents of the university, a job he held as governor. His complete conviction of the superiority of his own education prejudiced him against the extremes of freedom of expression on college and university campuses.

In later life he became more of a reader, grasping for the books that he was told to read in college but never did. On his adult list of reading priorities was *The Decline and Fall of the Roman Empire* and other books "of the type of thing they tried to force me to read then, outside reading and those sort of things." But his do-it-yourself education did not make him more sympathetic to the scholars of the state university and colleges. He was ill at ease among them and their students. He liked to lecture college students rather than participate in the give-and-take of ideas. When he addressed them, it was often in the nature of a dramatic confrontation from which someone had to emerge a winner and someone had to leave a loser.

He made visits to his alma mater and received honors from it. He returned in 1947 and was the grand marshal of the annual Pumpkin Parade. A decade later he visited the campus again, stood among the buildings, talked with old friends. On that day he put on an academic gown and walked over the green grass that covered the campus. He now was one of Eureka's most famous sons, a future member of the board of trustees, and he had come back to receive an honorary degree of Doctor of Humane Letters. As usual, his wife, Nancy, watched proudly as he accepted the degree and made a speech in reply. Like his scholarships, the degree was awarded more for outside activities than for intellectual attainment. It was given for "understanding and exposing Communists and their influence" while he was president of the Screen Actors Guild.

In 1967 he came back to Eureka once more on a cold September evening—this time as the conquering hero, Eureka's most prominent graduate. He was governor of California and, more important, a potential candidate for President. He had been invited to dedicate the college's new library, and the student body, the faculty and the townspeople were seated on chairs outside the new building to hear him. On the platform Illinois' most famous Republican politicians were with Reagan, Senator Everett Dirksen and Senator Charles Percy. The band played and the student chorus sang as people in the audience pulled their coats around themselves to keep out the cold.

For Reagan it was an important occasion. He was beginning a tour of three states, and this was to be a showpiece speech, one that would set the tone for a tour that his advisers hoped would start a serious Reagan for President movement. In it he addressed himself to one of his critics' favorite points—that he was out of tune with youth and hostile to education. He began with a joke, a reference to his own undistinguished grades in college: "Ten years ago, in cap and gown, I stood in this place to receive an honorary degree—a happening which only compounded an already heavy burden of guilt. I had always figured the first degree you gave me was honorary." The audience laughed. He went on to say, "As the day nears when classroom and playing field must give way to the larger arena, with its problems of inequality and human misunderstanding, it is easy to look at those in that area [adult life] and demand to know why problems haven't been solved." There was no recognition in this speech that the college students it addressed had already entered into adult life, that college was no longer a peaceful interlude between high school and a job. Students were manning the antiwar protest lines and serving in the civil rights movement. Some would soon leave school to fight in Vietnam or join the Peace Corps. These young people had accepted their responsibilities already, without waiting for the formality of a college diploma. They were participating in the "larger arena" of life.

The silence continued as Reagan rambled through a tortured explanation of why the older generation and the younger generation could not communicate. It was because of "horizontal stratification" —generations talked only to themselves. "This horizontal stratification has led to lateral communication, and it is highly essential that we restore vertical dialogue if not an outright recognition of the naturalness and rightness of a vertical structuring of society." Then he defended the older generation in a tone that was condescending to the students and as hackneyed as anything written in Hollywood by a script writer for a B movie. "That fellow with the thickening waist and the thinning hair who is sometimes unreasonable about your allowance or letting you have the car, his life seems a little dull to you now as he reports for his daily nine-to-five chores or looks forward to lowering a golf handicap or catching a fish no one wants to eat. I wish you could have known him a few years back on a landing craft at Normandy or Tarawa or on a weekend pass in Peoria. He was quite a guy." Reagan spoke in clichés that night, lecturing to an audience he seemed to think was composed of children. At the end there was an automatic bow to the books in the library as he urged the students to read Aristotle, Plato and Socrates, Maimonides and the "man from Galilee."

They listened while he lectured. Parents, he said, have given too much to their children. "We are the classic example of giving to you what we never had . . . from TV to wheels and dental care to Little League. But I am afraid we shortchanged you on responsibilities or the right to earn for yourselves. All too often, because we had to earn, we wanted to give. Our motives have been laudable, but our judgment has been bad. 'No' was either a dirty word or dropped from our vocabulary."

The students stood up and applauded politely when he finished. He might, after all, be the first Eureka graduate to become President. But Dutch Reagan, class of '32, had lost contact with the students of the sixties. His speech had shown the size of the gap between him and his college days and the college generation of the present. He had talked to them as if they were students of the Eureka of his day, when the drama club and football team were more important than studies and the world outside the campus.

5

HOLLYWOOD

Almost every afternoon between April and September in the mid-thirties, Reagan sat behind a desk in a six-by-eight studio on the first floor of radio station WHO, the National Broadcasting Company's affiliate in Des Moines, Iowa. In front of him was a big square microphone with the call letters—the *H* flanked by flashes of lightning—printed on the sides. Reagan, his hair still parted in the middle and combed back in the pompadour style of the times, waited impatiently for a Western Union operator in the next room, visible through a big window, to hand him a piece of paper through a slot. On the paper was written a brief description of the action in a Chicago Cubs or White Sox baseball game that was being played more than a hundred miles away. "Hartnett singles to right," might be typed on the paper, the bare outline of an exciting moment at Wrigley Field, and it was up to Reagan to reconstruct from this a vivid word picture of what was happening at the ball park. He had already described the pitcher, looking toward first, winding up and throwing the ball. All he had to work with was one brief sentence. From his imagination he filled in the rest.

The engineer, who also read the message, cracked a small bat on a piece of wood, imitating the sharp sound of Gabby Hartnett's bat hitting the baseball, and then turned up the volume of a phonograph record of crowd noises so it sounded like the thousands who were yelling at Wrigley Field. At the crack of the bat Reagan would tell how Hartnett scrambled down the first-base line, describing the chagrin of the opposing pitcher. His voice would rise in excitement as he told—still from his imagination—how the right fielder threw the ball back into the infield and Hartnett wisely held up at first base. Then Reagan would picture how the opposing manager walked out to the mound, held a worried conversation with the pitcher and returned to the dugout. Finally the Western Union operator would begin typing out another message he was receiving from Chicago, and Reagan would have the pitcher go into his stretch again, faking the action until he was handed news of the latest play. Some of those who heard Reagan "re-create" these games still recall his performances. "You would think from hearing those ball games you were sitting in Wrigley Field," said Republican Congressman H. R. Gross of Iowa, then WHO's top newscaster.

In this WHO studio, on the edge of downtown Des Moines, Reagan began the training that would eventually take him to Hollywood. Before television, major-league baseball was brought to most of the nation by talkative men who read Western Union's fragmented accounts of a game being played many miles away and re-created the action. This is how Reagan perfected his speaking ability and learned how to sell soap, cars and major-league baseball by the power of his voice.

Reagan was one of the best play-by-play men in the Midwest, a nonstop talker who was so garrulous that he wasn't even flustered when the wire occasionally broke down and he had to improvise until service was restored. Once when the wire failed in the middle of a game and Reagan was ad-libbing until it was repaired, the station manager ran downstairs from his office, looked into the studio and yelled, "When the hell are you going to get the game on?" Reagan signaled that the profanity was going over the airwaves and continued talking.

His success in the college play contest at Northwestern had stirred his ambitions to become an actor, and that led him into radio. Without prospects of a job following graduation, he returned to Dixon in the middle of the Depression for a final summer as lifeguard at Lowell Park. "After college, he didn't know what he wanted to do, not really," said his wife, Nancy, who has heard the story of his youth many times. "Becoming a sports announcer was not the career that he set out to follow. That just kind of happened." Radio was part of show business, an important part in small towns such as Dixon, and when the summer ended Reagan tried for a job in it. The big stations in Chicago, WBBM, WGN and the rest, turned him down, but he was advised to visit the smaller outlying stations. Most of his classmates, hoping for careers in more conventional fields, were unemployed, but Reagan, who has always been able to find work, was hired on his first stop. Peter MacArthur, the program manager of WOC of Davenport, Iowa, put him to work part-time to broadcast the remaining four University of Iowa football games. He was paid only $5 for the first game, between Iowa and the University of Minnesota, and $10 each for the remaining three.

By the beginning of 1933 he became a full-time staff announcer at $100 a month. In April he was shifted to WHO in Des Moines. This was the golden age of radio, and Dutch Reagan was a leading announcer at WHO, NBC's 50,000-watt prize in the area, a clear channel station that could be heard in Iowa, Missouri, Minnesota and the western Illinois country, where Reagan grew up. Besides re-creating baseball games, he covered track meets and football games. He also interviewed people outside the sports world, among them Aimee Semple McPherson, the evangelist, and Leslie Howard, the actor. On occasional Saturday nights he announced the station's big three-hour barn dance program in Shrine Auditorium, a country music show that was as popular as the WLS *Barn Dance* in Chicago, one of the most famous Midwestern country music shows of the era. Reagan's brother Neil, who was also with WHO, remembered that at one time "we had ninety-five hillbillies on the staff." Dutch also wrote a sports column for a newspaper that was published briefly, and during football season when Iowa was playing away from home, he handled the public address system for the Drake University football games.

Gross, the newscaster, remembers that even in those days Reagan loved to give speeches. So popular was he in WHO's big listening area that the station often sent him to talk to high school father-and-son banquets or before clubs. Gross, who also liked to make speeches and often accompanied him, recalls that Reagan, as he did in his later political talks, ended his speeches with a strong morality plea. "He would tell sports stories," said Gross, "plus some solid morality—

urging his audiences to stay away from drink, cigarettes and cheating."

Reagan lived in an apartment near the nurses' quarters for Broadlawn General Hospital. One night he broke up a robbery. "I heard a girl on the walk outside my window say, 'That's all the money I have.' I looked down and saw a guy poking a gun at her." Reagan had three guns in his room, but all were empty. But he pointed an empty gun out the window and yelled, "I have a forty-five in my hand, and I'm going to let you have it. Get going." The bandit ran away and Reagan put on his robe and escorted the girl back to the nurses' quarters. "I was shaking all over, and she wasn't even scared," Reagan said. "Just kept saying, 'To think, a little squirt like that trying to hold me up.' "

Neil Reagan said his brother was "probably the best on the staff" of the station. Neil was in advertising for many years, retiring as vice president of the McCann-Erickson agency in Los Angeles. One day he was asked to assess, as an advertising man and not as a brother, the single quality that Reagan showed in those days that was to make him successful in radio, films and later politics. "I would say it in one word. It is what you strive for in directing any dramatic show— credibility as far as the audience is concerned. If you have that, you don't have to worry about anything."

"I was doing pretty well in the sports announcing thing," Reagan recalled. "All the dreams down deep of being an actor had died." But in 1937 one of the hillbilly bands at the station stirred up the dreams again by signing a contract to appear in a Gene Autry movie. It was Autry's custom to hire for each film a country music band from a major section such as WHO, and when the movie played in the area, the local musicians would guarantee a large audience. The same year, Reagan accompanied the Chicago Cubs to Southern California for spring training on Catalina Island, which was owned by the same Wrigley family that operated the baseball team. "Suddenly the whole thing awoke," said Reagan. "It seemed more possible. I visited WHO's Western band on the set." Their agent, also a friend from Des Moines, arranged for Reagan to read for a casting director in Hollywood, who offered him no hope. He had lunch with another friend from Des Moines, Joy Hodges, a singer, who was more helpful. First she suggested that he remove his glasses in front of the camera, and then she introduced him to an agent, Bill Meiklejohn.

Reagan and Meiklejohn talked for a while, and then the agent called Warner Bros. and asked for Max Arnow, the casting director. "I have another Robert Taylor in my office," said Meiklejohn. Warners gave Reagan a screen test and was impressed enough to offer him a contract. Reagan had already left for the East with the Cubs, and when he arrived home, the news was awaiting him. "I thought I'd probably hear from the test by Thursday," he said. "When no word came I thought, Aren't they ever going to tell me I didn't make it? I was nervous as could be, but I couldn't explain why to those who asked me because I hadn't said anything about the test." Friday he received the telegram saying: SCREEN TEST OKAY. MAILING $200 A WEEK CONTRACT. Reagan leaped into the air and whooped with joy. "I didn't read the rest of the telegram until that night."

Joy Hodges jubilantly wired back to the Des Moines *Register* and *Tribune:* MAYBE SCOOP YOU DO HAVE POTENTIAL STAR IN YOUR MIDST DUTCH REAGAN LOCAL SPORTS ANNOUNCER SIGNED LONG TERM WARNER BROS CONTRACT FRIDAY THEY CONSIDER HIM GREATEST BET SINCE TAYLOR WITHOUT GLASSES I DON'T MIND TAKING SOME CREDIT MY OWN IDEA AND EFFORTS HIS TALENT CINCHED IT HOWEVER. The contract was important news in Des Moines, and the *Register* and *Tribune* recorded the event in a long story. Reagan told the paper, "I'd rather act than anything else. But I didn't think anyone would go home and give their husband arsenic after seeing me, so I turned to radio as a second choice." His contract guaranteed him six months' work at Warners, with options to extend it running over a seven-year period. "I may be out there for only six months," he said. "Of course I hope it doesn't turn out that way— but you never can tell." He added, "I've never had a thrill like this before. I'll admit it's got my head spinning like a top."

Despite Meiklejohn's enthusiasm, Reagan was no Robert Taylor. In his show-business career, which lasted until January 1966, when he formally announced he was running for governor, Reagan would never be a great movie star, a first-ranking personality like Taylor, Gary Cooper, Clark Gable or Errol Flynn. But given a good role, he was a believable actor, one who worked hard at his craft. He improved slowly over the years and did not fritter away his limited talents by dissipating, as so many of his colleagues did. Untemperamental and easygoing, he followed the advice of those more experienced, and as a result developed strong friendships with producers and with influential columnists such as Hedda Hopper. In many of his roles Reagan was a victim of the poorly written movies ground out by Hollywood's film factories in the thirties, forties and fifties by inept writers, directors and producers. The major studios owned their own theaters in those days and produced more than six hundred pictures a year for a receptive market, which did not face the competition of television. Most of the films were mediocre at best, and too often a success that should have boosted Reagan to stardom was followed by a disaster over which he had no control. In 1939 he was thoroughly convincing in his role in *Knute Rockne—All American,* an early success. But soon after, he was cast in a film appropriately called *The Bad Man* and found himself caught between two of Hollywood's most famous hams, Wallace Beery and Lionel Barrymore. "Sheer nickelodeon," said the reviewer for *Scribners Magazine.* "It is as crude and primitive as anything I saw in the old five-cent silent days in Bloomfield, Illinois, when I was a child in curls and pinafores." The reviewer for *Time* pinpointed Reagan's dilemma: "Both dialogue and action . . . are resolved into a prolonged contest between the stallion snorts of actor Beery and the crosspatch snuffles of actor Barrymore." As for the others, including Reagan, they "seem to walk through their parts in a mechanical daze."

Reagan treated his screen career with unusual objectivity. "He was never fooled by his publicity," said Taft Schreiber, who, as head of Music Corporation of America's Revue Productions, later brought Reagan into television. "The motion picture business was just a part of his evolution, as was radio before." Movies were never an art form to Reagan. Like Schreiber, he referred to movies as "the picture business" and there was always a heavy emphasis on the business end of it. When television came in, many of his more famous colleagues, out of work in the declining motion picture industry, were too proud to go on the new medium. But Reagan willingly switched as public tastes changed.

Personally he was, as he liked to confess when he was older, "a square." "He wasn't a night-club kid," said Robert Taylor. "When I first met him, he was vitally interested in athletics and keeping himself in great condition." He lived simply in an apartment, drove the convertible he brought out with him from Iowa and owned only four suits. Flynn, Bogart and other Warner players caroused at night, and Reagan occasionally joined the social life of Hollywood. But he also found time to make a speech to the San Fernando YMCA in those early days on "clean sportsmanship, health rules and the importance of team play." His home life was important to him. After his first movie he brought his parents to California, and Neil followed a year or so later. By 1939 he was ready for marriage, and that year he became engaged to Jane Wyman, twenty-four, an actress who had been divorced the year before from Myron Futterman, a manufacturer. They met while working on a picture, and she said at the time, "It was love at first sight." They were married on January 26, 1940, at the Wee Kirk o' Heather, a popular Hollywood wedding chapel, and then went on a short honeymoon to Palm Springs.

Hollywood, recalled Schreiber, was filled with all kinds of stars, but "talk to any actor," said Schreiber, "and all he can talk about is his box office." Reagan was a man apart with many other interests —horses, politics, sports. "He was knowledgeable," Schreiber went on. "He could carry on a conversation beyond acting—football, FDR; he was a totally interested man." He had another quality that endeared him to Schreiber and others at MCA: "He only had this one agency. This was it. It wasn't the agent's fault if things didn't go well. Most actors blamed their agents. He understood. He had a very sound grasp of the situation."

On the screen there was a certain sameness to his performances. As Schreiber saw it, there were two types of actors in Hollywood. Some had "screen magic that somehow on celluloid jumped out at the audience." Reagan was not that type. "He was not a Clark Gable," said Schreiber. Reagan developed slowly; as Schreiber said, "By the time he was doing great roles, he was doing a good job." His career, said his wife, Nancy, "wasn't a sudden skyrocketing that is followed as often by a sudden decline. It was a nice steady line." While not spectacular, he had staying power. Jeffrey Lynn, John Hodiak, Jon Hall and other young men who were more promising than Reagan in those days faded from major stardom, but Reagan continued as a leading actor.

His first movie at Warners in 1937 was a quickie that was noted briefly in a story in the Los Angeles *Times:* "A departure in the exploitation of talent is to be accomplished by Warner Brothers when that studio films a new subject called *Inside Story.* It seems this organization is to experiment with a radio sports announcer and news writer, one Ronald Reagan from Des Moines, Iowa, who will have the lead opposite June Travis." The movie was eventually called *Love Is on the Air,* and like some of his other early movies, it has disappeared into the vaults of Hollywood, so poorly done it has never been shown on television.

His parents were proud when they saw the movie in a special screening in Des Moines which was covered by the *Register* and the *Tribune*. The paper's reporter noted that his mother wiped away her tears with a lace-trimmed handkerchief as she watched him on the screen. "That's my boy," she said. "That's my Dutch." She added, "That's the way he is at home. He's just as natural as can be. He's no Robert Taylor. He's just himself." His father commented, "He doesn't change. He'll always be the same."

He made more than twenty B pictures during the early years of his career under his producer, Byrnie Foy, who was the eldest of the seven little Foys in the vaudeville act. In 1940 his break came when he persuaded Warners to give him his first good role, that of Gipp in the Rockne movie. He had wanted to do a film about the football hero since first going to work at Warners and had even considered writing it himself. He asked his colleagues how to write a screenplay. Some of Warners' writers liked his idea, handed in the story themselves and sold the studio on it. Reagan soon heard that the film not only was written but was being cast. When he asked the producer for the Gipp part, he was rejected on the grounds that he didn't look like a football player. Reagan protested that he had played the game and, as a matter of fact, looked more like a football player than the slouching Gipp. The producer still refused. Realizing that the man didn't believe anything until he saw it on film, Reagan went home and dug out a picture of himself in a Eureka football uniform. He got the part. The film was really about Rockne, the Notre Dame football coach, who was played by Pat O'Brien. Gipp died of pneumonia early in the picture, but his memory lived on because of a deathbed request he made of Rockne—that when Notre Dame was behind one day, he would ask the boys "to win one for the Gipper." Reagan played the Gipper as if he were Dutch Reagan at Eureka. Although George Gipp in real life was an undisciplined athlete who ignored the lessons of Reagan's YMCA lecture, Reagan portrayed him as a courteous, soft-spoken young man. In the film Gipper visited Rockne's home and talked over his troubles with the coach and his wife, just as Dutch Reagan used to visit faculty members' homes on cold Eureka evenings. As a result, Reagan gave one of his better performances.

The critics were not enthusiastic about the film, but they praised

Reagan. He remarked that the role "was the springboard which bounced me into a wider variety of parts in pictures. Before that I always played a jet-propelled newspaperman who solved more crimes than a lie detector." So convincing was he that he was chosen in the 1940–41 exhibitor's poll as one of the five "Stars of Tomorrow," the young players most likely to emerge from the season as successes.

In 1941 Reagan gave the best performance of his career in the movie that made him a star, *Kings Row*. In it he played Drake McCugh, the town sport. McCugh was injured in an accident and came under the care of Dr. Gordon, who disapproved of McCugh because he was dating his daughter. To punish McCugh, Gordon amputated his legs, and when the young man awoke, he looked down at his body and cried, "Where's the rest of me?," the line that provided Reagan with the title for his autobiography. Reviewers praised the whole cast, as well as Reagan. *Commonweal* called it a "splendid performance." *The New Yorker* said that the film will "give you that rare glow which comes from seeing a job crisply done, competently and with confidence." The picture was a success, Reagan's salary at Warners was tripled and a columnist for the Los Angeles *Times* reported that only Errol Flynn received more fan mail than Reagan at the studio. "It will behoove Warners to set about getting good roles for Mr. Reagan from this point on," the columnist said. "Incidentally, it should be remarked that his is an instance that should be of benefit to the psychology of younger players who figure they ought to soar right to the top. It took Reagan plenty of time to hit the pace that counted."

When he entered politics, his opponents would mock his ability as an actor, but critics throughout his career were often kinder. When he played a wartime serviceman in *Voice of the Turtle* in 1947, *Newsweek,* sharing the opinion of other reviewers, called his portrayal "sensitive." Bosley Crowther of the New York *Times* was generally unimpressed with the 1949 comedy *John Loves Mary,* but he said Reagan's performance in it had "dignity." *The Girl from Jones Beach* was a 1949 piece of fluff, but Richard L. Coe of the Washington *Post* said Reagan made his role "as painless as he can." Crowther admired him in it as "a fellow who has a cheerful way of looking at dames," and said he was "thoroughly capable of getting the most that is to be had out of the major comedy encounters that develop in the film." Some reviewers, such as Howard Barnes of the *Herald Tribune,* panned him: "Reagan's acting is so casual that it seems like mere improvisation for much of the time." But generally, when he was given good material, he would turn in a professional performance. He was working steadily, and in 1946 and 1948 he earned over $150,000 a year. While never a great actor, he was far from a failure.

In 1941, with *Kings Row* a popular success, his career once again slowed down—this time because of World War II. Lew Wasserman, his MCA agent and today one of the Democratic party's major financial contributors, negotiated another raise from Warners just before Reagan, a reserve second lieutenant in the cavalry, was ordered to active duty. On April 19, 1942, Reagan said good-bye to his wife and their infant daughter, Maureen, boarded a train at the Glendale station for San Francisco, where he reported for a month's duty at Fort Mason, and then was shifted back to Hollywood, where he spent the rest of the war. Reagan was one of the stars ordered into the "Culver City Commandoes," the First Motion Picture Unit of the Army Air Force, which harnessed the technology that produced *Hell's Angels, Dawn Patrol* and other airplane films to make training and combat movies for the Air Force and produce morale-boosting pictures for the home front. Reagan, George Montgomery, Arthur Kennedy, Clark Gable, Alan Ladd, Craig Stevens and Van Heflin were some of the actors who served among the thousand men in the unit. Most were skilled film technicians, brought together by the Air Force after the phenomenal success of two animated recruiting pictures, *Win Your Wings* and *Beyond the Line of Duty.* A half-million Air Force volunteers had written on their questionnaires that they had been persuaded to enlist by one or both of the films. So impressed was the Air Force that the unit was established. Like most of the unit, Reagan had two jobs—he was personnel officer and narrator for training films. For a while he was detached to play in the film *This Is the Army.*

The unit's first headquarters was the old Vitagraph studio, but in the fall of 1942 the men shifted to the nine-acre Hal Roach Studio in Culver City. Barracks and a mess hall were built, but it still was a most unmilitary post, called Fort Roach or Fort Wacky by the rest of Hollywood because of the way the stars chafed under military discipline. Reagan, on duty all night, filed a report to the commanding officer, stunt pilot Paul Mantz, which said of the post: "Very poor place to make pictures. Recommend entire post be transferred as near to 42nd Street and Broadway as possible. Also suggest several

Westerns be made to round out the program." Under irregularities and disturbances Reagan wrote: "3 A.M.—post attacked by three regiments of Japanese infantry. Led cavalry charge and repulsed enemy. Quiet resumed." One afternoon after a military-minded officer had marched the Hollywood soldiers four abreast to the flag-pole, Reagan, who was watching, shouted, "Splendid body of men. With half this many, I could conquer M-G-M." General H. H. Arnold, the Air Force chief, saw a studio gag film put together from all the mistakes made during the year and asked the unit to make him one for a party in the Pentagon. Reagan played a general, with a cigar in his mouth, briefing a bomber squadron. As he pointed to the target, the map rolled up, uncovering a pretty girl.

The unit, however, did work the Air Force considered vital. Reagan was the narrator for one of its most difficult projects, *Target Tokyo*. It was a training film to prepare the pilots of B-29 superfortresses for the fire-bombing raids on Japan. Special-effects men went to Washington and studied the landmarks the pilots would follow from Saipan to the target of Ota, the site of a plant producing new fighter planes. The files in Washington, along with newspaper photographs, travel brochures and books, provided the details for a ninety-by-ninety scale model of the route to Ota, built of cheesecloth, plaster, matchsticks and piano wire. Above the model was a camera crane, and the camera moved over the set as if it were a B-29 on a bomb run. Reagan, playing the briefing officer, described the route, and to the pilots watching it on Saipan months later, it gave an invaluable glimpse of what faced them.

The unit made the classic film about a flying fortress, William Wyler's *The Memphis Belle*. That was one of the best-known Fort Roach productions, but just as valuable were briefer films about B-17s. Midway through the war, absenteeism hit the Boeing plant at Seattle, Washington, where the B-17s were made. The First Motion Picture Unit made two ten-minute films, which were shown with the newsreels at civilian theaters, telling how the planes from Seattle were helping win the war, and soon absenteeism decreased. Secretary of War Henry Stimson, concerned over the failure of women to volunteer for work in Connecticut Valley ball-bearing plants, asked the unit to make a civilian recruiting film for the area. Other home front films urged women to become bus drivers and asked Americans to open their homes to war workers who couldn't find housing.

The First was often called in for emergency situations at the war front. Pilots were afraid the extra gas tank on the speedy new P-38 lightning fighter plane would explode in flames if hit by enemy bullets. The unit's film convinced the pilots that the plane was safe. Flying and ground crews discovered that the American P-40 fighter and the Japanese Zero looked practically alike at 1,000-yard distances, and American crews were shooting down their own planes by mistake. When a Zero was captured, it was brought to San Diego and flown side by side with a P-40. Film-unit crews filmed the planes from all angles, showing how to tell them apart, and the prints were rushed to the South Pacific to clear up the confusion.

As part of the unit, Reagan performed a useful job, but later on he magnified it into one of his qualifications for the governorship. When his experience was questioned, he would reply that he had served in World War II as adjutant of an Air Force base. Never did he explain that the base was located in the film community, within driving distance of his home.

By 1945 the war was nearing an end. The final months of the war brought two developments that would have a profound effect on Reagan's thinking. One was the personnel situation at Fort Roach, where Reagan was growing restive under the government's command. Civilian workers had been ordered to serve at the post, which was chronically understaffed with servicemen, and Reagan was unhappy with federal regulations that prevented him, as personnel officer and adjutant, from firing the incompetent or unneeded ones. Another development was the troubled Hollywood labor conditions of the postwar period. Two powerful union groups—the Conference of Studio Unions and the International Alliance of Theatrical Stage Employees—were fighting for control of the studio workers, and Reagan's union, the Screen Actors Guild, was trying to help settle the dispute. Reagan would re-join the board of the Screen Actors Guild after his discharge on September 12, 1945, and become one of the union's most vocal leaders.

He was thirty-four years old and ready to move on to another stage in his life. The movie career, which had seemed important when he was twenty-six, now did not satisfy him. The union soon occupied much of his life. His career suffered and his marriage failed. But in the end he would find a new career, more promising than the one he had begun at Warner Bros. less than a decade before.

6

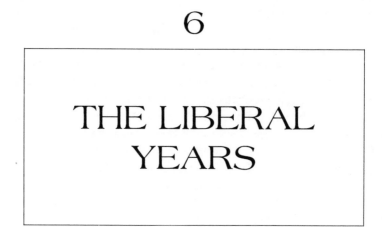

THE LIBERAL
YEARS

Ronald Reagan—like a man sheepishly confessing a boyhood indiscretion—enjoyed recalling his youthful days as a "bleeding-heart liberal." He often told a story of how he joined left-wing organizations after World War II and learned, almost too late, that he had been duped. It was a convincing confessional to his conservative audiences of later years. They loved him even more for his frank admission of early mistakes. The story, however, was an exaggeration. Reagan was a Democrat; he was a union leader. But never, by the standards of postwar Hollywood, was he a militant participant in the liberal causes of the time.

In 1947 five hundred members of Hollywood's liberal community rose to protest against the House Un-American Activities Committee investigation into Communism in Hollywood. Reagan was not among them. Reflecting a liberal view, the "Talk of the Town" section of *The New Yorker* said: "If the producers in Hollywood are sincere in their belief in America, they need not worry about Communists. All they need to do is make a good picture. A movie man who has made a good picture, a newspaper publisher who has put out a good issue, can walk through aisles of Communists on his way to work in the morning and when he sits down the chair will feel solid under him and the room will not go round and round." Reagan, however, was worried about Communism. He supported the committee investigation and appeared as a friendly witness. He also favored the blacklist imposed by the producers on writers who refused to testify. As a union leader, Reagan led the Screen Actors Guild across picket lines to keep the studios running in the face of a strike by a union that he considered Communist-dominated.

It is a fact that Reagan flirted briefly with an organization that was later accused of being a Communist front. But he scurried out of it as soon as he was informed of its leftist orientation and his joining seems born more of naïveté than true belief. This was just months after the long war in which the Soviet Union had been the United States' ally. For years everyone had loved the Russians. Children sent their dimes to help Russian refugees. Public schools taught Russian history. Even the conservative boss of Reagan's studio, Jack Warner, had made a movie friendly to Russia during the war— *Mission to Moscow.* When criticized for the film afterward, Warner replied, "This picture was made when our country was fighting for its existence, with Russia one of our allies. It was made to fulfill the same wartime purposes for which we made such pictures as *Air Force, This Is the Army, Objective Burma, Destination Tokyo, Action in the North Atlantic* and many more."

Politically unsophisticated, Reagan returned to a civilian life full of the idealism generated by the war. He eagerly joined organizations that advertised the humanitarian goals of preserving world peace, ending poverty and opposing such postwar exponents of racism as Gerald L. K. Smith. Like many veterans, Reagan worried about the danger of Nazism in postwar America.

There is no doubt that he was more liberal in his younger years than he is now. As a young man he had been committed to Franklin D. Roosevelt, whose New Deal had given his father a job and who was the nation's Commander in Chief during the war. But it was a personal and emotional loyalty, and Reagan said he thought little about the social programs Roosevelt advocated. When Roosevelt died in 1945, Reagan recalls he was left without political roots. He supported Democrat Harry S. Truman for President in 1948, choosing Truman's Fair Deal domestic program over the Republican alternative offered by Thomas E. Dewey. He campaigned for Helen Gahagan Douglas, a liberal Democrat who lost to Richard M. Nixon in California's United States Senate race in 1950.

But beneath the surface there was a strong conservative streak, the legacy of Reagan's Midwest boyhood. His support of Truman, for example, was not the act of extreme liberalism. That was the year the most ardent liberals bolted the Democratic party and worked for the Progressive party candidate, Henry A. Wallace, a critic of President Truman's strong stand against Communist aggression in Europe. "Progressives want a genuine two-party country and not a country operated by a fake one-party system under the guise of a bipartisan bloc," said Wallace, the former Vice President of the United States. Praising Truman for his anti-Communist stand, Reagan remained with the Democratic party. Two months before the election of 1948, Reagan sounded like a sedate businessman when he told the Rotary Club in Los Angeles how his union fought the Communists. "We are for the free-enterprise system," he said. Then, in words that would not be out of place in a Reagan campaign speech almost two decades later, he added, "We are against statism. We have fought our little Red brothers all along the line."

His later opponents would have done well to study his record in those postwar years, for it shows him to have been a knowledgeable and articulate spokesman for his point of view. He was in the middle of day-to-day battles and testified at length before congressional committees. His basic political instincts were sharpened during this period, and he emerged from it a battle-hardened and polished advocate of the conservative cause.

Reagan's first taste of Hollywood politics had come in 1938 when he was a reluctant recruit for the Screen Actors Guild. The young man from the Midwest had seen no need for unions when he came to Hollywood, but an actress, Helen Broderick, persuaded him that the guild was needed to improve the salaries and working conditions of the screen players. The union was unique. It was organized and later run by rich men and women, the actors and actresses who sometimes made more than $100,000 a year. These wealthy people set the tone for the union, and as a result it has always been conservative. Unlike the auto workers, the miners, the steelworkers or other unions, the guild did not campaign for Democratic candidates. It couldn't. Too many of its leaders and members were conservative Republicans. Among its past presidents are United States Senator George Murphy, who has been active for years in Republican politics, and Robert Montgomery, who was the television adviser to Republican President Eisenhower.

The guild's main interest was bread-and-butter issues. It was formed in March of 1933 when producers forced contract players to take a 50 percent pay cut from their $15-a-day pay and free-lancers to accept a 20 percent reduction. There was no overtime or premium pay for holidays, and an actor who was promised pay for nine days of work often found that those days were stretched over many weeks. The guild was incorporated on June 30, 1933, and by the time the first meeting was held on July 12, such well-established stars as Alan Mowbray, James and Lucille Gleason, Leon Ames and Boris Karloff had joined. Other prominent actors soon followed. Among them were Robert Montgomery, Groucho Marx, Ralph Bellamy, George Raft, Chester Morris, Fredric March, Gary Cooper, Spencer Tracy, Miriam Hopkins, Paul Muni, James Cagney and Eddie Cantor. "I am not here because of what I can do for myself, but to see what I can do for the little fellow who has never been protected and who can't do anything for himself," said Cantor at one of the first meetings.

Reagan became active quickly. He was appointed to the board of directors to fill a vacancy in the young contract player category, and when he attended his first board meeting, any doubts he had about joining a union were dispelled. Seated there were the stars with the greatest prestige—the men and women Reagan looked up to, whose example he wanted to follow. Being in the same room with them was an impressive experience for the young man. At first he sat and watched the senior leaders of the union who were in the middle of the fight to rid Hollywood unions of hoodlum influence.

At the center of the controversy were two union leaders, George Browne and Willie Bioff. Browne was president of the International Alliance of Theatrical Stage Employees, which represented everyone from movie projectionists to stagehands. Bioff was his personal representative. These two men, who controlled most of the studio workers, were accused of extortion by the federal government in 1941. They were charged with taking more than $550,000 from five major studios under a threat of "you pay us or we'll break your business." They were convicted and sent to prison. The fight against Bioff and Browne began long before the trial, and in 1939 the guild withdrew from the AFL's Central Labor Council in Los Angeles because, according to *Daily Variety*, the actors objected to the support that council leaders gave to Bioff. Bioff was resisting extradition to Illinois, where he still had time to serve on an old six-month jail sentence for pandering in Chicago. "For some time, it has been apparent to the Screen Actors Guild that the officers and controlling faction of the Los Angeles Central Labor Council have not conducted affairs along the lines of democratic, honest unionism," said Kenneth Thomson, the guild's executive secretary. The action was supported unanimously by the board of directors.

In 1941 the long fight over hoodlum control of the unions resulted in a development that was to cause even more bitter labor troubles after the war. A union leader who had opposed Browne and Bioff, Herbert Sorrell of the painters union, formed the Conference of Studio Unions. This was the beginning of the fight between the conference and the alliance. It would have been easy for the movie labor force to take sides if it were a simple choice between a gangster-dominated union and an honest one. But by the end of World War II the picture was hopelessly confused. Sorrell himself provided much of the controversy. He was, remembered an acquaintance, about five feet eleven inches tall, with "a busted nose and cauliflow-ered ears. . . . I think he told me he used to be a heavyweight boxer at one time." Even before he formed the conference, Sorrell had been praised for his opposition to the extortionists, Bioff and Browne. It took courage to oppose those two in the late 1930s when their power was almost unchallenged. "Sorrell let Bioff know that this town would not be big enough for both of them if Willie tried any monkey-shines," the trade newspaper *Variety* said in an editorial on Decem-ber 18, 1939. But years later the California legislature's Joint Fact-Finding Committee on Un-American Activities was to say in an official report filed with the legislature: "Herbert K. Sorrell is a secret member of the Communist Party. The Conference of Studio Unions, headed by Sorrell, on strike for over a year, is Communist dominated, inspired and directed for the purpose of capturing the American Federation of Labor unions in the motion picture indus-try." Sorrell denied the charge and told the United States House Education and Labor Subcommittee in 1948: "I am not now nor ever have been a member of the Communist Party."

By the end of World War II the International Alliance, now rid of Brown and Bioff, and Sorrell's Conference of Studio Unions were locked in a struggle for control of the studio work force. The alli-ance's new Hollywood boss was Roy Brewer. He and Sorrell were implacable foes and this complicated the situation. In March 1945 the conference, a coalition of painters, janitors, machinists, guards, office workers and others, called a strike when it was denied jurisdiction over seventy-seven set decorators' jobs. It was a violent strike. The International Alliance, which also controlled many studio jobs, claimed jurisdiction over the set decorators, too. The alliance sent its workers through the conference's picket lines, supplying the manpower to keep the studios operating. Pickets fought with other employees at the Warner lot. Bricks were thrown, cars overturned and men injured. The conference charged that the alliance was corrupt and too friendly with the producers. The alliance replied that the conference was dominated by Communists.

In October 1945, less than a month after Reagan was discharged, the guild pulled its members off work because it feared they would be injured by crossing the Conference of Studio Union picket lines. Twenty days later the strike was temporarily settled. But in July 1946 the dispute over control of the set designers resumed again. This time Reagan took an active role in the Screen Actors Guild's efforts to end the strike, which lasted only two days. As he later told the House Education and Labor Subcommittee:

"We again found ourselves with the prospect of actors that were going to be unemployed by reason of the slowdown in production. . . . I suggested that it was about time we forget all the rules and regulations and red tape and go back to the town hall meeting idea, that the guild take the lead and try to get all the leading parties to sit down at a table in one room and hammer this out . . . instead of talking through the newspapers. If we couldn't succeed, we would at least know which side or what individuals had failed to cooperate, which was more than we had been able to learn up to then. We formed this committee, and as testified here, it was largely as a result of this committee the meeting in Beverly Hills was called and the strike was settled."

Despite Reagan's optimism, this settlement was only temporary. Under the Treaty of Beverly Hills, neither union was given final control of the set decorators. Negotiations were merely postponed. Differences became deeper. In August 1946 an AFL arbitration board issued a new ruling. Sorrell interpreted it to mean that the Conference of Studio Unions was given jurisdiction over the set decorators. In September he pulled his men out again—maintaining that they were striking over more than the control of the set decorators. Wages and hours were involved, Sorrell said. Brewer of the International Alliance called it a jurisdictional strike and supplied men to take over the jobs vacated by the conference strikers. The guild tried once again to arrange a settlement, but failed. Finally, as Reagan recalled later, "We decided we had done everything we could do, and on that basis we decided that it was a jurisdictional strike, and we so reported to the membership." On October 2 the guild voted 2,748 to 509 to cross Sorrell's picket lines and join the International Alliance in keeping the studios going.

Reagan later said that he was threatened with disfigurement if he gave to the guild a report that was favorable to the International Alliance. Testifying in a 1954 lawsuit that grew out of the old labor troubles, Reagan said, "I was out on location in the country when I was called to the telephone at an oil station. I was told that if I made the report a squad was ready to take care of me and fix my face so I would never be in pictures again." For a time, police guarded his home and he carried a gun. During this period he was one of several actors preparing to board a bus that would take them across the picket lines. Just before they climbed aboard, the bus was bombed and burned.

The Screen Actors Guild leaders made another attempt to settle the strike by traveling to Chicago to the AFL convention to ask for a resolution to set up permanent arbitration machinery in the motion picture industry to settle future labor disputes. Reagan, Jane Wyman, Walter Pidgeon, Dick Powell, Alexis Smith, Gene Kelly, Robert Taylor, George Murphy and Robert Montgomery arrived at the convention with plenty of fanfare, but as Reagan told the House Labor Committee, the stars found it a frustrating experience.

"We descended on Chicago by plane and train," Reagan testified. "I might add we realized, being a small union, at the AF of L convention, that our greatest weapon, which happens to be the one weapon which goes with our type of work, was publicity. We knew if we could drop ten or fifteen actors or actresses on any city in America they are bound to get their names in the papers and this we did."

There was something almost comic about the picture he drew before the investigating committee, as he told of the rebuffs given the stars by labor leaders obviously unimpressed by the Hollywood contingent. "We found, when we arrived there—speaking of confusion —that we had made a mistake and did not have our resolution before the resolutions committee in time, under the rules, for it to be considered." This blow was followed by a desperate search for help. "We saw several international presidents, trying to find out what we could," said Reagan. "We were told on several hands that we were helpless. The upshot was, however, they did accept our resolution. They put it before the convention . . . and it was unanimously passed by the convention." But the American Federation of Labor never put the resolution into effect, and when the House committee's counsel, Irving G. McCann, asked Reagan in 1948, "What is wrong with the AF of L?," Reagan replied, "Sir, that is calling for a conclusion of the witness." As the years passed, his loyalty to the Screen Actors Guild never wavered, but he became more and more hostile to organized labor's national leadership.

Reagan was becoming better known as a union leader than as an actor. At the studio he was working in a soon-to-be-forgotten film, *Night Unto Night.* But at union headquarters he was at the center of the industry. Watching Reagan, Harpo Marx, Gregory Peck, Robert Taylor and Franchot Tone participate in board deliberations during the strike, columnist Hedda Hopper admiringly wrote: "I thought never had so much glamour gone out on a limb for so many fellow players." Years later Peck would be one of Hollywood's most enthusiastic campaigners against Reagan in the 1966 election. Governor Edmund Brown was so appreciative that he suggested Peck run for the U.S. Senate, but Peck declined.

In May 1947 a glimpse of Reagan's philosophy was provided in an interview with Miss Hopper. "Our highest aim should be the cultivation of the freedom of the individual for therein lies the highest dignity of man," he said. "Tyranny is tyranny, and whether it comes from right, left or center, it is evil." The way to fight Communism, he said, is to improve America. "The Reds know that if we can make America a decent living place for all of our people, their cause is lost here. So they seek to infiltrate liberal organizations just to smear and discredit them. I've already pulled out of one organization that I joined in completely good faith. One day I woke up, looked about and found it was Commie-dominated. You can't blame a man for aligning himself with an institution he thinks is humanitarian, but you can blame him if he deliberately remains with it after he knows it has fallen into the hands of the Reds. I can name you one organization that is so obviously controlled by the Communists that all members must be aware of it. So I must believe that any who choose to support it must be, at least, Communist sympathizers. Otherwise, knowing what they must know, why don't they get out?"

The organization from which Reagan resigned was the Hollywood Independent Committee of the Arts, Sciences and Professions, one of the social action groups that abounded in Hollywood during and just after World War II. In addition to his membership in this organization, he joined the liberal American Veterans Committee and the United World Federalists, which advocated world government. But he quit the veterans committee quickly. And the United World Federalists was a dreamy sort of organization—far removed from the main currents of political thought.

In 1947 the California legislature's Joint Fact-Finding Committee on Un-American Activities said that the Hollywood Independent Committee of the Arts, Sciences and Professions was one of "two key Communist fronts in California." But by that time Reagan had left. His disillusionment began, in fact, at his first board meeting, when James Roosevelt, son of the late President, proposed a declaration repudiating Communism. A fight followed and Reagan spoke on Roosevelt's behalf. John Howard Lawson and Dalton Trumbo, two screenwriters, criticized Reagan. Later in the evening Reagan, Roosevelt and a few others met to plan strategy. Reagan recalls proposing that "we reaffirm our belief in free enterprise and the democratic system and repudiate Communism as desirable for the United States." The proposal was rejected by the executive committee, and Roosevelt and Reagan quit the organization.

Reagan and congressional and legislative investigators contended that Communist influence prevented the organization from condemning the Communist party. But Mrs. Ellenore Abowitz, an official, gave another reason to the California legislative committee: "Our theory is that in these days, the immediate danger to our form of government is fascism."

Arguments over Communism were becoming increasingly bitter by 1947. The House Un-American Activities Committee sent a subcommittee to begin a new investigation on Communism in the film industry. Jack L. Warner told the subcommittee that he had fired six writers because "what they were doing was taking your money and supposedly writing your scripts and trying to get these doctrines into the films, working for the party or whatever the term is." Many Hollywood personalities bridled at the committee's methods. *Life* magazine reported that John Garfield, Paul Draper, Lauren Bacall, Humphrey Bogart, John Huston, June Havoc and Danny Kaye were among those who flew to Washington to protest the committee's next round of hearings. "The whole procedure is as if I came out before an audience of five thousand and before I'd said a word the audience shouted 'You stink,' " Kaye said. Bogart later recanted and said, "I went to Washington because I felt fellow Americans were being deprived of their constitutional rights. I see now that my trip was ill advised, foolish and impetuous, but at the time it seemed the thing to do."

As president of the Screen Actors Guild, Reagan joined two past presidents, Montgomery and Murphy, in telling the committee how Hollywood had resisted Communism. The hearings were a circus, for the publicity-conscious chairman, J. Parnell Thomas, had called some of the biggest stars to testify. One of the committee members was a young congressman, Richard M. Nixon of California, who was building a reputation as a Communist-hunter. Every day, lines of women waited outside the committee room for a chance to see Robert Taylor, Gary Cooper, Robert Montgomery and others. While the stars brought the publicity, the committee's real targets were a group of screenwriters and directors who had decided they would not answer any questions dealing with their political beliefs or memberships in organizations. They cited the First Amendment, guaranteeing the freedom of Americans to speak, write or assemble.

According to one witness, the Communists, like the committee, considered the actors as window dressing to help obtain publicity. Howard Rushmore, a journalist who said he had belonged to the Communist party from 1938 to 1939, testified before the committee that the party didn't have much use for actors. "The general line would be that the stars were, 99 percent of them, political morons, and they added some other uncomplimentary things, which I wouldn't care to repeat, but the Communist party per se had great contempt for the stars of Hollywood," he testified.

When Reagan appeared before the committee he answered the questions in a clear, concise way, even though he was angry with the committee counsel, Robert Stripling. Stripling had come to his hotel room the night before and demanded that Reagan tell him what he planned to say on the witness stand the next day. Reagan later claimed he was "conditioned as a liberal to think of the committee as a pretty venal bunch"—even though he cooperated fully with the investigators and did not join others in criticism of the committee. He was unhappy with Stripling's request, but he answered his questions, anyway, telling how the guild had fought the Communists.

Apparently that was not what Stripling wanted to hear, for Reagan said the counsel did not ask him the same questions on the witness stand.

Reagan was a contrast to some other friendly actor-witnesses, like Gary Cooper, who testified it would be a good idea to outlaw the Communist party "although I have never read Karl Marx and I don't know the basis of communism, beyond what I have picked up from hearsay. From what I hear, I don't like it because it isn't on the level."

Reagan testified: "There has been a small clique within the Screen Actors Guild which has consistently opposed the policies of the guild board and officers of the guild, as evidenced by votes on various issues. That small clique referred to has been suspected of more or less following the tactics that we associate with the Communist party."

Counsel Stripling asked: "Would you refer to them as a disruptive influence within the guild?"

Reagan: "I would say that at times they have attempted to be a disruptive influence."

Stripling: "Has it ever been reported to you that certain members of the guild were Communists?"

Reagan: "Yes, sir; I have heard different discussions and some of them tagged as Communists."

Stripling: "Have you heard that from any reliable source?"

Reagan: "Well, I considered the source as reliable at the time."

Stripling: "Would you say that this clique has attempted to dominate the guild?"

Reagan: "Well, sir, by attempting to put over their own particular views on various issues, I guess in regard to that you would have to say that our side was attempting to dominate, too, because we were fighting just as hard to put over our views. . . .

"I would say of these people, the best thing to do is make democracy work. In the Screen Actors Guild we make it work by insuring everyone a vote and by keeping everyone informed. I believe that, as Thomas Jefferson put it, if all the American people know all of the facts they will never make a mistake. Whether the party should be outlawed, I agree with the gentleman who preceded me that it is a matter for the government to decide. As a citizen, I would hesitate, or not like, to see any political party outlawed on the basis of its political ideology. However, if it is proven that an organization is an agent of a power, a foreign power, or in any way not a legitimate political party, and I think the government is capable of proving that, then that is another matter." Several years later, after his thinking had shifted more to the right, he would conclude that the Communist party was not a political party but part of a Soviet Union conspiracy.

Stripling questioned Reagan about another experience he had had with one of the groups of that era. Reagan told how he had been duped into sponsoring a recital that was under the auspices of the Joint Anti-Fascist Refugee Committee, a group that both the counsel and Reagan felt was too far to the left. "I was called several weeks ago," Reagan said. "There happened at the time in Hollywood to be a financial drive on to raise money to build a badly needed hospital in a certain section of town, called the All Nations Hospital. I think the purpose of the building is so obvious by the title that it has the support of most of the people of Hollywood—or of Los Angeles, I should say. Certainly of most of the doctors, because it is very badly needed.

"Some time ago I was called to the telephone. A woman introduced herself by name. Knowing that I didn't know her, I didn't make any particular note of her name and I couldn't give it now. She told me that there would be a recital held at which Paul Robeson would sing and she said that all the money for the tickets would go to the hospital and asked if she could use my name as one of the sponsors. I hesitated for a moment because I don't think that Mr. Robeson's and my political views coincide at all, and then I thought I was being a little stupid because, I thought, here is an occasion where Mr. Robeson is perhaps appearing as an artist and certainly the object, raising money, is above any political consideration—it is a hospital supported by everyone. I have contributed money myself. So I felt a little bit as if I had been stuffy for a minute and I said, certainly you can use my name.

"I left town for a couple of weeks, and when I returned, I was handed a newspaper story that said this recital was held at the Shrine Auditorium in Los Angeles under the auspices of the Joint Anti-Fascist Refugee Committee. The principal speaker was Emil Lustig. Robert Burman took up a collection, and remnants of the Abraham Lincoln Brigade were paraded up to the platform. I did not in the newspaper story see one word about the hospital. I called the newspaper and said, 'I am not accustomed to writing to editors, but I would like to explain my position,' and he laughed and said, 'You needn't bother, you are about the fiftieth person who has called with the same idea, including most of the legitimate doctors who also had been listed as sponsors of that affair.' "

Mr. Stripling: "Would you say from your observation that this is typical of the tactics or strategy of the Communists, to solicit and use the names of prominent people either to raise money or gain support?"

Reagan: "I think it is in keeping with their tactics, yes, sir."

Stripling: "Do you think there is anything democratic about these tactics?"

Reagan: "I do not, sir."

Following the hearings, the ten witnesses who had refused to answer the committee's questions were cited for contempt of Congress and eventually convicted. On the following day the Motion Picture Association of America blacklisted the ten. It promised to fire any of the witnesses under contract, and said: "We will not employ any of the ten until such time as he is acquitted or has purged himself of contempt and declared under oath that he is not a Communist." Reagan agreed with the association.

Compared to some of his colleagues, he was a moderate on the Communist issue. He did not storm into the committee hearing like Sam Wood, the producer of *Kings Row,* who testified that Communists were making a constant effort to subvert pictures. "If you go back into the pictures, you will find frequently the banker or the man in public life, the doctor, any one of them would be the heavy in the picture. I think it is particularly bad if that is constantly shown, if every night you go into the pictures you see a dishonest banker or senator, you begin to think the whole system is wrong. That is the way they work on it." Nor did Reagan go after the Communists with the enthusiasm of Adolphe Menjou, who said, "I am a witch hunter if the witches are Communists. I am a red baiter. I make no bones about it whatsoever." Menjou obligingly described his clothes to reporters before he testified: "A brown chalk-stripe suit, a tie made for me by Mr. Sulka, a Clark Gable shirt that he kindly let me copy and my hat is Homburg." Then he described for the congressmen how Communist propaganda could be injected into movies. "I believe that under certain circumstances, a communistic director, a communistic writer, or a communistic actor, even if he were under orders from the head of the studio not to inject communism or un-Americanism or subversion into pictures, could easily subvert that order, under proper circumstances, by a look, by an inflection, by a change in the voice. I think it could be easily done. I have never seen it done, but I think it could be done."

In today's ideological scale, Wood and Menjou would be to the far right, nervously looking for Communists under every rock—as do many of Reagan's present supporters. On the other side were the stars who attacked the committee. They formed the Committee for the First Amendment, which condemned the investigation and defended the writers cited for contempt, the Hollywood Ten. Although many members of this committee in later years disavowed it, claiming they had been tricked into joining by Communists, its roster in 1947 contained some of Hollywood's biggest names—actors, actresses, writers and directors who were active in liberal causes then and now. Another sixty personalities took part in hour-long broadcasts entitled *Hollywood Fights Back* that sought support for the blacklisted witnesses.

Reagan's replies to the committee were restrained. "I do not believe the Communists have ever at any time been able to use the motion picture screen as a sounding board for their philosophy or ideology," he said. *Life* magazine, impressed with his testimony, and that of Robert Montgomery and George Murphy, said they "made their points neatly, with a good deal of restraint and common sense, and left the stand without dragging their feet."

After the hearings Reagan returned home and faced the fact that his marriage was breaking up, and that his interest in politics was at least in part to blame. At the time, the breakup of what was considered one of Hollywood's happiest couples was big news. In December 1947 Reagan told Hedda Hopper, "We had a tiff. That's right. But we've had tiffs before, as what couple married eight years hasn't. But I expect when Jane gets back from New York, we'll get back together all right."

He was wrong. In February, Miss Wyman's attorney, Lloyd Wright, Jr., said she was suing for divorce. There was a brief reconciliation in April, but the following month Miss Wyman filed a complaint in Los Angeles County Superior Court charging Reagan with extreme mental cruelty. In June the story of the divorce hearing was told in the Los Angeles *Times*. Miss Wyman, hatless, with her hair in a pageboy bob, explained to Judge Thurmond Clarke what had happened to the eight-year marriage. Reagan was not in the courtroom. She said the Screen Actors Guild was now occupying much of his time, and she did not share his interest. Reagan, she said, insisted that she attend meetings and be present during long discussions with his friends, but her ideas "were never considered important. Most of their discussions," she said, "were far above me."

It was not a matter of disagreeing with him, but simply that she could not match his interest. "Finally, there was nothing in common between us, nothing to sustain our marriage." She was awarded custody of the couple's two children, Maureen, seven, and Michael, three.

A bachelor again, Reagan moved into an apartment. He was kept busy with some good parts in undistinguished movies. He played in *John Loves Mary* with Patricia Neal and in a musical comedy that was a box-office success, and then went to England for a part in *The Hasty Heart.* Later he would remember it as a lonely period, a time of working and waiting for something better to come along.

7

A TIME FOR CHOOSING

In 1949 Reagan completed work in London on *The Hasty Heart,* a touching story based on a popular play by John Patrick. Great Britain, trying to restore its economy, had forbidden American firms from removing their money from the country, and the only way the movie studios could use their big deposits in British banks was to make movies in England. Reagan had reluctantly accepted the part of Yank, an American soldier, for he had wanted to play in a Western. But *The Hasty Heart* turned out to be one of his better films. The stars were Patricia Neal and Richard Todd, who appeared in his first major role. He had to learn to play a bagpipe for the film, and Reagan suggested Todd wear earmuffs during the lessons. Todd politely turned down the suggestion. Much of the action took place in a hospital in Burma, and *Newsweek* commented that "Reagan and his fellow patients achieve an offhand naturalness that maintains them as distinct individuals." The *New Republic* disliked the plot— "one of the most barefaced tearjerkers ever concocted"—although it thought the film had "an admirably directed cast." *Christian Century* said the movie was "simple, effectively done."

But as before, this success was followed by a series of poor roles that robbed Reagan of whatever reputation he had as a proficient actor and box-office attraction. The next fifteen years would be a time of great change for Reagan. His movie career was failing and, what was more significant, his views on life and politics were changing. This period marked the transformation of the actor into the politician.

His career had a setback soon after his return to America. On a June night he was playing with some other stars in a benefit softball game for the City of Hope, a research hospital. "Bob Hope was pitching, and Bill Demarest, the umpire, had called two balls and one strike on me when I bunted," Reagan remembered. "The fellow on first stepped in front of the bag to block me off, and I hit him with all stops open. Anyway, my leg came apart like a wet cigar." His leg broken in four places, Reagan was hospitalized through most of the summer, lost a screen role and was limping for almost a year. "Funny thing about this accident," he told Al Wolf, sports columnist for the Los Angeles *Times.* "In three years of college football I played all but two minutes. And at guard, what's more. I had plenty of water wrestling matches while pulling out hysterical swimmers, but had no serious mishaps. And just a week before this softball game, I was taking a jumper over a hurdle only to have it smack the barrier good. Horse and I went head over heels into a lot of trees. But we were both lucky, just a couple of scratches."

At the studio, Reagan was arguing with Jack Warner over movie roles. Warners had promised him a part in a Western, *Ghost Mountain,* after he completed work on *The Hasty Heart.* But the box-office receipts for his film *That Hagen Girl* were low, and the studio replaced him in the Western with the more popular Errol Flynn. Reagan was angry and Warners was in no hurry to make peace. Like other studios, the company was trying to trim overhead by reducing the number of players who were working on expensive long-term contracts. As a result Lew Wasserman negotiated a new deal. Warners would pay Reagan $75,000 a film for one picture a year over a three-year period. In addition, Reagan signed with Universal for one picture a year for five years at the same price. But there was no security in such contracts. If an actor turned down a bad role, he would not receive any money. When Reagan was a regular contract player, he was paid whether or not he worked.

In politics Reagan would often talk about personal freedom. But he was lost and unhappy when he was given his own freedom by Warners. "A star doesn't slip," he told Hedda Hopper. "He's ruined by bad stories and worse casting. I think if the producers would close up their private projection rooms and see pictures in regular theaters, they'd get some idea of what they're doing to our business." As good parts became harder to find, Reagan's unhappiness with the men who ran the studios intensified. At a meeting of the Screen Actors Guild he complained that producers were reducing advertising budgets despite the drop in theater attendance. "No industry has ever been able to survive business reverses by cutting down advertising," he said.

Accustomed to accepting every role that came along at Warners, Reagan started out doing the same as a free-lancer. As a result he starred in a series of failures. *Storm Warning* with Ginger Rogers and Doris Day was a quickly forgotten film about the Ku Klux Klan. *The Last Outpost* at least gave him a chance to ride horses in a Western. He was aging and new faces were coming along. So, at the age of thirty-nine, he was cast as the father of a teen-ager in the movie *Louisa.* His daughter was Piper Laurie, eighteen, then a starlet on the Universal-International lot. "I thought they'd make me up to look old, maybe whiten my hair at the temples," said Reagan. "But they just washed my face and shoved me in."

Reagan remained active in the Screen Actors Guild, and if his interest in the union cost him one wife, it soon brought him another. Director Mervyn LeRoy telephoned, not to hire Reagan for a film but to ask his help as president of the guild. A young actress at Metro-Goldwyn-Mayer, Nancy Davis, had been receiving mail from left-wing organizations and had found her name in the *Hollywood Citizen News* among a list of people who, she recalls today, "had rather exotic political feelings." She brought her problem to LeRoy, and he suggested calling Reagan. As she tells the story, it looks as though Reagan was the victim of a plot—not Communist but matrimonial. "Well, I knew Ronnie, but not personally, and Ronnie didn't know me from Adam, but I thought that was a dandy idea so I said, 'Yes, Mervyn, you do that, you call Ronald Reagan.'" After two days she hadn't heard from Reagan and she reminded LeRoy, an old friend of her family. As she stood next to him, he telephoned again. Reagan checked through files at the guild office, convinced himself of her loyalty and discovered that her name had been confused with that of another woman. He reported this to LeRoy, but LeRoy insisted that he take her out to dinner and tell her personally. Reagan began dating Nancy steadily, and on March 4, 1952, they were married. Reagan's friend William Holden was the best man, and Mrs. Holden was matron of honor.

Associates in Hollywood said the marriage influenced Reagan's political thinking. Mrs. Reagan is a conservative. Her father is Dr. Loyal Davis, a wealthy and politically conservative surgeon who retired after a long career in Chicago. Reagan still deeply admires Nancy's parents.

Miss Davis' career—like Reagan's—was in the doldrums. She had never been a star like Miss Wyman, but merely a young actress in some unimportant films. To her, acting was something to do between college and marriage, and she all but retired after the wedding. Later, though, she would return to the studios for an occasional performance with Reagan. In 1956 they co-starred in Reagan's last movie, *Hellcats of the Navy,* a low-budget film about the submarines in World War II. The *National Parent Teacher*—the only magazine to review it—said: "This black and white melodrama authentically, if routinely, portrays courage and initiative" in World War II. The magazine pointed out that the movie was technically well produced but complained that neither the director nor the cast made any effort at characterization. Reagan's movie career had come full circle. In the early days at Warners, making B movies for Byrnie Foy, Reagan had played in an undersea quickie, *Submarine D-1.*

A few months after the wedding, Mrs. Reagan announced that she was pregnant. The Reagans were living in a big new house in Pacific Palisades and were worried about making the mortgage payments. The Hollywood slump was at its worst, caused mainly by the competition of television, high labor costs and poor movies. Producers who couldn't have met his price in more prosperous days were calling him with free-lance offers for work in hastily made films. Actors and actresses more famous than Reagan found themselves out of work. "I grabbed everything," he said—accepting parts in movies he hated to see when they were shown in the theaters. His career was collapsing. "When I realized it, I feared it was too late," Reagan said. As a drastic solution he began refusing all bad parts in an attempt to salvage his star ranking. He refused a Universal picture and lost $75,000. Universal offered him two more films—$150,000 worth of work—and he turned them down. "I went fourteen months and turned down half a million dollars' worth of film, not counting percentages," he said. His wife remembers it as a difficult time. "You know, Ronnie didn't get into the so-called big money until after big taxes, so there was no residual, you had to keep on working. And it was hard. For any man it is demoralizing and for any wife watching him. Your heart breaks."

With Lew Wasserman now president of MCA, Art Park became Reagan's agent and tried hard to find him work. Park and others suggested he try a Las Vegas night-club act. The Reagans felt out of place amid the bright lights of the gambling city, but he accepted, anyway. Reagan was not, commented a columnist, "a typical night-club entertainer." He was the master of ceremonies for a variety act that included the Continentals, a comedy dance team, and two other acts. He worked with the Continentals in a comedy routine and finished up with some semihumorous comments.

His two weeks at the Last Frontier were a success. "He broke the record," said Mrs. Reagan. "They wanted him to extend and we could use the money." Offers came from night clubs in other parts of the country, but the Reagans declined. They didn't like the smoky rooms, the drinking and the late hours. "I'm sure that by most standards we're probably considered squares," said Mrs. Reagan, "and frankly I'm happy to be one. We're not night-club people." At the Last Frontier they went back to their hotel room after Reagan's performances and relaxed with books they had brought from home. They only went into the gambling casino once, on their last night, cautiously bringing only $5 with them.

Reagan also rejected offers to appear in plays in New York or in television series. Finally help came from an unexpected area, his union activities. As president of the guild he had become an unofficial spokesman for the movie industry, often acting as the toastmaster at banquets, giving speeches pleading for a tax break for actors and promoting Hollywood. He would say, "I know the public has been fed a lot of drivel under the name of publicity, so we can understand their false ideas about us. But believe me, I have found this place to be pretty much a cross section of the U.S.A." He donated his time for much of this, but finally it paid off. In 1954 the General Electric Corporation was looking for a host for its new half-hour television series—a man who could act, sell General Electric products, help build the company's corporate image and visit G.E. plants to improve employee morale. "I could think of only one man, Reagan," recalled Taft Schreiber, who was in charge of Music Corporation of America's Revue Productions at the time. General Electric agreed, and Reagan's drought was over. Schreiber negotiated a $125,000-a-year contract for him, and later it was boosted to $150,000. G.E. was delighted, for Reagan was a superb television salesman. There was a joke in Hollywood about someone who watched him delivering an institutional advertisement for General Electric's nuclear submarine and remarked, "I really didn't need a submarine, but I've got one now."

Reagan's eight years with General Electric were important to his political development. He visited 125 plants, met 250,000 General Electric employees and spent hours in serious conversation with the conservative businessmen who ran the company. It was like a political campaign. He would shake hands with the workers in the plants. At lunch and dinner he spoke to clubs or other groups. At first his speeches were simple Hollywood boosting, but in his conversations with executives and workers he began to find, for the first time in his life, a coherent political philosophy. The people he met, he felt, were dissatisfied with the bigness of their union, their company and their government. General Electric's management complained of government harassment and expansion. Reagan began thinking about the huge federal projects that had been started under Roosevelt and realized that he did not approve of them. To General Electric's embarrassment, Reagan singled out one such project for special attention, the Tennessee Valley Authority, to which the company sold millions of dollars' worth of electrical equipment. Company officials came to Schreiber and said, "Doesn't he know what he's saying?" But Schreiber said that G.E. did not try to censor Reagan. He voluntarily deleted the reference to the TVA and substituted an attack on another aspect of big government.

In 1952 Reagan—still a Democrat—supported the Republican candidate for President, Dwight Eisenhower, and backed him again in 1956. By this time his philosophy was much what it is today. Typical of Reagan's speeches during his association with G.E. was a talk in May 1958 to the Executives Club of Chicago. He began with a discussion of the troubles of the movie industry and concluded with a rousing attack on the government. Censorship, high taxes and government harassment had been wrecking the movies because studio chiefs had let "the planners and regulators get a foot in the door. This superstructure of government imposed on our original form is composed of bureaus and departments and is unchanged by any election," he said. "This hierarchy threatens to reverse the relationship of citizen and civil servant."

In Amarillo, Texas, a few years later, he said, "Medical care for the aged is a foot in the door of a government takeover of all medicine." When the American Medical Association was fighting Medicare, Reagan eagerly helped the doctors. He made a phonograph record which the physicians used to whip up enthusiasm for their battle against the health-care plan. He criticized the income tax, "this progressive system spawned by Karl Marx and declared by him to be the prime essential of a socialist state." He became a campaigner against farm price supports and opposed urban renewal. He favored voluntary Social Security "so those who can make better provision for themselves are allowed to do so." He wanted the government out of the power business, opposing the needed rural electrification program of the New Deal.

He questioned every social program enacted since 1932, programs that had come into being under Roosevelt and Truman and had been continued by Republican President Eisenhower. Except among the die-hard right wing, debate had ceased in American life over such accepted plans as Social Security and the progressive income tax. Reagan was now intent on reviving that debate.

Often after these talks, someone from the audience would approach him and suggest that he run for public office. In California, when he spoke before Republican groups, listeners asked him to run for governor or U. S. senator. He always replied that he was an actor and could do more good for the nation speaking as a private citizen. "I think he sharpened his wits and saw what it might be like to be a politician—to be confronted with issues he had no total involvement in," Schreiber said of these days. "He began to speak out, and I think this is what made him a politician."

His association with General Electric did more than sharpen his political philosophy. *The G.E. Theater* was an extremely successful show. It relied on the veteran big names of Hollywood as guest stars. Charles Laughton made his television debut on *The G.E. Theater*. Fred Astaire appeared in a nondancing role. Tony Curtis played a bullfighter, and James Stewart starred in a Western version of Charles Dickens' *A Christmas Carol*. The show introduced more famous movie stars to television than any other series. But ratings dropped when *Bonanza* moved against it at 9 P.M. on Sunday nights. Reagan's show, in black-and-white, was no match for the appeal of the hour-long color Western. In 1962 General Electric dropped the show.

The long years with General Electric and the acquisition of valuable ranch land in the Malibu Hills north of Los Angeles had made Reagan wealthy. He had stepped down as Screen Actors Guild president, although he remained on the board of directors. In 1959 he was brought back as president during a time of crisis for the union. The guild was trying to win for its membership a share of the profits that studios were making from selling post-1948 movies to television. These films were bringing in large amounts of money, and the guild was prepared to strike for a percentage. Howard Keel, the president, was leaving Hollywood for a part in a New York play, and the guild needed a dynamic leader to keep the membership enthusiastic in case they walked off work. "We needed somebody who could speak, excite the membership, stir them up," said one guild worker. In the opinion of the nominating committee, Reagan was the best qualified, and so John Dales, the executive secretary, called him. Afraid that more controversy would hurt his career, Reagan consulted MCA, but Lew Wasserman advised him to go ahead, and Reagan took over as president. There was no conflict in his mind between his conservative speeches on the road and his position on a union negotiating team. The guild, with its 14,000 members, remained a mixture of liberals and conservatives interested only in economic goals.

The producers rejected the guild's demands, and on March 7 the actors and actresses struck. Millionaires joined bit players in walking off the job. Alan Ladd, who was acting and producing, left the set of *One Foot in Hell,* from which he would receive 10 percent of the profits. Marilyn Monroe, Yves Montand and Tony Randall quit *Let's Make Love.* Clifton Webb looked around a quiet movie lot and said, "It's so awful, everything has stopped. In the barbershop, no one even talked." Most guildsmen supported the strike. Frank Sinatra summed up what many felt: "For the good of the entire motion picture industry, the Screen Actors Guild has compromised greatly from its original contract demands. I personally believe it is now time for all motion picture producers to do a little compromising."

But not everyone backed the strike—the first in the guild's history. John Wayne, who had originally joined Kirk Douglas, Lauren Bacall, Bing Crosby and some others in signing a pro-strike newspaper advertisement, later said, "I don't know what the hell they're striking about." The strike lasted six weeks and Reagan frequently was called upon to boost morale. In the end, the studios granted the actors payments for the television sales of their old films, and part of the money was used for a pension fund.

There was a two-year lapse between jobs after *The G.E. Theater,* but in 1964 the United States Borax Company needed a new host for its weekly dramatic show, *Death Valley Days.* Neil Reagan, who was then vice president of the McCann-Erickson advertising agency which handled the Borax account, suggested his brother, and Reagan was hired at about the same salary he received from G.E.

At the same time he plunged actively into Republican politics. In past years he had made speeches to help candidates raise money and draw crowds, but had not held an important position in any of the campaigns. In 1962 he changed his registration from Democratic to Republican, and in 1964 he was appointed state co-chairman of Citizens for Goldwater-Miller. Few of Goldwater's supporters were angrier than Reagan at the refusal of the moderate Republicans to support Goldwater in the general election. In a bitter speech to Los Angeles County Young Republicans after the election, Reagan said, "We don't intend to turn the Republican party over to the traitors in the battle just ended. The conservative philosophy was not repudiated" in the election. "We will have no more of those candidates who are pledged to the same socialist philosophy of our opposition."

These were impressive words to a few wealthy Goldwater Republicans who were beginning to recover from the disaster of 1964 and were looking toward the gubernatorial election of 1966. There were several reasons Reagan appealed to them. His philosophy was the same as theirs, and therefore the state would be in safe hands for business if he were in charge. He was the California Republican party's best orator. In the closing days of the Goldwater campaign, when even the die-hard supporters of the senator were conceding defeat, Reagan had made a televised fund-raising appeal that attracted wide attention. The speech, "A Time for Choosing," was along the same lines as the one he had been giving for years on the G.E. banquet circuit. This time he borrowed a line from Franklin Roosevelt and used it to emphasize his conservative message of desperation and despair. "You and I have a rendezvous with destiny. We will preserve for our children this, the last best hope for man on earth, or we will sentence them to take the last step into a thousand years of darkness." The speech was to party conservatives what William Jennings Bryan's "Cross of Gold" speech had been to the farmers and workers of the Democratic party in 1896, a rallying point, a promise of hope for the future. Bryan left the national convention a presidential candidate. When conservatives flicked off their television sets that night in 1964, Reagan was as good as a candidate for governor.

His entrance in the race was assured by the victory in the 1964 U.S. Senate election of his old friend George Murphy, who defeated Pierre Salinger, the former press secretary to Presidents Kennedy and Johnson. Murphy had proved that an acting career was more a help than a handicap. His old movies, still on television, made him seem like an old friend to the crowd and quickly established a rapport that made it easy for him to deliver his speeches. His performing skill permitted him to defeat Salinger, who was overweight and a poor speaker, in a television debate.

Thinking about all this were two wealthy men, Holmes Tuttle, an auto dealer who had known Reagan since 1947, and Henry Salvatori, an oil developer who had met Reagan socially in the late 1950s. "In 1965, after the Goldwater debacle," Tuttle said, "I called Henry Salvatori and some others, and we went to Ron and discussed the idea of his running for governor." Others also asked him to run. One supporter called Reagan while he was on location with *Death Valley Days*. Reagan declined, but several months after the 1964 election Tuttle came to Reagan's house and made another approach. "Holmes came up to the house specifically to see me," Reagan remembered later. "I gave him the usual thing about running for office." Finally Tuttle asked just one thing—"Would you agree not to give us a flat no? Just kick it around in your mind." Reagan agreed, and thus was born the Friends of Ronald Reagan, a group of supporters who mailed out thousands of letters signed by A. C. (Cy) Rubel, the former president of Union Oil Company. "Ronald Reagan, out of a deep sense of duty and dedication, is willing to serve as Republican candidate for governor, providing a substantial cross section of our party will unite behind his candidacy," the letter said. "To this end, Mr. Reagan has agreed to exhaustively explore the depth of feeling and the possible commitment to such an endeavor."

This was not, however, the humble effort of a few admirers. The address on the letterhead was 1300 West Olympic Boulevard, Los Angeles, the office of Bill Roberts and Stu Spencer, the founders of the political public relations firm of Spencer-Roberts and Hafner. Roberts was tall and chubby, Spencer short. Both were nervous, the proper emotional state for men whose livelihood depended on something as uncertain as winning a political campaign. Spencer and Roberts got their start in the business by managing a Republican congressional candidate's campaign after the Korean War. They first made a name in the state by handling U.S. Senator Thomas H. Kuchel's successful re-election campaign in 1962. In 1964 the firm was in charge of New York Governor Nelson Rockefeller's unsuccessful primary campaign against Goldwater. When Reagan's friends began looking for professional advice, Goldwater told them he would never run a campaign in California again without Spencer and Roberts.

In April 1965 Ralph Townsend, a Los Angeles–area businessman who was friendly with both Reagan and Stu Spencer, asked Spencer and Roberts if they would handle the Reagan campaign. They did not immediately agree. First they lunched with Townsend, Reagan and Neil Reagan at a private club in Los Angeles, the Cave de Roy, and then had two more meetings with Reagan at his house. But before Spencer and Roberts would take the account, they had to be assured of one thing. On record—made in scores of speeches— Reagan was as conservative as Goldwater. And his fighting words to the Young Republicans after the 1964 election made it clear that he did not approve of taking the moderates back into the Republican party. Roberts did not believe an ultraconservative would win the governorship in California. He told Reagan that neither he nor Spencer wanted to be associated with another futile Goldwater crusade. Reagan replied that neither did he. Without specifically saying so, he implied he would agree to moderate his conservative statements— and work with more liberal Republicans—in the interests of winning an election. From then on he began moving toward a more moderate position in his speeches. He was, said Roberts, "a reasonable guy with a sense of humor who didn't take himself too seriously."

"By September," said Roberts, "his feet were in concrete on running for governor. He had made a mental commitment," even though the formal announcement would not be made until early the following year.

Since Reagan, Roberts and Spencer had decided against selling Reagan's conservative ideas, something else had to be offered to the voters, a framework that would allow him to appeal to Californians of varying political beliefs. It was the Creative Society, a vague hodgepodge of ideas put together under a title obviously inspired by Lyndon Johnson's Great Society. It was concocted by an ultraconservative minister friend of Reagan's, the Reverend W. S. McBirnie, who is a radio commentator in addition to being the spiritual leader of a church. His fifteen-minute radio program, *Voice of Americanism*, sponsored by his Center for American Research and Education, is heard throughout California, often on small radio stations that feature fundamentalist radio ministers who mix religion with right-wing politics. He describes himself as a "hard-line conservative," and on his broadcasts he warns each day of the "international communist conspiracy." He preaches an uncompromising message against any accommodation with the Soviet Union. He denounces as leftist such established institutions and people as the National Council of Churches and George Kennan, former ambassador to the Soviet Union and Yugoslavia.

During the campaign one of McBirnie's letters of political advice to Reagan came into Governor Edmund Brown's possession. Reagan charged that the governor's aides had stolen it. Brown seized upon the letter as evidence to back up his claim that Reagan was an extremist. Brown said of McBirnie, "He appears on the same platform with Robert Welch [founder of the John Birch Society]. He has said our newspapers are infiltrated by Communists, and he has called Senator Tom Kuchel a California disgrace. Mr. McBirnie has also accepted an award from Billy James Hargis' anti-Catholic, anti-Semitic Christian Crusade, an organization that described the National Council of Churches as 'guilty of treason to God and Country.' " McBirnie replied that Brown was lying. He acknowledged, however, that Hargis once offered him an award, but he did not accept it, although he considers Hargis' group a patriotic organization. As for the newspapers, McBirnie said that testimony before the House Un-American Activities Committee had convinced him that Communists had infiltrated them.

McBirnie, in short, became a spokesman for ultraconservatives in California. Yet when the Friends of Ronald Reagan began meeting in Reagan's house with Bill Roberts to begin planning the campaign, McBirnie was there. "Late in the spring of 1965," said McBirnie, "I wrote Ronnie and I talked to him about having worked on the inside of the Nixon campaign, and we talked about Nixon's speeches."

Finally, McBirnie said, Reagan "asked me to be a member of the initial circle of counselors."

It was after one of the meetings that McBirnie thought up the phrase Creative Society. There was some grumbling among the advisers that the Reagan campaign needed a slogan. While McBirnie was driving back to Glendale on the freeway, the idea of the Creative Society was born. In essence it was this: Politicians should be catalysts to harness all the resources of the private sector of the nation to solve America's problems. "How do you get that creative energy loaned to government? You get businessmen to volunteer as one-dollar-a-year men as during the war. . . . I sat up all night," McBirnie recalled. "I wrote him a long letter, formulated the whole thing as a structure." Reagan liked the idea and began using the phrase in his speeches. Brown strongly criticized Reagan for accepting advice from McBirnie, but Reagan replied, "I'm very proud to have had the help of Dr. McBirnie, and he has been of inestimable help in expressing the philosophy of the Creative Society. But it is the same philosophy which I have held and expressed for the last fifteen years many times in speeches." McBirnie, too, said, "I did not create the Creative Society; I gave it formulation. The Creative Society is Ronnie's."

Once elected governor, Reagan would no longer rely on McBirnie's advice. McBirnie, however, still kept in touch with the Reagans and even arranged for them to be presented with a baby elephant from the son of the deposed King of Albania, an admirer of the governor. The Reagans donated the elephant—named G.O.P.—to the Sacramento Zoo.

In the fall Reagan talked to the Tulare County Industrial Management Association in Visalia, in the farm country, and a volunteer worker reported to Democratic headquarters: "Polite applause greeted his introduction, and he was more warmly applauded after he concluded. Spontaneous applause greeted his responses to several questions." More important, the Democrat said, "I talked with a member of the Republican Central Committee . . . who was in attendance at a small meeting of the Central Committee addressed by Reagan prior to the luncheon. He tells me that some obviously unfriendly questions were asked. He considers that Reagan handled himself very well and made a very favorable impression on some liberal Republicans who had previously viewed his candidacy with considerable coolness." This report was filed—and ignored by the Democrats.

There was a triumphal visit to a Republican state convention in San Francisco, when Reagan's reception drew hundreds more party workers than those of his rivals. Without making a speech, he was the center of attention. Salvatori, Tuttle, Rubel and the rest of California's conservative Republicans had themselves a candidate.

8

THE FIRST CAMPAIGN

Norwalk is one of the bedroom communities that stretch in a dreary row along the Pacific Coast south of Los Angeles. It is a formless city, encompassing ten square miles of suburban tract houses, one looking very much like the next. Without tradition, it is a new city that was incorporated in 1957 for a reason that seemed particularly appropriate for the times—a revolt against big government. Businessmen and residents of these subdivisions believed that the Los Angeles county board of supervisors, their governing body at the time, was too far away to understand their problems; they couldn't get a street repaired without a long hard fight with the county bureaucracy. "The larger your government becomes, the more cumbersome it becomes," said a resident of Norwalk in a statement that could have come from one of Ronald Reagan's campaign speeches.

In 1966, the year Reagan first ran for governor, Norwalk was a perfect example of his constituency. It was not a city of the rich; the modest houses cost about $16,500 and were generally built on 60-by-100-foot lots. Only a few of the residents were in medicine, law or other professions. The overwhelming majority were skilled laborers, with an average yearly income of $6,200. Many of them worked on the Apollo project at the nearby North American plant or in other government-supported industries. Government spending was important to Norwalk in another way. Metropolitan State Hospital for the mentally ill employed fourteen hundred of its residents. It was, by every traditional indicator, a Democratic city, and, not surprisingly, three out of four voters were registered Democrats.

But by 1966, registration no longer meant much to these blue-collar, working-class suburbs around Los Angeles. Anger at the county in the mid-fifties had turned into a revolt against the government in Sacramento and Washington, and these people wanted a change. After the incorporation of their community, taxes were still too high and paychecks dwindled in the face of a bewildering array of taxes by the county, the fire district, the recreation district, the school district, the state and the federal government. When Norwalk residents discussed taxes, they would inevitably condemn the expensive state welfare program, supported by tax money, and this in turn brought the discussion to black demands for racial and social equality. Norwalk itself was a white city. Only three of its approximately twenty-four thousand families were black in 1966. In 1963 Governor Edmund Brown and the Democratic legislature had offended these suburbs by enacting into law the open-housing bill that prohibited discrimination by property owners against blacks and other minorities in the sale, lease or rental of property.

A year later Norwalk showed how it felt about the law and voted for the statewide ballot measure that nullified the open-housing law. The people, in the words of a Democratic strategist, were "the non-minority wage earners here from the Southwest or South. The party is too liberal for them." The proposition was subsequently overturned by the state supreme court and later by the United States Supreme Court. Neither decision was popular in this area, and the rulings did much to reinforce the common dislike of the judiciary, another remote branch of big government. A short distance to the south a big sign overlooking the freeway proclaimed "Impeach Earl Warren," and in these suburbs were chapters of the John Birch Society, which sponsored the right-wing crusade against the then Chief Justice of the United States. In 1968 George Wallace, the segregationist former governor of Alabama, found supporters in these areas when he was trying to qualify his American Independent party for California's presidential primary election, and Richard M. Nixon ran ahead of Hubert Humphrey for President in the area that fall.

In April 1966, when Reagan was running in the primary election, he toured these suburban communities, and the reception was enthusiastic wherever he went, especially in the shopping centers. These were the Main Streets of a society that lived by the automobile and freeway, and every afternoon and evening such centers were crowded with shoppers. Political reporters considered the reaction of the crowds almost as sound a test of public opinion in the area as a scientific poll. At the Lakewood Shopping Center, where dozens of stores were built along a long, wide mall, customers from both the working-class communities such as Norwalk and the more affluent subdivisions in neighboring Orange County to the south awaited Reagan. Although he was there during a relatively light midweek shopping period, Reagan was surrounded by more than five hundred people yelling "Good luck" and "Give 'em hell about the unions!" Standing on a concrete ledge near some trees in a planter box, Reagan grinned modestly and said, "I guess there's no secret about what I'm doing here."

On the face of it, they were yelling for the wrong candidate. Yet in spite of their modest incomes and dependence on government contracts for jobs, these people were conservatives. Why? Theories abound: They had made some money, and they were frightened of losing it. They were lonely, insecure, rootless people, moving from suburb to suburb, from job to job, and they were reaching back to old-time values for stability. Or perhaps they were influenced by the wealthy established families of the area. Maybe, because so many were transplanted from the South and Southwest, they were conservatives or even bigots at heart. Whatever the reason, they had voted for Nixon for governor in 1962 when most of the state backed Brown. And in 1964 these people had come very close to giving Goldwater a majority in their area.

Later in 1966, when Brown came here, he was surrounded by teen-age members of an ultraconservative political group who shouted their opposition to him. He managed to finish his speech and leave unharmed, but one reporter, to protect himself from the crowd, locked himself in the Pacific Telephone communications car to phone in his story without interruption from the young people. When Senator Robert Kennedy, campaigning for Brown, visited Lakewood, the teen-agers and some of their parents were even more vicious. Earlier in the year Kennedy had become involved in an argument with Samuel W. Yorty, the mayor of Los Angeles, over

Yorty's handling of black slums. Yorty, who ran against Brown in the Democratic primary, was admired in this area for his strong defense of the police during the racial violence in Watts the year before, and when Kennedy appeared, the teen-agers waved signs praising the mayor and telling Kennedy to go home. Obscene slogans were scrawled on many of the signs, and the senator had difficulty speaking as the mob milled about him. Robert Kennedy was no hero to the youngsters at the Lakewood Shopping Center.

After the Lakewood appearance Reagan stopped at a smaller shopping center and talked to about a hundred women and a few men. It was still midafternoon. The women, standing near their station wagons filled with children, listened intently. At night he spoke to a packed crowd at a dinner that followed what was becoming the typical pattern for a Reagan appearance—show business personalities to warm up the crowd, followed by the candidate's speech. Reagan did not gloss over his movie background. In fact, he advertised it. He was introduced by Andy Devine, the froggy-voiced comic sidekick in Gene Autry cowboy movies, who said, "I don't know why an actor can't get into politics. What's wrong with an actor who wants to do something for his country and state? I haven't run into a crooked actor yet, I'll tell you that." The Voices of Faith Choir sang the "Ronald Reagan Pep Song" to the tune of "California, Here I Come": "Ronald Reagan, here we are. You're the one we're hoping for." (The Voices of Faith weren't seen again on the campaign, but Devine, Edgar Bergen, Chuck Connors and other Hollywood people became fixtures. Connors was so popular with the audiences that some people suggested he run for the U.S. Senate. Flattered, the television cowboy star finally said he couldn't afford to leave show business.)

With much fanfare Reagan was at last brought out, and he told stories about his days in the movies and about his work in the Screen Actors Guild. He even reminisced about broadcasting the Cubs games. It was a show, and the audience enjoyed it all, the jokes and the serious part. Welfare and unemployment insurance were Reagan's targets that night, and when he finished speaking, people crowded around him, as they had earlier in the day. Finally the rally was over, and Reagan left Lakewood and returned home.

It had been a typical day for the candidate, and in the eight months that followed—first in the primary election and then in the fall campaign against Brown—neither his routine nor his speech would substantially change. It was a simple campaign, designed by Roberts and Spencer to display their candidate's best qualities and hide his weak points, setting the pattern for all Reagan campaigns to come. His greatest weakness was inexperience, but the strategists quickly turned this to their advantage. Roberts knew that Reagan could not match Brown's knowledge of state government. "We decided not to show brilliant knowledge, which he did not have," Roberts said later. "We tried to operate on the level that he is not a professional politician, that he is a citizen politician, Joe Doakes running for office." The use of the term "citizen politician" was masterly strategy, for, as Roberts realized, "the term 'professional politician' does not conjure up a good image with the general public." Reagan's boast that he was a citizen politician, Roberts said, "was one of the best ways he could compete with Brown on knowledge of the issues. It was a defense measure, but later on it turned into a real asset. At the end, Brown was defending himself against being a professional politician."

Roberts understood the issues. "I'd say that our three main ones in this campaign were, first of all, morality; then taxes, spending, that whole ball of wax; then the eight years of incumbency." He also knew how to avoid an issue. He was aware that his opponents would try to link his conservative candidate with extremist right-wing groups such as the John Birch Society. He knew that Reagan would be asked to repudiate support from members of the John Birch Society. Richard Nixon had done this when he ran for governor in 1962, and as a result he lost the support of much of the party's conservative wing. Roberts did not want this to happen to Reagan. Thus Reagan stopped short of repudiating the Birchers and avoided offending ultraconservatives who wanted to join his crusade. But out of respect to moderates who disliked and feared the Birchers, Reagan expressed strong disapproval of Robert Welch, the founder of the society. "I wanted a strong enough statement disavowing Welch," said Roberts. He opposed telling "a whole segment of the party to go to hell" because it would deprive his candidate of financial support and the help of some of the party's most enthusiastic volunteer workers.

Reagan's tendency to tire easily forced the strategists to rely more on television than personal appearances. "He doesn't hold up well," said Roberts. "Give him three or four days of three or four meetings in a row and he gets real irritable." Roberts and Neil Reagan put together a series of television spot announcements that took the place of many of the traditional personal appearances. They were unique because of their simplicity—Reagan standing or sitting in front of the camera, just talking to the viewers. Expensive sets and clever writing were avoided. "We had to stay away from Hollywood productions," said Roberts. "To Reagan it was an extreme danger. People would have said: 'Oh, for Christ's sakes, Darryl F. Zanuck stuff.' We did it in a very simple manner and cut costs." A University of California film producer, Ernest Rose, agreed that Roberts had succeeded. He said Reagan's television films were "almost intentionally awkward, crude and bumbling." The spots were essentially illustrated lectures with what seemed to be "an intentional effort not to make [them] slick and commercial."

Personal appearances were an essential part of the campaign, however, for they helped raise money and build up the enthusiasm of party workers. But they did not serve the traditional purpose of directly winning the votes of hostile or unconvinced voters.

Spencer-Roberts' success in displaying their candidate to advantage was first revealed the night of January 4, 1966, when Reagan announced in a televised speech that he was entering the gubernatorial primary. Stu Spencer said that it was basically written by Reagan, and reworked and revised in cooperation with his advisers. It dealt knowledgeably with all of the major state problems, and it convinced thousands of viewers that Reagan was not, as his opponents insisted, an empty-headed actor mouthing someone else's lines. Just as important, the speech was carefully given a moderate tone to show that he was not another Goldwater. Instead, Reagan held up the vision of a better California and asked his fellow citizens to help him attain it. "As of now," he said, "I am a candidate seeking the Republican nomination for governor . . . California's problems are our problems . . . it won't matter if the sky is bigger and bluer out there if you can't see it for smog, and all our elbowroom and open space won't mean much if the unsolved problems are higher than the hills." His speech was hopeful. "Our problems are many," he said, "but our capacity for solving them is limitless."

The speech also contained something for the Goldwater fans and for the working-class residents of Norwalk and similar communities, a well-aimed appeal for morality and law and order. This, along with the moderate tone, would become a basic part of the campaign. "Our city streets are jungle paths after dark, with more crimes of violence than New York, Pennsylvania and Massachusetts combined." Im-

mediately after his discussion of crime were these words about
Berkeley: "Will we meet [the students'] neurotic vulgarities with
vacillation and weakness, or will we tell those entrusted with administering the university we expect them to enforce a code based on
decency, common sense and dedication to the high and noble purpose of the university? That they will have the full support of all of
us as long as they do this, but we'll settle for nothing less." And
finally, there was the condemnation of welfare, heavily self-right-
eous: "Working men and women should not be asked to carry the
additional burden of a segment of society capable of caring for itself
but which prefers making welfare a way of life, freeloading at the
expense of the more conscientious citizens."

Now he needed a formal staff to run the campaign. Even the most
experienced candidate needs trustworthy assistants—men who provide him with the material and the advise for the long campaign,
schedule events, arrange trips, assure him of a place to sleep while
on the road. A California campaign is like a presidential campaign,
for the population centers that must be covered comprise a wide area:
a morning in Los Angeles, lunch in San Francisco, an afternoon rally
in Oroville one hundred and fifty miles to the north, dinner in Oakland across the bay from San Francisco; four speeches or more a day,
hundreds of hands to shake, dozens of party leaders to recognize
with a smile and a familiar word. Reagan needed guides through the
forest.

An important addition was Lyn Nofziger, the press secretary, who
is still one of Reagan's most important advisers. He is a short, plump,
balding man who, unlike Reagan and other men in Reagan's entourage, has never cared much about how he looks. In the beginning his
sports coats, shirts and slacks were always wrinkled. By the 1980
presidential election he had abandoned coat and tie, as if to tell the
world he would not be bound by the conservative dress code followed
by the others. Politically, however, he has been conservative since his
youth. Just after World War II he testified before the California
legislature's Joint Fact-Finding Committee on Un-American Activities that one of his teachers at Canoga Park High School in 1941 and
1942 "was always on the side of the left. She argued one side with
some of the kids, and some of us argued the other side. There was
no impartiality on her side."

Although Nofziger loves puns, he is not a jolly fat man. Looking
around with suspicious eyes, he is quick to sense potential enemies,

often among political reporters, most of whom he believes are too liberal. He began as a reporter for an obscure and low-paying suburban newspaper near Los Angeles and worked himself up to national political reporter for the conservative Copley newspapers before joining Reagan in 1966. He was guarded with reporters, handing out news he thought would help his candidate and blatantly withholding anything that would put Reagan in an unfavorable light. That foreshadowed Nofziger's conduct during the 1980 campaign, when he became famous for cutting off the infrequent press conferences before too many difficult questions were asked.

His main goal was to see Reagan elected President. Often, in the years that followed the 1966 campaign, he was apart from Reagan, a loser in interstaff combat. But Nofziger always returned, and on election night 1980 he had the satisfaction of being at Reagan's side as press secretary.

Entering the Reagan campaign at about the same time was Philip Battaglia, a successful attorney. He started as Southern California chairman, a figurehead position, but in the end would be the state campaign chairman and, finally, for a time, Reagan's executive secretary and "good right arm." To Battaglia, life had been a struggle to succeed, to acquire wealth, power and social position. At the age of thirty-two he was a partner in one of Los Angeles' most respected law firms, Flint & MacKay, and a member of the University of Southern California's board of trustees.

Other staff additions were two college professors, Dr. Stanley Plog of the University of California at Los Angeles and Dr. Kenneth Holden of San Fernando Valley State College. These two men would be the brain trust, the intellectuals who supplied the layman candidate with all of the information he needed to convince the electorate that he was capable of being governor. They would write the position papers and research the complicated state problems, some of which Reagan scarcely knew existed. Spencer and Roberts, who had picked the two, did not tap the traditional campaign sources of intellectual advice. For Plog and Holden were behavioral scientists—men who combined the traditional disciplines of psychology, sociology, statistics, political science and other social sciences to find out why men behaved in a certain manner. Plog and Holden owned a small research firm, the Behavior Science Corporation of Van Nuys. Some of their assignments were prosaic, such as setting up a complete psychological testing service for a school system. But others dealt directly with subtle relationships between people. They would be assigned by a troubled business to go into a plant or office, interview the workers and supervisors, find out how they got along together, and deduce from their behavior the reason for the business problem. Perhaps a supervisor was insensitive to the complaints of his workers. He would be shifted. Perhaps an executive was not, in the opinion of Holden and Plog, psychologically sound enough for promotion. He would be told. When the stock market slumps, businessmen look for economic causes, but Holden said, "We think it's largely psychological." Plog and Holden are both psychologists. Holden has his doctorate from Ohio State University. Plog's is from Harvard.

Plog and Holden first met Reagan at the candidate's house. To someone with Holden's neat academic mind, the scene at Reagan's home was distressing. "He didn't have a secretary, and he was assimilating stacks of material on state issues, clipping newspapers and magazines. It was a monumental task." Quickly Holden and Plog, ever the behavioral scientists, analyzed their prospective client. Some of Holden's observations: "Charismatic personality. Knows his position and the position of others . . . He is not a map reader, he is not a reactor. Reagan knows who he is and what he stands for. His library is stacked with books on political philosophy. He can take information and he can assimilate it and use it appropriately in his own words."

Holden and Plog talked with Reagan about the campaign. "He liked the cut of our sails and we liked the cut of his," Holden said. They joined the Reagan team, and Holden proudly claimed it was probably the first time in American history that a major political candidate has taken on intellectual advisers from a firm specializing in approaching the voters in psychological terms. "We looked at the campaign as a problem in human behavior, a very complex problem." The idea was to find out why the voter would mark his ballot for Reagan or for someone else. The Behavior Science Corporation decided that it would try to pinpoint the issues that concerned the voter and offer Reagan methods of approaching them. As an example, Holden and Plog, along with Reagan, became aware shortly after the campaign began of the voters' intense interest in the University of California. Reagan, at that period, always concluded his speeches by asking for questions from the audience, and there was always a question about the university. It soon became clear to Holden that the voters were especially unhappy about President Clark Kerr's handling of the student demonstrators, and that Reagan would have to offer a constructive alternative that would not be attacked by the Democrats as political interference with the university. Holden came up with the idea of proposing an investigation of the university by a nonpartisan commission headed by John McCone, former chief of the Central Intelligence Agency. McCone was a Republican, but Governor Brown would have difficulty criticizing him, since he had enthusiastically chosen McCone the year before as chairman of the commission that investigated the Watts riots. Holden recalls that Roberts was unenthusiastic about the plan, but Holden flew to San Diego, where Reagan was resting, and sold the candidate on the idea. Reagan used it for campaign speeches, but the commission never materialized. Another of Holden's ideas was turned down—that Reagan be flanked by university professors when he proposed the commission, including two Nobel Prize–winners who supported his candidacy.

The main job of Behavior Science was to supply the candidate with information—volumes of it. Holden and Plog singled out eighteen main problem areas and began gathering information, for neither man was, himself, an expert in any field of state government. One of the most complex issues was school finance, a field fully understood only by a few school administrators. Plog and Holden invited such educators from the San Fernando Valley to their office and asked them to talk about their problems. The two psychologists put the information in a growing pile of black books. These books—there would be eight of them before the campaign ended—contained 5-by-8-inch cards on which basic facts were written. From these books Reagan would take the information for his speeches, which he wrote on 3-by-5-inch cards. In addition, Behavior Science gave him position papers on issues that "he could react to and sharpen up his own philosophy."

Either Holden, Plog or an assistant—and the black books—would accompany Reagan on every campaign trip. If Reagan didn't know the answer, the behavioral scientist and the black books would be consulted. And if the answer wasn't available on the road, a phone call would be made to Behavior Science's office in Van Nuys, where an assistant would look it up. This technique permitted Reagan to counter the skepticism with which his candidacy was greeted and to become a convincing candidate. He would adopt a similar method with the mini-memos after he took office.

For George Christopher, Reagan's primary opponent, the campaign was a disaster. He was a bulky, rough-featured man with two successful terms as mayor of San Francisco behind him, but he was little known in Southern California and was a poor campaigner for the age of television. He was effective and even dominating in a small group, but he had little feeling for the language and in speeches he became entangled in such sentences as: "I am cognizant of two philosophical thoughts which perhaps pertain to this election." He was the candidate of the moderate Republicans who had supported Nelson Rockefeller against Barry Goldwater in California in 1964 and who were trying to regain control by backing a successful gubernatorial nominee.

Reagan's chances for the nomination looked good. Only once in the primary did he falter, in an argument over civil rights. In March he and Christopher appeared before the state convention of the National Negro Republican Assembly in Santa Monica, attended by the few blacks who, for reasons that are hard to understand, still clung to the Republican Party after it had nominated a presidential candidate in 1964 who had voted against the United States civil rights bill in the Senate. Ben Peery, a Los Angeles businessman, rose to ask a question he had asked at GOP meetings in the past. To Reagan he said, "How are Negro Republicans going to encourage other Negroes to vote for you after your statement that you would not have voted for the civil rights bill?"

Reagan is not a bigot, but he is unusually sensitive when anyone questions him about race relations. He is defensive about the subject even at the best of times, and he was even more so at this meeting, for he had been trying to win support from the black community without success and was frustrated by his failure. Christopher also irritated him. The mayor's criticisms of Reagan had been mild, but Reagan and his wife kept track of all of them until they were magnified out of proportion. And he was sick with a virus that had weakened him for most of the primary campaign. Reagan gave his standard reply—he favored the aims of the bill, but it was "a bad piece of legislation." He defended Goldwater's vote against the bill, saying, "If I didn't know personally that Barry Goldwater was not the very opposite of a racist, I could not have supported him."

It was Christopher's opportunity, and he rose to take advantage of it. "Contrary to my opponent, I would have voted for the bill if I had been in Congress." He added that "the position taken by Goldwater did more harm than any other thing to the Republican party, and we're still paying for that defeat. This situation still plagues the Republican party, and unless we cast out this image, we're going to suffer defeat."

Weeks of tension took their toll when Reagan stepped up and said, "I want to make a point of personal privilege." Then he shouted, "I resent the implication that there is any bigotry in my nature. Don't anyone ever imply I lack integrity. I will not stand silent and let anyone imply that—in this or any other group." He slammed his fist into his hand, mumbled a few words and stalked out of the hall, followed by concerned assistants. One newsman reported him as saying, "I'll get that S.O.B."

It was the first time the candidate had become unstrung. Reagan got into a car and was driven to his home in nearby Pacific Palisades. Holden was afraid the campaign would be destroyed by a moment's anger. Very upset, he persuaded Nofziger to follow Reagan home and bring him back. He called the Reagan house and talked to the candidate, who had just entered the door. Holden advised him to come back, and Reagan finally agreed. Accompanied by Nofziger, he returned to the convention and told the president, the Reverend Lawrence C. Thomas, that his anger wasn't directed at the delegates.

Christopher tried to use the incident as evidence of mental instability. "Mr. Reagan, of course, has been ill, and I extend my sympathy in this moment of his emotional disturbance," he said. But Reagan's quick return to the meeting took away much of the sting. "Frankly, I got mad," he said. He felt Christopher had implied he was a bigot. "There was no outright charge . . . I felt in the manner of answering, there were inferences that placed me over in that category. It was the sum total of the afternoon. I'm not a politician. There are just some things you can't take as a man." A newsman brought up a central issue: he wondered if the incident would raise questions about Reagan's "emotional stability under stress." He asked if Reagan was emotionally fit for the campaign ahead. It was a blunt question, but Reagan merely smiled and said "Yes." Hollywood columnists, he recalled, had said he was a "Boy Scout and a square," and he told the reporters, "Fellows, you can't have it both ways. You can't be a wild-eyed kook and a square."

Reagan carried 53 of the 58 counties in the state, and Christopher did well in only two, his home county of San Francisco and in San Mateo, which adjoins it to the south. Reagan's margin was overwhelming—1,417,623 to 675,683.

From then on, Reagan and his advisers were confident of victory. "To me, it was a matter of staying alive from the primary to the general," said Roberts. "Most of the issues were ours to pick and choose." For the next few months it was necessary only to avoid mistakes and stick to the pattern established early in the year. Soon Reagan was so certain of winning that he began to put together his new administration.

The man who won the Republican nomination for lieutenant governor and who became Reagan's running mate was Robert H. Finch, an accomplished politician who was much more moderate than Reagan. Finch had managed Richard M. Nixon's campaign for the presidency in 1960, which came close to winning. Two years later he advised Nixon, his close friend, to stay out of the California gubernatorial election, but Nixon ignored him and lost embarrassingly. Traditionally, the candidates for governor and lieutenant governor do not run on the same ticket in California, as the President and Vice President do. Reagan, overcoming his reservations about Finch's moderate philosophy, assisted Finch by including him in many of his campaign events, but the two were never comfortable together. In 1968 Finch re-joined Nixon, first as an unofficial adviser on his presidential campaign, and then, after resigning as lieutenant governor, as Secretary of Health, Education and Welfare and later a White House counselor.

In the fall campaign Reagan faced a politically vulnerable opponent. Edmund Brown had been one of California's good governors and some of his accomplishments would make life better for future generations in the state. His greatest accomplishment was the beginning of construction of the great water project. When he had been in office for less than a year, he successfully campaigned for a $1.75 billion bond issue to finance it. "It is all very well to work for all the other necessary programs," he said. "But without water, California is without a future." He had put through a master plan to control the jumble of university branches, state colleges and junior colleges being built in the state, and as a result, California's system of higher education was a model for the rest of the country. Brown also had proposed and later signed the state's first fair employment practices act in 1969. And in 1964 he had sacrificed much of his personal prestige on another civil rights issue, losing a fight against Proposition 14, the ballot measure that nullified the open-housing law.

He was an optimistic man, convinced of the goodness of his fellow human beings. His nickname was Pat—and it suited him perfectly, a plain name for an unpretentious man. There was no regal air of command about him. He was forever telling stories about his social blunders. One of his favorite pictures showed him spilling coffee over himself while John F. Kennedy, whom he revered, laughed uproariously. It hung in his office for everyone to see, along with a political cartoon picturing a confused Pat Brown looking through his horn-rimmed glasses. When he met someone, he always said, "I'm Pat Brown," just in case he wasn't recognized. Sometimes he wasn't. A few months after he had been sworn in as governor, Brown wanted to swim. The pool closest to the governor's mansion was across the street at a motel. Carrying his swimsuit and a towel, the governor of California courteously introduced himself to the clerk at the desk, explained his situation and asked if he could use the pool. The clerk didn't believe him, but the manager finally allowed him to use the pool. Mrs. Brown was upset at the loss of dignity and asked some of Brown's old friends to build him a swimming pool at the mansion.

His notable achievements in his eight years in office were obscured by his greatest flaw, indecisiveness that prompted even some of his supporters to call him "a tower of jelly." He wanted to be remembered as a compassionate governor, but if anything, he was too compassionate. He liked to listen to both sides of a story, and unfortunately, he saw merit in each. When he was governor, some of his appointees to an important state board were discovered to have accepted favors from men with criminal connections. Brown fired them but then granted them time to explain their case in a hearing open to the press. After listening to their stories. Brown admitted in public that the men had made a good case for themselves, and he withdrew their dismissal. His action added to his image of indecisiveness.

By the end of his first term, public opinion polls showed that voters were tiring of his familiar face. "The people don't appreciate my greatness," he would say half jokingly.

Nevertheless, he was convinced he could defeat Reagan. He and his staff underestimated the challenger, sharing the view of an aide who, after attending a Reagan speech in December 1965, reported:

"He will fall apart when he gets attacked from the floor and is asked leading questions, hounded and the like . . . His attacks on LBJ and Governor Brown . . . won't make it with those who don't think the President is a dictator and those who realize the necessity of close state and federal cooperation. The real issue always boils down to what Reagan would do as governor, and given the present situation and our close working with Washington, he could do nothing."

The error of that prediction was quickly evident. On Labor Day, only half the expected union members attended a rally to begin the incumbent's fall campaign. Agriculture, which had benefited from Democratic-sponsored water projects, was angry at Brown because growers believed he was sympathetic to the farm workers union and favored too much welfare. Some of the most liberal Democrats were refusing to support the party because of their opposition to Lyndon B. Johnson's war policy, which Brown was backing. It was an early manifestation of the anti-war troubles that would face Johnson in California in 1967 when thousands demonstrated outside the Century Plaza Hotel in Los Angeles during his appearance there in midsummer. Brown continued to talk about the accomplishments of his two terms in office, but this constructive approach was submerged by the virulence of his anti-Reagan attacks. Brown charged that Reagan was an extremist, but with little success. The liberal San Francisco weekly paper, *Sunday Ramparts,* concluded that while Reagan was conservative, "The Democrats have been unable to show genuine connections to the John Birch Society, to any other rightist organization or even to decidedly right wing opinions."

And finally, on September 27 there was a riot in San Francisco's black Hunters Point slum after a white policeman shot a black youth who was fleeing in a stolen car. Looting and burning began, and by midnight Brown had called out the National Guard; it evoked memories of Watts the year before and inflamed devisive racial feelings just as Brown's campaign should have started to move. In midafternoon the next day Brown decided to fly from Southern California to San Francisco. Only four people were in his plane, the *Grizzly II,* for the flight north—Brown, his press secretary Jack Burby, his travel secretary Tom Hickey and a reporter. Brown, slowly realizing the immensity of the blow his campaign had suffered, looked out the window at the storm clouds and the ice forming on the wings of the plane. He was slumped in his favorite seat, toward the front of the plane, his coat off. Finally he talked of the riots, puzzled at why they happened in "the most affluent nation in the world." He also talked about how he was now disliked by blacks as well as whites. He had met with fifty black leaders recently, he recalled, and "all they said was 'You sold us out, Governor.'"

Brown wondered aloud if he should tour the riot zone. Hickey told him that Mayor John Shelley of San Francisco was hit by a rock when he went there the night before. Burby insisted it wouldn't be safe for Brown to tour the area. The governor leafed through a newspaper, filled with stories of the violence, and paused at a picture of the police carrying away the body of the dead boy. "This is what does it. This little boy." It was, some of his advisers thought later, the time when all hope for victory vanished.

A bus rather than an airplane was the symbol of Reagan's Southern California campaign. Thirty-eight percent of the registered voters lived in Los Angeles County—2.96 million people—and they, along with voters in neighboring Orange and San Diego counties, would to a large extent determine the election. Reagan's comfortable Greyhound bus was loaded each morning with sweet rolls and coffee for breakfast; soda, beer, sandwiches and fried chicken for lunch, and whiskey and gin for the long drive back to headquarters. It was a self-contained home, with a lavatory, for the long days on the freeways. In the mornings the bus would leave Reagan headquarters and bring the six or seven members of the traveling press, the staff and the candidate to the first event of the day, which was sometimes a coffee hour with women or a stop at a television station to tape a show for future broadcast. After that there would be a noon stop for a speech at a luncheon. In the afternoons there would be a rest stop at a motel. After Reagan's blowup over civil rights some months before, the afternoon stop was seldom missed. His nap over, the candidate would rise refreshed for a dinner speech, which would end the day. By ten o'clock he was usually in bed.

For reporters his campaign was a pleasant change from traveling with Governor Brown, who was out every day from seven in the morning to midnight. But from the way Reagan talked, his public never guessed that his schedule was restricted. When campaigning in the south, he spent many of his evenings and nights at home, but whenever he and Mrs. Reagan appeared together at a luncheon or dinner, they would hug each other on the platform and remark to the audience how long they had been separated by the campaign. It was a sour sight to the traveling reporters from Northern California who had been away from home for two weeks at a time.

To those who watched the 1966 campaign and the Reagan elections that followed, the strategy, speeches and day-to-day routine never seemed to change. In 1966, as in 1980, Reagan consolidated his base with the Republican right and moved toward the center, a political strategy that gives a mistaken impression of a moderate Reagan. Then as now he was prone to tire and his advisers insisted on a daily schedule that allowed him plenty of rest. Their manipulation of television in 1966 anticipated the television-oriented strategy of 1980 when TV news organizations were favored in the timing and arranging of news events and even in the distribution of seats on Reagan's plane. "The most effective thing we can do is put him on television whenever we can," said Nofziger.

The 1966 campaign also marked a major change in American politics. Two years before, the Republican party, ignoring all but ideologically pure GOP conservatives, had seen its presidential candidate, Goldwater, overwhelmingly defeated. Spencer and Roberts understood the importance of expanding the Republican base, and how to do it. Their targets were the working families, such as those who lived in Norwalk, the men and women who became "the forgotten Americans" of Reagan's speeches, "the man in the suburbs working sixty hours a week to support his family and being taxed heavily for the benefit of someone else."

For the most part Reagan's campaign was aimed at the white majority. Seldom was a stop made in a black community, although Reagan made a conscious effort to win the Mexican-Americans away from the Democrats. "*Ya basta!*" he cried—"We've had it." He was followed by a mariachi band when he went into Mexican-American communities, and the violins, trumpets and guitars made his appearance exciting. He concentrated on a sore point, charging that Brown had neglected these people in appointments and in social programs. In October, Mervyn Dymally, a black assemblyman for the Watts area and now a congressman, said the Mexican areas "are usually nine-to-one Democratic, but Reagan will make some dents in it."

He was surprisingly successful with the labor vote, demonstrating that the union leaders had lost their old-time hold on the rank and file. Standing in the yard of a plant, among union members, he said, "Even though I knew the upper crust of labor is opposed to my candidacy, I wasn't prepared for the extent they would lie about my record." With great effect he told about how he had opposed the right-to-work initiative that was backed by William F. Knowland, the Republican candidate for governor in 1958. He was warmly applauded when he said, "As long as we say a person must belong to a union, we must protect the union membership with a secret ballot." That position was opposed by organized labor.

"We've tried to support you a little bit," one union member told him. Another—with an "I'm a Democrat for Reagan" sign pasted across his bare stomach—said, "I'm shaking the hand of the next governor of the state of California."

By and by, even old friends began to desert Governor Brown and he realized he was going to lose. All the bounce vanished from him at the end of each day. Late in October he sipped Scotch on his plane and looked across at his wife. "Tired old governor," he said. "Tired old wife."

During the last two weeks of the campaign Reagan, who had been sitting in the back of the bus writing his speeches or studying, relaxed. It seemed that the crisis was over; the rest of the campaign was a triumphal march to the capitol. In these last weeks there was even some hilarity in the winner's circle—merriment that was part of traveling with a winning team. One afternoon when the campaign entourage flew to San Francisco, the party was met by Sue Warschaw, who had been assigned by the Brown campaign to heckle Reagan and tape-record his speeches. She had brought water pistols to "put out the prairie fire" with which Reagan usually ended his speeches, and she gave the weapons to the press covering Reagan. The reporters squirted water on one another the rest of the afternoon and on the commercial airliner that Reagan and the campaign party took back to Los Angeles that night. But by then the pistols had been filled with gin, and those who were aboard the plane recall that Reagan determinedly read a book, trying not to appear part of the group firing gin-filled water pistols in the cabin of a United airliner.

The Reagan team was confident and their confidence was well founded: on election night it was over quickly. Reagan and his wife were driving to their party at a hotel in Los Angeles when a radio newscaster announced that Reagan was the new governor. "It can't be over," Nancy said. We're not at the party yet." Reagan had won easily, by a margin of 993,739 votes. That night there were victory parties at the Biltmore and Ambassador hotels in Los Angeles. It was at the Ambassador that Brown was dealt the final blow. Hurrying over to congratulate Reagan was Mayor Sam Yorty of Los Angeles, who had refused to support Brown. After losing to him in the primary, Yorty had become a leader—and a symbol—of the Democrats who had left their party and gone over to Reagan.

9

THE GOVERNOR
AT WORK

As a chief executive Ronald Reagan keeps himself aloof from much of the conflict and interplay of ideas that shape an administration. The evidence of this lies in the archives which hold the records of his eight years as California's governor, and it is supported by the recollections of veterans of those Sacramento years. In the Hoover Institution's Reagan archives, box after box contains the story of an administration full of controversy and often rich in ideas. But Reagan initiated few of them. With each issue, the pattern is the same. There is the mini-memo, reducing the issue to a page, often backed up with a thick stack of documentation—papers and reports created by months of research, struggle between various interest groups, and fierce arguments between factions of the administration. But not much is seen of Reagan's participation in those struggles, nor is his imprint on the vital internal debate that shaped his administration's policies. The issue was presented to Reagan usually only when the battle was over, the ideas reduced to paper, and the sharp edge of controversy smoothed away. Then he would read the material, usually at home or while traveling on a plane.

He was exposed to the nature of the debate briefly, when the issue was presented in the structured atmosphere of the cabinet meeting.

Reagan presided at these meetings, but not as a dominating chief executive. His style was as one of a group of equals, part of a board of directors he referred to in a folksy way as "the fellas." The cabinet secretary would go through an agenda, calling on cabinet members seated at a table to present their proposals. Other cabinet members would then add their opinions, as would lesser administration aides seated in chairs along the wall. If things got tense, Reagan would lighten the atmosphere by telling an anecdote from his movie days or by mentioning how the situation reminded him of something that happened when he was president of the Screen Actors Guild. Finally, Reagan's most trusted adviser, the strong arm of his administration, Edwin Meese III, would sum up the arguments. Only then would Reagan make his decision, sometimes on the spot. Once the decision was made, Reagan would quickly formalize it, writing "OK, RR" on the mini-memo.

Such relaxed uninvolvement with detail is unusual among the leaders who run society. Corporate executives tell of weekends on the job. Press secretaries for Presidents Johnson, Nixon and Carter gave reporters accounts of their boss' desk-bound lives. But Reagan and his aides boast of their approach. "You show me any executive who doesn't delegate, and I'll show you a failure," said Meese. To him, Reagan's uninvolvement in detail was a virtue: "He had many out-standing traits from the beginning, the ability to delegate, the ability not to worry about things that are inconsequential. He did not worry about things until there was a time to worry. He didn't worry un-necessarily. He was the type of person who, if he had to make a tough decision on Friday, didn't worry about it all week long. He prepared, but he didn't worry. In other words, he had an amazing capacity to concentrate on what's important and not be worried about things that are unimportant. Once he made the decision, he made it and he'd pass on to something else."

Reagan preferred restricting discussion of pending issues to cabinet meetings. "When somebody tried to buttonhole him in the hall or someplace," Meese explained "he'd say, 'Well, I've got to talk that over with the fellas,' meaning that he'd bring it to the attention of the cabinet. The cabinet was well established as the focal point for decision making, which was a very important thing. It was a very organized, disciplined way of decision making."

One veteran of the cabinet meetings recalled the atmosphere: "It was all very low-key, you never raised your voice at anybody, and you didn't want to burden the governor with details and minutiae. So you thrash all those small things out in advance. You bother the governor with major things. In theory that's absolutely right. You can't burden a governor or a President down with minutiae. The question becomes what's minutiae and what's important."

Meese was important to the cabinet system. Like Reagan, he is an unpretentious man, not much different from when he was a young deputy district attorney in Oakland, dashing between the crowded old municipal courtrooms to file charges against murderers, robbers, burglars, rapists and drunk drivers. His father was Oakland's treasurer–tax collector. Traditional values and stability marked their family life: until moving to an apartment in 1980, his parents had lived in the same house for forty-four years. It was located next door to the house in which his grandparents had lived for decades. Meese's wife, Ursula, a county probation officer when they married in 1959, had known him for thirteen years before their marriage.

When the administration took office in 1967, Meese was clemency secretary, advising Reagan on whether to grant clemency in death-penalty cases, and in two years rose to executive secretary, top assistant to the governor. At cabinet meetings, recalled one former official, "Ed would think of himself as the facilitator. He was very adept at talking. We'd have these arguments around the table, and Ed would finish by summarizing what everyone had said, and he's excellent at that."

Ideas for Reagan's programs usually came from his subordinates. "I think he looked for people who had ideas and acted on those ideas as they came before him," said Meese. "But he also originated a lot of ideas himself." Meese had trouble remembering just what ideas Reagan contributed. "I can't remember specific ideas, but he would say, 'I've been thinking about this. What do you think of that?' He developed a lot of ideas himself, ways of doing things, specific programs. I wish I could remember all of them, but it was not unusual for him to come in clutching a magazine article or saying, 'What about this, let's see if we can't do that.' Or giving some idea to a department head to do something.

"He thought of family visits for prisoners. When he appointed Ray Procunier director of corrections, Ray came in to see the governor, and he asked Ray to take the job. As Ray was leaving he said, 'Ray, there's one thing. For a long time I've read about this, and I've always felt there ought to be family visits or conjugal visits for prisoners. I think we're doing the wrong thing the way we handle it now. I'd like you to experiment and try it. Not being a bleeding-heart liberal, perhaps I have a better chance to do some of these things in prison reform than a person who is perceived as more liberal.' And that was the start of the family-visitation program in California prisons."

But while he would delegate authority and leave innovation to others, Reagan was not a totally passive executive. Occasionally, in moments of great crisis, Reagan intervened. He would be the big gun, brought in by aides when all else had failed. There were a few occasions when he sat for hours with legislators, negotiating details of complicated tax and welfare legislation. When important legislation was bogged down during the night sessions that occurred in the final days of a legislative session, Reagan would sometimes come to the capitol and call legislators off the floor to lobby them. One year an important tax bill was one vote short of passage. Democratic Senator Tom Carrell of Los Angeles had promised his vote, but at the last minute he suffered a heart attack. According to William Bagley, Reagan came to the capitol at about seven-thirty in the evening and tried to round up another vote. When he failed, Bagley said, "The governor called Mrs. Carrell, and she said, 'If you need him, Governor, he's OK, he's resting. It wasn't that serious.' Then he [Reagan] talked to the doctor. The idea was that we could have had an ambulance plane ready in fifteen minutes. But he [Reagan] decided not to [bring Carrell back]. So we lost the tax-reform bill that year."

The opinions of trusted, unofficial advisers have always been an important part of Reagan's decision making. Then, as at the start of his presidency, it was the "kitchen cabinet," financial backers whose advice Reagan respected and often followed. It was a diverse group, and the only common denominator was wealth and maturity. The latter quality made their advice more important in Reagan's mind than that of some of his staff members who, although rich, lacked the experience he respected. Henry Salvatori was one member of the kitchen cabinet. So were Holmes Tuttle and the late A. C. "Cy" Rubel. Through the gubernatorial campaign and into Reagan's administration, they were viewed as mystery men by Democrats—ultraconservatives who exercised undue influence on the governor. Salvatori scoffed at that—there was no mystery to him. Always accessible, he liked to talk frankly of the role that he and the others played in the administration—adviser and counsel to Reagan, who, he insisted, always made up his own mind. To Salvatori, the wealth of the unofficial cabinet members was a virtue, for they were so rich that they asked no special favors in Sacramento. It made the Reagan administration unique because "not in the history of America has an administration come in without a single obligation. None of these fellows were after anything."

Most, like Salvatori, Tuttle and Rubel, were deeply conservative and among the original Reagan backers. They were Jaquelin Hume of San Francisco, the president of Basic Vegetable Products, Incorporated, one of the first members of the Friends of Ronald Reagan; Edward Mills, an old Goldwater supporter and also one of the first behind Reagan; Taft Schreiber, vice president of Music Corporation of America, who had been vice chairman of Reagan's statewide campaign committee. The two others were Reagan's personal attorney, William French Smith, who had been active in the Republican party, and Leland Kaiser, a San Francisco investment banker.

Over the years, the kitchen-cabinet's roster changed, but Tuttle and Smith remained powerful. Tuttle helped make key political decisions and raised large amounts of money for Reagan's campaigns and those of other key Republicans. Smith also helped guide Reagan's political career, and the governor appointed him to the University of California board of regents. Smith moved to the forefront after Reagan was elected President. Each day, during a period late in 1980, he and other kitchen-cabinet members met in Smith's downtown Los Angeles law offices. Constituted as an unofficial appointments committee, and with Smith as chairman, they began the work of choosing the top officials of Reagan's Administration, making sure the appointees were as conservative as were the kitchen-cabinet members.

Smith had graduated summa cum laude from UCLA in 1939 and from Harvard Law School. After service in the Navy in World War II he returned to Los Angeles and joined the major downtown law firm of Gibson, Dunn & Crutcher, where he specialized in the management side of labor law. He met Reagan through Republican politics in the 1960s, and along with Tuttle and others, urged Reagan to run for governor in 1966. Even philosophical opponents praise his ability. "He is highly intelligent, with a good analytical mind," said Fred Dutton, a Washington attorney who often opposed Smith when both served as university regents. But even his friends concede his manner is aloof and icy. A lawyer who knew him well once was asked if there was a warmer side to the Smith personality, one that was not seen in public. "There may be," he said, "but I ain't seen it."

When Smith was appointed Attorney General by Reagan, another kitchen-cabinet member, William A. Wilson, took over the chairmanship of the appointments team. Wilson was a California cattle rancher, a member of the boards of large businesses, and a University of California regent. He moved into an office in the Executive Office Building next to the White House for a time after the inaugural and continued to screen appointments. The surprising idea of a private citizen such as Wilson having a key role in making presidential appointments emphasizes the importance of the kitchen cabinet. These men viewed the Reagan presidency as an opportunity for them to have an important role in shaping foreign and domestic policies in a way that fitted their own political philosophies and the needs of their many business interests.

In Sacramento, however, their interest had not been as intense. State legislation exerted little effect on their businesses or lives and they were not especially interested in state politics—except as a vehicle for getting Reagan into the White House. Power in Sacramento went to official advisers, who appeared to share the kitchen cabinet's contempt of government. These aides' knowledge of government seemed to come from *Reader's Digest* articles on bureaucratic waste, and they arrived in Sacramento intending to clean up the mess and then move on to something more worthwhile.

They were, commented one old government hand, convinced they were the sole repository for goodness in the world—that everything that had gone on before was bad and everything the administration did would be right. So new to government were they that a guidebook was prepared for them in October 1966 by the assembly minority leader, Robert T. Monagan, and his staff. It was a thick book, a sophisticated civics course containing an outline of the historical development of the role of governor; a list of all the positions in the governor's office, with salaries; and a summary of the legal requirements of Reagan's relations with the legislature, including the date on which he must submit his budget.

But the book was ignored, as was much other good advice during the first years of Reagan's administration. Those years were marred by his bad relations with the legislature and some embarrassing mistakes by inexperienced assistants. In the minds of some of Reagan's advisers, Sacramento was merely on-the-job training for the presidency. Their main goal was winning the Republican presidential nomination in 1968. Early in the administration Henry Salvatori, in an interview with Doris Klein of the Associated Press, hinted of the new team's priorities. "People criticize Ronnie for having no political experience," he said. "But he has a great image, a way to get through to people. Look at the Goldwater experience. His philosophy was sound, but he didn't articulate it moderately. The governor has a similar philosophy, but he can express his thought. Look at John F. Kennedy. He didn't have much of a record as a senator. But he made a great appearance—and he had a beautiful wife. So does the governor. Nancy Reagan doesn't have to take a back seat to anyone. And the governor has plenty of time between now and the nomination to make a record as an administrator. But I don't believe people in other states really care much about what's happening in California."

But Reagan did not win the nomination in 1968. Richard Nixon had worked too hard for the prize, assuring himself of the support of the South long before the convention began. Reagan dashed from one Southern caucus to another, but he knew he had failed when Senator Strom Thurmond told him that he would honor his pledge to back Nixon.

Reagan returned to Sacramento, embarrassed by the failure. Resigned to a Nixon presidency, with the White House probably out of their grasp for eight years, Reagan and the others settled down to running the state.

Reagan's successful campaign for re-election in 1970 was noteworthy for its use of highly refined polling techniques that now dominate American politics. The crude briefing books used by Reagan in 1966 were abandoned in favor of a much more sophisticated system developed by his campaign managers. Stuart Spencer and Bill Roberts' pollster for the 1970 campaign, Richard Wirthlin of Decision Making Information, had included all of the important ingredients of computerized politics. Among them were the results of public opinion polls; studies of political behavior in thousands of election precincts; histories of voting patterns; all the small details of the census, such as income, race, sex, education, family size, numbers of television sets in households. From that he made up a political profile of the state, which was kept timely with daily telephone polls of several hundred people. This permitted the campaign to shift to meet new issues. For example, when a Decision Making Information poll showed that the environment had become the No. 1 concern among

Californians, the administration emphasized its environmental record. Wirthlin is an important member of the Reagan team. His polls continued to shape Reagan's policies during the next four years of his governorship, through the presidential campaigns of 1976 and 1980 and into his presidency.

The final four years of Reagan's governorship were the most important in the development of attitudes and work habits that would shape the presidency. In those years, as an experienced governor, he faced the domestic issues that would confront him as President: poverty, the economy, the environment, and the appointment of judges who, in the end, would determine how laws affect Americans. Reagan faced these issues in the arena of a large state, as complicated economically, socially and politically as any nation. By going back to those days, by examining the records of his administration and by drawing on the recollections of those who were there, we are able to probe the mind and understand the character of the man who is the Fortieth President of the United States.

10

A CITIZEN POLITICIAN MEETS THE PROFESSIONALS

Gaslights flickered on the walls of the garish red-and-gold room that housed the state senate of California in 1967. It was an unusual arena for the biggest triumph of Ronald Reagan's first year as governor, but this was where victory came, amid the gaudy splendor reminiscent of a luxurious Gay Nineties house of prostitution. Only the desks and the state seal woven into the red-and-gold carpet were evidence that this room was a solemn chamber of state government. And they were hardly noticed among the red shutters, the red-and-gold marble columns topped by gold leaf, and the big senatorial chairs covered in bright blue. The politicians who were members of the inner circle of the senate had spent $100,000 of the taxpayers' money two years before to redecorate the room to their own personal tastes, which ran to shiny silk suits, two-tone shoes, and martini and steak-sandwich lunches paid for by special-interest representatives. It looked like proof—in living color—of Reagan's campaign charge that "They've been in power so long, these professional politicians, that we're beginning to see a denigration of moral standards."

This was the den of the enemy, and it was here that Reagan would send his lieutenants to bargain and trade for passage of a bill he needed to make his first year a success. It was the first of his several tax increases. Passage would provide his first real test of fitness for high office. Success would give the state a financial cushion and allow Reagan the leisure to travel and participate in national politics. Failure would keep him at home trying to finance the operations of state government, dogged by the local difficulties that have overcome other governors. The tax bill was especially important to Reagan because of the troubles that had overtaken the rest of his legislative program. Many of the bills he had requested had been rejected by the Democratic-controlled legislature. Even some of his own Republicans had deserted him and left bills buried in committee. A few weeks before, Nofziger had correctly stated that a defeat on the tax bill would hurt Reagan's national reputation.

The difficulties he faced were great. His main problem was the Republican party's failure to win control of the senate and the assembly when Reagan was elected governor. As big as his triumph was, it did not carry along enough candidates to take over the legislature. If all the votes given to the Republican legislative candidates in November 1966 had been totaled, they would have exceeded the Democratic votes. But these representatives are elected from districts, and a Democratic reapportionment had drawn the individual districts so skillfully that the Democrats still managed to hold on to the assembly 42 to 38. In the 40-seat senate, reapportionment allowed the Democrats to remain narrowly in control. But Democrats held back from using this majority to openly challenge Reagan. His victory of almost a million votes frightened them. Instead they decided to fight a holding action, preserving the liberal programs they had created under Governor Brown and limiting Reagan's retrenchments.

By simple mathematics, Reagan needed Democratic votes if any of his programs were to become law. Without Democratic support he would have nothing to show for his first year as governor. But for most of the legislative session he had refused to negotiate. And until his need for the tax bill, he had not come to terms with the most powerful man in the legislature, Jesse Unruh, the Democratic speaker of the assembly. That was another reason for Reagan's troubles.

Then forty-four, Unruh was one of the most pre-eminent state legislators in the United States. During the 1960 presidential campaign he had been John F. Kennedy's man in California, and after Kennedy's assassination he gave his loyalty to no one else. With

Brown defeated, Unruh waited for a chance to move on to higher office. But sometimes he looked back on his childhood as the son of a poor Texas sharecropper, afraid, a friend said "that he'd wake up one day and find out he was going around without underpants again." He was built like a football guard, a powerful-looking man with a thick neck and broad shoulders. When he had come to the legislature thirteen years before, he weighed about two hundred and eighty pounds and was called "Big Daddy" after the domineering father in Tennessee Williams' play *Cat on a Hot Tin Roof.* He quickly acquired power in the legislature and in the political life of Southern California. As speaker he had jealously fought Brown, convinced he was more qualified to be chief executive. The fighting hurt both men and left Unruh with the reputation of a bully. With the determination of a poor boy who would not be denied fame, he worked to repair his image, dieting away almost a hundred pounds, swearing off political brawls and building a legislative program upon which he could one day run for higher office. He acquired polish, grace and skill and now lectured at Rutgers, Yale, Berkeley and other campuses. But occasionally he would slip into an auditorium and hear a country-and-Western band. C&W-music fans cheered him as one of their own when he was introduced at a concert in Sacramento.

Unruh ruled the assembly with the same sort of strength and guile that Lyndon B. Johnson had used in the U. S. Senate in the fifties. In the next few months the relationship between Reagan and Unruh often resembled Johnson's relationship with another Republican Chief Executive, President Eisenhower. Like Johnson, Unruh was afraid to challenge the popular chief executive publicly. Sometimes he would even work with him. But in private he yearned for the governorship and cursed the fate that had given it to Reagan. In 1970 Unruh ran for governor, but Reagan defeated him easily.

In the past few years Unruh had spent much of his time trying to improve the image of his colleagues in the legislature. Neither he nor the other legislators liked Reagan's attacks on professional politicians. For despite the senate's gaudy décor and the remnants of lobbyist control, the California legislature had become one of the nation's best. In 1966 a *Saturday Evening Post* article on state house corruption had singled out California for praise, saying that the legislature "has shown ability and willingness to initiate."

Only two decades before, the stench of corruption had been heavy in Sacramento. It was still the era of the "cinch" bill, a peculiar measure directed against a specific industry or group. Once he had introduced it, the author would wait patiently for the industry to pay him off, and then he would drop the bill. In those days the assembly public morals committee took its orders from the most famous of the California lobbyists, Arthur L. Samish, the fat representative of liquor, beer and race-track interests. Meeting in a hot, overcrowded little room with its members underpaid and ill-informed, the committee waited for instructions from Samish's messengers before making decisions. So powerful was Samish that he even mocked California's popular and respected governor, Earl Warren. Warren might be governor of the state, said Samish, but "I am governor of the legislature." Samish's boasting finally resulted in an investigation, and he was sent to jail for income-tax evasion.

The legislature had cleaned up and gained self-respect since then. It had added, for example, a new twist to the inevitable conflicts between the executive and legislative branches. Instead of merely obstructing the governor's programs, it proposed alternatives.

Unruh believed in equipping legislators with a capable staff so they would no longer have to rely on lobbyists for much of their advice. He supplied assemblymen with more help to free them from the time-consuming job of answering mail from their constituents. Fringe benefits were improved. With Unruh's help the legislature became so independent that the assembly sent its own lobbyist to Washington to round up federal support of its projects. Finally, in 1966, the voters recognized the legislature's new status and voted the senators and assemblymen a $10,000-a-year pay raise in exchange for legislative acceptance of conflict-of-interest rules.

These men did not forget Reagan's past criticisms, and at that early stage he found it difficult to participate in the back-slapping camaraderies of politicians. They found him pleasant, witty, humorous—and remote. "He makes an effort to be one of the boys, but never lets the bars down," said someone who had watched him at the regular parties he and his wife gave for small groups of legislators. "Meanwhile the legislators are running around acting like legislators, drinking, baring their souls, talking."

Another reason for Reagan's problems was the old division between moderate and more conservative Republicans, a split that was evident among GOP legislators. The moderates did not agree that the Creative Society was the only answer to California's problems, and while they carefully kept their disagreements to themselves, they were reluctant to help the governor.

Reagan was not, however, without advantages. The first was his big vote, the evidence of a popular mandate. Another was the nature of party politics in California. The Democratic control of the legislature was, in a sense, a mathematical deception. In Sacramento, as elsewhere, the representatives paid more attention to the wishes of their constituents than to the orders of party leaders. In California, party leadership was weak. "There is no Democratic party in California," Unruh once said. Hiram Johnson and the progressive reformers had wrecked party strength when they threw out the political bosses in 1910. The direct primary replaced conventions. And to weaken the party structure even more, candidates were permitted to "cross-file": they could seek the nomination of their party and the other party at the same time. Many times, candidates would win both the Democratic and Republican nominations. This blurred party lines and gave an advantage to the candidate best known to voters, the incumbent. Democrats eliminated cross-filing in 1959, but official party organizations remained weak, unable to exert pressure on legislators. In the assembly, Unruh could influence votes, but even he had to respect the pressures from local districts. A Democrat coming from a suburban district whose residents—concerned with taxes, black militancy and crime—voted for Reagan in 1966 would not quarrel publicly with the governor. To do so would invite the possibility of defeat.

Reagan knew his political problems could be overcome, and his tax increase approved, if he could come to terms with Unruh. Not only had Unruh control of the assembly but he held a balance of power in the senate. Some senators were his friends and had been helped by campaign contributions he had directed their way. And strangely enough, Unruh's ambition forced him into an alliance with Reagan, for Reagan and Unruh had something in common. Both understood that political advancement in California depended on the votes of the growing white middle class of conservative suburbanites. Unruh needed an issue to win these people away from the Republicans, to make them realize that their economic interests—a determining factor in their vote—rested with him, not Reagan. Unlike Reagan, he could not appeal to them with veiled criticisms of the civil rights movement or promises of a drastic reduction in welfare costs. That would have lost him the support of minorities in the

Democratic party. Instead, he decided to appeal to the pocketbooks of the middle class. He would shape the tax bill to his own taste, make sure the governor was blamed for the big increase—and take credit himself for whatever was popular in the plan.

Shortly before the vote on the tax bill, Reagan and Unruh talked for an hour in Reagan's office. This was not a meeting place of Unruh's choosing. He liked to deal in his own office, safely seated behind his desk, in a room decorated with Kennedy mementos and souvenirs of trips to the Orient and Europe. But the protocol of government required him to go downstairs, be ushered into Reagan's office and sit across from the governor. It was Reagan who seemed irritable. He made a strong statement in favor of his version of the tax bill. He insisted on paying back a $194 million debt from the Brown administration. He also wanted to put a tax on such services as shoeshines and auto repairs, but Unruh told him, "Your tax on services is so incredibly bad that I'm tempted to keep it in the program, but in the interests of good government, I'll take it out."

In the middle of the conversation Reagan interrupted Unruh and gave him a lecture on the economy of the nation and the state— something that seemed unnecessary to Unruh, who operated an economic consulting business as a sideline. But he listened politely until the subject was changed and the conversation returned to the tax bill.

Unruh and Reagan finally agreed on terms for a bill. Unruh promised to speed the bill through the assembly, and then help Reagan round up votes in the senate. There was an unexpectedly tense moment in the assembly. Democrats refused to vote for the tax increase until every Republican voted first. One first-year Republican refused, and it took personal persuasion from Reagan to change his mind.

The assembly vote was a preliminary step before the real drama —the fight in the senate. This was where Reagan's aides would meet their greatest test. They went upstairs to the senate chamber, following the same path Reagan had taken six months before on the day he delivered the budget message. The intervening months had taught his assistants much about government, and they were ready for the administration's most crucial day. Battaglia—now with so much influence that some of Reagan's other friends jealously called him "Governor Battaglia"—led the group. He was followed by Vernon Sturgeon, an aide who, until his defeat the year before, had been a favored member of the senate. There was also Jack Lindsay, an assistant with the looks, enthusiasm and lack of sophistication of a junior-chamber-of-commerce president, and Paul Beck, the glowering, dark-complexioned press secretary—a former reporter who always seemed guiltily ill at ease when confronting his former colleagues of the press corps in the heat of daily battle. They greeted the sergeant at arms and walked into the chamber. Unruh soon joined them. He walked into the hall and through the big wooden doors that guarded the colorful room. Reagan wasn't in the capitol. After sending his troops into the fight, he had flown south to have a bladder stone and a nonmalignant growth on his lip removed.

In the need for victory, the Reagan men forgot all the old campaign promises of no political deals. Where once the administration scorned legislators' appeals for patronage, they now listened. Through his aides, the governor asked recalcitrant senators if they wanted to make a deal. Several, rebuffed for months, were delighted, and Battaglia, standing quietly in back of the senate chamber, talked to them. One senator was told that Reagan would now sign his appropriation bill, despite the administration's economy goals. Two more were told that, by coincidence, the men they were backing for judgeships would now get the appointments. Power was also used. The legislature's only member of the John Birch Society, John Schmitz, whose conservative constituency provided some of Reagan's most enthusiastic and wealthy supporters, refused to vote for the tax increase. Brought into a side room by Battaglia, Schmitz was told that every one of his bills would be vetoed if he refused Reagan a vote. He wouldn't surrender.

Despite Schmitz's refusal, the bill passed and was flown to Reagan's hospital room, where he signed it the next day.

Reagan's political maneuvering was resented in the senate, where Battaglia was ordered off the floor just before the vote. And Unruh so offended the old-guard senate leadership by the way he went from desk to desk calling in old debts that George Miller, chairman of the senate finance committee, later said, "I am sickened by the presence of this little Nero on our floor. Let him restrict his wheeling and dealing and politicking to his own den and befoul his own aisles." Looking back on it, one of the participants in the difficult negotiations remarked, "It was the first time the Reagan administration showed any signs of any normal wheeler-dealer ability."

It was an unusual experience for those first uncertain years. For the most part in that time, Reagan was a prisoner of inexperience and of the rigid, cumbersome system he used at the beginning of his governorship. There were many more failures than successes. And none of the failures was more embarrassing than Reagan's fumbling with a bill liberalizing the state's abortion law.

In the late 1960s, abortion had not yet become a major national political issue. The right-to-life movement was just beginning. But the Roman Catholic Church, the main opponent to liberalizing the law, was influential in the capitol. Reagan tried to please everybody —the church and the doctors who supported the liberal proposal. So badly did he handle the issue that he ended up doing the impossible, antagonizing both sides. For a while he seemed to be doing his best to kill the reform and please the opponents who were writing him at least a hundred letters a day. But he later angered the Catholics by signing it, and when the fight was over, he had only one souvenir —a picture of himself putting his signature on the bill after a day of confused indecision. As one critic commented, the widely printed picture would quickly go on the bulletin board of some Catholic churches at election time.

Although abortion reform had been an issue in California for years, it became more important in 1966 when a state board charged nine respected San Francisco physicians with unprofessional conduct for aborting women who had contracted German measles in the early months of pregnancy. The ailment can result in the birth of a deformed child. Before the action, many legitimate physicians had been performing abortions in German measles cases, with the unofficial approval of their hospital surgical boards. The fight for reform of the law was taken up by one of the young men who had been responsible for the improved quality of the legislature, Senator Anthony C. Beilenson, a Democrat from Beverly Hills. He had introduced the reform in the past, but had been laughed at as a dreamer. Now, with the charges pending against the San Francisco doctors and the enactment of abortion reforms in Colorado and North Carolina, his chances looked brighter. But first Beilenson needed Republican support, for the Democrats were split.

As it turned out, Republicans would not back the bill either. Reagan informed senate Republicans that he would not support it because he did not approve of the German measles section aimed at preventing the birth of a potentially deformed child. He said: "I cannot justify morally . . . taking of the unborn life simply on the supposition that it is going to be less than a perfect human being, because I don't see very far . . . from that to some day deciding after birth that we will sort out those people who should be allowed to live or not, and I don't see any difference between that and what Hitler tried to do." He approved, however, the provision allowing abortions to prevent pregnancies caused by rape or incest or to prevent a birth that, in the judgment of a panel of physicians, would gravely impair the mental or physical health of the mother. Beilenson agreed to Reagan's changes, and Republicans were free to vote for the bill. It narrowly passed the senate.

When the liberalization law reached the assembly, Reagan unexpectedly started another fight. On the morning of the assembly debate he said he had new objections. The deal he had made with Beilenson was off, and he would not support the bill unless new changes were made. Opponents, expecting assembly passage, were suddenly given new hope. Their last-minute attempt to kill the bill appeared to be succeeding. One of the opponents had, through Battaglia, placed in the governor's hands a legal opinion declaring that there was a loophole in the bill. Possibly, the opinion said, abortions could be used to prevent the birth of a potentially deformed child, despite the Reagan revisions. A doctor could evade the intent of the law by convincing a supervising panel of physicians that the birth of such a baby would injure the mental or physical health of the mother. The information in this legal opinion should have reached Reagan days before. But it came late and was a complete surprise to him.

How did Reagan explain his ignorance of the implications of the bill? "For one thing," he told reporters at his weekly news conference, "I've been out of the city and I've only just received an analysis from the legislative counsel." Television cameras, as usual, were recording the weekly meeting with newsmen. Reagan usually sparkled during these sessions, but this time he was not prepared. "These are fast-moving days," he said, "and I have been—I left the city Friday morning, and I've been involved in other activities. I haven't been vacationing. I've been pretty busy and just arrived back. . . . There are some five thousand bills or so up there, and we have had frequent meetings and do keep as close contact as possible, and I don't think there has been any lapse at all." Obviously there had been a lapse in the channeling of information to the governor by his staff. When the possible loophole in the bill had been debated in the senate two weeks before, Reagan either had not heard of it or had not understood its implications. The blame had to fall upon the governor's inclination to isolate himself from outside contacts and news, and the inherent inadequacy of the mini-memos.

Beilenson was furious at Reagan for his latest hesitations. So was the Republican who was his floor manager for the bill in the assembly, Craig Biddle. Further amendment would have the effect of killing the bill. The senate was required to approve the amendments, and there was little chance that senators, having voted for the bill once, would risk criticism by voting for it again. The issue was too controversial.

But as it turned out, the assembly paid no attention to Reagan. Biddle opposed Reagan's changes and informed his fellow assemblymen that Reagan had promised him "he would sign it in its present form." In a rare open Republican break with the governor, he told the assembly it was his duty "to pass legislation of this house" no matter what the governor said. Biddle and other Republicans joined Democrats in approving the bill 48 to 29 without the amendments Reagan had asked for. When Reagan signed it, he smiled dutifully for photographers while Biddle and Beilenson stood next to him. He jokingly threatened not to sign the bill before he finally wrote his signature at the bottom. To refuse would have caused a deep split between him and the Republican legislators who had voted for the bill. With the bill now law, they were satisfied.

Reagan had liked to criticize his predecessor, Governor Brown, for being indecisive, but Reagan's own wavering on the abortion bill showed that he too had difficulty in making up his mind on an emotional issue. For the first time he was faced with a problem that did not fit the neat partisan pattern to which he had grown accustomed. The debate cut across party lines, and with his surprise objections, Reagan antagonized both conservative Republicans and liberal Democrats. Several special-interest groups who had been following the bill were angry and disappointed. The matter was, however, more a topic of conversation in the capitol than anywhere else —something for insiders to speculate about. Public opinion polls showed his popularity high, and none of the legislators who complained privately about him would challenge him in public. The mistakes might hurt him later, but for the present even Unruh held back from fighting Reagan in the open. The strength of his mandate was shown a few months later, when every single Republican legislator stood behind him and defeated Democratic attempts to overturn his vetoes of more than $30 million in appropriations—including money for some Republican projects.

Reagan faltered on the abortion bill, but he showed the beginning of an ability to deal with political realities on the tax bill—which was vital to the success of his first year in office. He could compromise with his enemies. He would boldly announce a controversial program, quietly modify it in the face of criticism and then hail the compromise as a complete victory. He was described as "a man who charges up a hill in the daytime and retreats under the cover of darkness"—a description that irritated him. "You can't win," he said. "You set your feet in concrete and say, 'Here I stand or fall'; then you are being stubborn and unreasonable. You try to indicate the world is a fallible place. You do your best and you make decisions on certain facts, but you try to keep yourself with an open mind."

The adoption of the philosophy of the "open mind" was an important development in Reagan's political career. His willingness to negotiate with his foes on the bill that was most important to his administration, and his ability to get it through the legislature, provided arguments for his supporters who contended he was not another Goldwater; he was not bound to a rigid conservative philosophy that he would not modify. Reagan's new ability to compromise made him appear more moderate—and more acceptable as a potential candidate for President.

11

REAGAN AND THE POOR

On May 22, 1970, an idea was proposed to Ronald Reagan that was unusual even for his private-enterprise-oriented administration. It was a revolutionary plan to turn the administration of the troublesome and increasingly expensive welfare system over to private enterprise. Neighborhood welfare corporations would be created in two counties to run a system that was originally designed to provide short-term help for the most needy but had grown over the years into a cumbersome, multibillion-dollar bureaucracy. The corporation—private, profit-making enterprises—would decide welfare eligibility and amounts of grants. Before the grants were delivered to recipients, they would first be invested by the corporations on a short-term basis. Then, increased by profits from the investments, the money would be used for welfare payments and for the financing of income-producing businesses in the neighborhoods. The businesses would create jobs and provide a way to end the hopeless cycle of one generation following the other on welfare.

As was his custom, Reagan presided over the discussion of the plan at a cabinet meeting and then wrote "OK, RR" at the top of a cabinet mini-memo, agreeing to let his social welfare director go ahead. But it was never put into effect. The following year Robert

Carleson, a new social welfare director, took over the department and studied the proposal. "I didn't think it was going to work," he recalled. "First of all, there were a lot of federal constraints. I figured it was not a viable solution."

Many solutions were proposed and abandoned during this period as Reagan tried to reduce the size of the growing welfare system, one of the most important efforts of his eight-year governorship. It was a struggle that tells much about Reagan, his attitude toward the poor, his methods of making policy and his political skill. It pitted Reagan, the critic of big government, against the ultimate in government bureaucracy, a ponderous, expensive welfare system run by administrators who talked in their jargon. Their clientele, mostly the minority poor, was rapidly losing political power. Public opinion polls showed the voters disapproved of welfare; it made a perfect target.

Records of cabinet meetings portray a governor trying to clear the welfare rolls of those he considered undeserving while rejecting some of the harsh proposals of more militant assistants. He had no sympathy for young women who he believed became pregnant just to escape parents, then going on welfare. Parents should be made responsible, he said, because "only in this way can we remove a tax-paid incentive to immorality and imposition of the welfare cycle on a new generation." A similar lack of sympathy was expressed by his human relations agency, which saw the problem in a slightly different light. On October 9, 1970, they told the cabinet that "at the present time, there is an increasing number of girls coming into the program simply as a way of financing therapeutic abortion. Thus eligibility is granted to kill the eligible."

Reagan initialed his approval for an order to deny abortions to welfare recipients. But an even sterner measure was rejected, one that would have banned any state medical care until the 24th week of pregnancy. As the proposal put it, no pregnant woman would be eligible "until after the normal period of abortions, which would be 20 weeks, and [it] still allows for some pre-natal care as well as delivery." Another proposal that was too harsh for Reagan was a particularly heartless solution to the unwed-mother problem. His social welfare board had proposed that a welfare mother who had a third illegitimate child be considered unfit and morally depraved and that her children be taken from her. James Hall, Reagan's secretary of human relations, said it was "a very good report. I welcome it."

But the governor, rejecting the proposal, said, "I think the laws we have regarding the fitness of a household, the ability to take a child away from a household on the basis of moral unfitness is sufficient if it is properly enforced." However, Reagan did propose a bill to eliminate aid to welfare mothers if they refused a state offer that would return them to their home states for available jobs.

In the 1966 campaign and throughout his governorship Reagan attacked welfare, speaking in a hostile, simplistic manner that reflected his small-town roots and, in the view of his critics, showed a lack of sympathy for complicated causes and effects of urban poverty and unemployment. From the beginning, audiences applauded the attacks, even when they were based on wrong information. "Great numbers of people are coming to California simply because they know that in twenty-four hours they can be taken care of by the rest of us," he said during his first campaign. His statement was erroneous. There was only one category of welfare that provided immediate eligibility and that was aid to the blind, involving a relatively small number. Most recipients—unwed mothers and their fatherless families—had to live in California for at least a year before receiving aid. After a few months in office, Reagan recognized his error. "We have some pretty sound residency requirements here," he said. "My criticism during the campaign was a lack of enforcement . . ."

But despite his preoccupation with welfare, Reagan's piecemeal solutions during his first term did not accomplish his main objective, a fundamental change in welfare policy. Reagan wanted to give welfare only to the unemployable needy, a philosophy well expressed by Dr. Martin Anderson, a Reagan adviser, who wrote: "If persons are capable of self support, both for themselves and for their families, they should not expect to receive any money from other members of society who work and pay taxes." That was completely contrary to the policy of national, and previous California state, administrations which had been moving toward a policy of eliminating dire poverty by providing minimum guaranteed grants to the poor, whether or not they were employed or employable.

Only in his second term, when Reagan's political skills improved, was his administration able to change the direction of welfare policy through new laws and regulations.

One reason why it took him so long was that the welfare issue in California was more complicated than he first suspected, a political, economic and social puzzle that was shaped by the peculiar nature of poverty in California, a state which has always been notable for its islands of extreme poverty surrounded by the most ostentatious wealth. The ever present contrast between poverty and wealth led to the creation of powerful political and social movements that shaped the debate over welfare.

Since the Depression, when the government actively began to give money to large numbers of the poor, welfare has been at the center of the state's economic conflict, used at various times for the benefit of both conservative business interests and by liberals.

The most famous example of welfare as an economic tool of business interests came during the Depression, when it was used to provide low-paid workers for the state's agricultural industry. In his book *Factories in the Field,* Carey McWilliams, the great California historian, reported how in the 1930s federal and state relief payments to the unemployed were withdrawn from workers to force them to accept low piecework wages. A committee appointed by government relief administrators decided that the prevailing rate for farm work in Los Angeles County should range from 22 1/2 cents to 30 cents an hour, and recipients were told to accept those wages or be deprived of relief. That effort, backed by the state's powerful farm organization, the Associated Farmers, kept wages low and crippled union organizing efforts.

During the Depression, aid to the poor was also a valuable political organizing tool for liberals. The cities, unlike the farmlands, were ready for radical solutions. Unemployment was high, a situation worsened by the disintegration of the high hopes that had brought the immigrants to California. The elderly retired, for example, could no longer live on income from investments that were suddenly worthless. The despair produced solutions that were often so radically visionary that they enhanced the state's reputation as a place of strange ideas. Confronted by poverty amid plenty, the troubled searched for help in evangelical religious groups and with experimental social theories.

One of the most influential of the radical social and economic theorists was Upton Sinclair, the social reforming novelist who, decades earlier, had exposed corrupt and oppressive business practices in *The Jungle* and other popular books. Gladwyn Hill, in his book *Dancing Bear,* wrote of Sinclair: "The name Upton Sinclair sounds almost ominously imposing, and Sinclair has sometimes been represented as an ogre bent on bomb tossing. Actually, he was a slight, bespectacled man of exceptional gentleness and good will— a man who, but for an extraordinary mind and a gift for commercially lucrative writing, might have been just another of the obscure people who frequent health food stores."

Sinclair had run for office as a socialist for many years. In 1934 he won the Democratic nomination for governor on a platform of Production for Use, in which the urban unemployed would live on communal rural land colonies or work in shut-down factories, where they would produce food and goods for the state. Significantly for future politics, Sinclair also proposed higher welfare payments of $50 a month for the aged, widows and the disabled. So ready were Californians for radical change that the old socialist received 879,537 votes, not far behind the conservative Republican winner's 1,138,620. More important, his campaign helped give the Democrats the registration majority in the state and solidified a welfare constituency that has been a powerful force ever since.

Welfare was not a great issue during the prosperity of World War II. But afterward a changing economic structure brought welfare back to the center of political debate. Postwar prosperity was generally for the educated and skilled. The manufacture of aircraft, aerospace equipment, high-technology computers, electrical equipment and communications supplies became leading industries, and today California is the No. 1 recipient of contracts from the Defense Department and the National Space and Aeronautics Administration. Meanwhile, old inner-city plants that manufactured tires and automobiles were laying off workers and closing.

California developed a great system of public higher education, and its highly trained graduates were important to the new industries. In addition, the state was part of an important trend in American life, the shift in population from the Northeast and the Midwest to the South and the West. But besides contributing to the prosperity, the immigration helped create a frightening new kind of poverty, with a wide, uncrossable gulf between rich and poor. The state's newcomers preferred to live outside the cities, and industry followed them there. This further isolated the poor from jobs, and government in turn began spending billions to assist them.

In 1961, California's Democratic legislature had radically changed the state's welfare law, making many more people eligible for government aid. Reflecting the liberal era, neither the Democratic administration nor the legislators gave much thought to the long-range financial implications of what they were doing. In fact, the bill was so complicated that only the author, Philip Burton, and a few of his staff really understood it. A brilliant, extremely liberal tactician, Burton was smart enough not to explain it to many of his colleagues. As a result of the legislation, the number of Californians receiving welfare payments increased from 620,000 to about 2.3 million between 1961 and 1970. Most were children and mothers receiving Aid to Families with Dependent Children, a controversial category that provided aid to unwed mothers and their children. More than 300,000 of the recipients in other categories were aged, and the rest suffered from blindness and other disabilities.

Government programs were launched to help the inner cities, but few succeeded. For example, there was the Watts Industrial Park in Los Angeles, a federally financed project conceived to bring jobs to the scene of the 1965 ghetto riot. But even good intentions and federal aid could not bridge the gap between white and black and rich and poor. It took ten years to sign enough leases with employers to fill the park. "A lot of employers are afraid for their personal safety," said Jack Karp, president of National Industrial Properties to Los Angeles *Times* reporter Martin Baron. Karp, who is familiar with the real estate market in the area, said, "If you drive around there during the day, you see a lot of unemployed young men, and that scares the hell out of people."

Welfare administrators, academics and both liberal Democratic and Republican politicians abandoned the idea of eliminating the permanent layer of unemployed and instead centered attention on revising the welfare system to provide for a minimum income for all. And in response to complaints from state and local officials over welfare costs, they proposed that the federal government both finance and administer the system, shifting the burden to Washington with its broader taxing power.

It was at this point that Ronald Reagan, with his hope for reducing welfare rolls, became governor. In 1968, after Reagan had been governor for a year, the new Republican President, Richard M. Nixon, proposed a huge welfare reform called the Family Assistance Plan. It was the heart of Nixon's first-term domestic program and would guarantee a national minimum benefit for welfare families. It would also have made more people eligible for welfare, and it would have given control of the welfare system to Washington. Although the proposal was surprisingly liberal for the President, it was not strange that Nixon endorsed it. It reflected the influence of the Secretary of Health, Education and Welfare, liberal California Republican Robert H. Finch. Nixon, bored by domestic affairs, left them in the hands of subordinates while he was absorbed by his main interest, foreign policy.

Reagan opposed the program. His advisers told him in a cabinet memo that "the free enterprise position, simply stated, is that the continued growth of government operated welfare under [the Nixon proposal] is malignant. The more it grows, the worse the problem becomes." Agreeing with the advice, Reagan told his assistants to come up with a strategy to thwart the Nixon plan.

It was more than a philosophical dispute. Although Reagan always spoke highly of Nixon and defended him almost to his resignation, it was an alliance of pure political convenience. Neither had forgotten that Reagan opposed Nixon for the 1968 Republican presidential nomination and might have taken the nomination away had it not been for Senator Strom Thurmond's support of Nixon. Also increasing tension between Reagan and Nixon was Nixon's appointment of Finch, then California's lieutenant governor, as Secretary of Health, Education and Welfare. Even when Reagan and Finch headed the California Republican ticket in 1966, Reagan distrusted and disliked Finch. And it rankled Reagan that Finch had written the Nixon Administration's welfare policy.

Eventually Finch left Washington. Nixon, preoccupied with the Vietnam war and wanting to solidify his conservative support for the 1972 election, abandoned the Family Assistance Plan. Reagan thus became the party's chief advocate of welfare reform. It was an important step in his political career. His dominance of the difficult issue helped convince Republicans in other states that he was more than an actor, that he had the ability to understand policy and push it in a conservative direction. As a result, Reagan's concentration on the welfare issue allayed doubts about his competence and became a major factor in his winning the party's nomination and the presidency in 1980.

The welfare program which Reagan advocated nationally was prepared when he and his assistants agreed that a new, more politically sophisticated attempt was needed to change welfare laws. Work started in 1970 after Edwin Meese and his assistant, Michael Deaver, listened to the finance department's projections of next year's budget and decided to talk to Reagan. "It was clear that unless we did something about welfare, we'd have to raise taxes," Meese said. "We went back to his office and we talked about what needed to be done. That was when he said, 'We've got to have a program to solve this welfare problem.' "

Task forces were formed to write new welfare laws and regulations. The purpose was to reduce the welfare rolls. In particular Reagan wanted to put a ceiling on yearly welfare appropriations, though he was willing to increase aid to the most needy. Political experts on the governor's staff prepared a grass-roots campaign to mobilize anti-welfare feelings among voters and channel them into pressure on the Democratic legislature.

Reagan assembled a group of conservative state officials, headed by Meese, to take charge of the new program. Typical of the officials was Robert Carleson, then public works director but later welfare director, who, in discussing the poor, once said there was a great resentment against someone who presents food stamps at a supermarket checkout stand "and buys something you can't afford to buy and then goes out and gets into a nice car."

Despite the rhetoric, Carleson and the other aides were effective conservatives and not like the businessmen who were recruited for cost-cutting task forces early in the Reagan administration. Those early and unsuccessful Reagan reformers had ranted against "welfare fraud" without understanding the system. Carleson, who had been a city administrator for years, understood that information was the key to mastering government and that the only way to beat the officials who ran the system was to know more than they did. "I was in my office a minimum of ten hours a day each day, seven days a week," said Ronald Zumbrun, an attorney who worked on the welfare reductions. "We went down in the bureaucracy, and there were stacks of hearing-officer decisions six feet high. I read those and we started reversing things that were legally incorrect."

In addition, a statewide citizens committee was formed to speak and to stimulate a letter-writing campaign to influence the legislature. Reagan was the star speaker, but county officials and community leaders also carried the message, stimulating the anti-welfare feeling that had shown up in public opinion polls.

"I spoke at Rotary clubs, women's groups, the Lions, the Elks, two or three times a week," said the committee co-chairman, Neil Papiano, a Los Angeles attorney. "I didn't feel strong resistance anywhere. Some legislators told me they were surprised at the depths of their constituents' feelings."

Another move to use the popular antagonism to welfare to influence the legislature was Reagan's threat to place on the 1972 ballot a voter initiative which would have enacted his program even if the legislature turned him down. "We called it Operation Crossfire," said Carleson.

Arguing for the initiative, cabinet member Hall wrote Reagan: "During the last four years, we have learned some basic lessons. Unless restrained, welfare and education expenditures will destroy our economy. The legislature cannot and will not deal effectively with the problems of welfare and education finance. Administrative reforms are often hampered by the existing civil service system." The threat of the initiative frightened Reagan's opponents. "I was afraid of class warfare," said Republican Assemblyman William Bagley, one of the influential opponents of the Reagan plan. "The initiative would have pitted the taxpayer against the poor, and the taxpayer would have won."

The most important part of the effort was the attempt to reach a compromise with legislative Democrats. If successful, it would give Reagan at least part of what he wanted, without the political turmoil of an initiative campaign.

His main antagonist was the speaker of the assembly, Bob Moretti, who was Reagan's opposite in many ways. His political philosophy was liberal. He loved the rough and intricate maneuvering of the legislature, and his greatest enjoyment was sitting with friends gossiping about politics and plotting for the next day's session. He was a skilled and intelligent politician who inspired great personal loyalty from colleagues and his staff. But unlike the mannered and controlled Reagan, Moretti seemed to have come directly from the streets. When he was first elected to the assembly, he spoke in incomplete, ungrammatical sentences that belied his degree from the University of Notre Dame. In the East or Midwest, where political skill and friendships can move you up through a party organization, Moretti would have been a mayor or perhaps a governor. But in California, where candidates tend to look like TV-news anchormen, Moretti would be at a disadvantage in statewide elections.

Reagan and Moretti had much at stake. Both needed to emerge from the 1971 session claiming a record of accomplishment. Moretti had decided to run for governor in the next primary election, but he knew he could not match the better-known name, intriguing personality and campaign funds of Edmund G. Brown, Jr., who would be a major opponent. Instead, he would run a campaign conceding his abrasive aggressiveness while portraying himself as the most effective Democrat. Meanwhile, Reagan and his staff were troubled by polls showing that while he was popular, California voters did not consider him effective. Looking ahead to the 1976 presidential election, they knew they had to change that impression.

Strategy was planned far in advance. "We determined that the way we had to get a welfare reform package was to play one house against the other, that it could not be the governor against the legislature," said one Reagan assistant. "The guy who obviously was the prime candidate was Bob Moretti . . . the theory was that you couldn't push Bob Moretti around; you could talk tough with him, and you could talk directly with him, but you weren't going to beat him. We didn't want to beat him, we wanted him on our side."

Relations between the two were not especially friendly. At one point Reagan's assistants heard that Moretti planned to confront Reagan in the governor's office over a welfare issue and that the speaker had told the press so there would be a public confrontation. Reagan was advised to beat Moretti to the punch by going to the speaker's office to see him in private and avoid the confrontation. Reagan followed the advice.

Reagan's first attempt to convince Moretti failed. "He thought he could get Moretti's support, initially," said Meese. "He called Moretti in, asked him to come in for a briefing. Moretti came in and listened in kind of a disinterested manner. But the governor really thought he had something here. Moretti said he would think about it, and then he called later on and said he couldn't buy it."

At the outset, the Democrats made a serious blunder. They turned down Reagan's request to present his program to a joint session of the senate and the assembly. That provided Reagan a chance to play the outraged victim of a stubborn legislature. "Having been denied the opportunity to address the legislature in person, I will, of course, submit a written message. But it now appears that I will have to seek other means to inform the people first-hand of the specific reforms we will be proposing [to the legislature]," he said.

He told Meese, "Find a forum where I can do this as a speech. This will be like the books that were banned in Boston. We'll get more attention this way than by just speaking to a joint session."

The forum Meese selected was Town Hall, a business-oriented civic luncheon group in Los Angeles. The fact that Reagan had been denied access to the legislature made his speech big news in the city, and it was extensively reported in the newspapers and on radio and television, reaching far more people than he would have in a routine speech to the legislature. That speech and others by Reagan were important in mustering public support and aided the citizens committees in gathering popular backing.

As the summer of 1971 approached, compromise seemed far away. Reagan insisted on placing a ceiling on welfare appropriations. And he insisted on a "tightly controlled qualification program to provide only for those entitled to participate" in welfare. The governor insisted his plan was the best. "I think the task force has really thought of every contingency," he said. County government representatives, fearing the Reagan plan would deprive them of needed state funds, supported a Democratic alternative. That prompted Reagan to write every county supervisor in the state that the Democratic bill is "not true welfare reform but amounts to nothing more than a giant tax increase." Nor were the Democrats willing to talk at this point. Liberal Democratic Assemblyman John Burton, younger brother of Philip Burton, wrote to Reagan in April: "As a member of the state legislature who represents a district made up of a cross section of society including individuals on welfare, I consider your present attack on welfare a base canard. You, sir, are either a liar or a fool."

But a month later, with the stalemate between Reagan and the Democrats receiving unfavorable publicity, both sides began to consider further compromise. Cabinet member Hall, who had been one of the hard-liners, wrote: "Even under ideal circumstances, it is unlikely that [our] bills can reach the Senate floor before the first week in June. An inflexible posture on the part of the administration will be taken as a sign of bad faith . . . bipartisan cooperation is probable if [our] bills are amended. Timing is crucial if we are to regain momentum for welfare reform." Hall recommended dropping the divisive statewide initiative proposal. "OK, as per our discussion," Reagan wrote on the memo. Publicly he continued to urge on the anti-welfare voters. He said, "Well, you sent your legislators to Sacramento to enact your desires, not ignore them. So if you want welfare reform you keep right on demanding it." But by early June, even Reagan admitted publicly he was willing to compromise, although he would not say how far.

"There is one thing I learned when I was negotiating for the [Screen Actors Guild] union against these tycoons in the motion picture business," he told reporters. "If you are going to sit down and negotiate out a welfare program, you are not going to tell anybody in advance what you might or might not be willing to compromise on. And gentlemen, you just have to realize you have me in the position right now of willing to sit down and meet on the basis of welfare reform legislation. But I ain't tipping my mitt."

Finally, Moretti was ready to talk. On June 28, 1971, he sent a letter to Reagan which said: "Although it is obvious that you and I have a great number of honest differences, I think it is important during this week and the coming weeks that we set aside our personal and philosophical disagreements and work to assure the people that our state will prosper. As we have both said publicly on a number of occasions this year, if we do not act positively on at least a few of our major state issues, the people of California will properly hold us accountable.

"In the spirit of reasonable compromise and agreement, therefore, I would propose as an initial step an early meeting, perhaps later today between you and me to resolve the difficult questions that are immanent."

Moretti visited the governor's office and had a memorable conversation, which he later related to Bill Stall, then Associated Press bureau chief in Sacramento and later a reporter for the Los Angeles *Times.* He told Stall he had "said exactly what was on my mind. I said 'Governor, I don't like you and you don't like me. I understand that. I know you say bad things about me and I say bad things about you. There are no secrets in this building. But I don't have to like you to have to work with you. If you really want to get something done about the issues, let's sit down and start working on it. If you want to keep it [welfare] as an issue, that's one thing. If you really want to get the job done, let's start working on it.' And that's how it [the negotiations] all started."

Moretti recalled that Reagan had basically agreed that "What I said was true . . . he agreed that all could be put aside, and we could start trying to work out some compromises on these various political positions of ours."

The negotiations that followed told much about Reagan's willingness to work long hours, to master tedious detail and to compromise.

He was the main negotiator on his side and Moretti the lead

spokesman for the Democrats in sessions that often lasted six to eight hours. Reagan was briefed by attorney Ronald Zumbrun, who, at the governor's request, gave him four sheets of paper each day. The governor, Zumbrun said, asked for "one sheet that has all the items we have to have. The next one, what we'd really just like to have. The next one, the ones that are nice to have and one with the ones that don't mean much."

Speaking of Reagan's conduct during the negotiations, Robert Monagan, who was a participant, remembered: "They [Reagan's staff] would give him the background paper and he'd read up. He's a quick learner, he's no dummy. He knew as much as they did about the issues that were going to be discussed at the moment. Maybe not the whole total broad picture, but when issues were argued about, he'd pick up on them and go. He gave up some things, of course, but he won more than he lost [in the negotiations]."

Sometimes, Monagan said, Reagan would get angry. "There would be a few profanities, 'Goddamn it, we aren't going to horse around with this crap anymore, that's it, you don't want to do anything, the hell with you. We just won't do it.' Fifteen minutes later he'd be telling some kind of anecdote, something about James Cagney, movie stories and things. He'd have a gag or something to tell. Then pretty soon everyone was talking easier again."

William Bagley, participating as chairman of the assembly social welfare committee, recalled a dispute Reagan had with a Democratic negotiator, Assemblyman Leo McCarthy, over how much personal property welfare recipients should be allowed before it disqualified them for benefits. "Leo was adamant," Bagley said. "I remember walking out in the hall and Leo said, 'I'll go this far, the guy has [to be allowed to have a car worth] fifteen hundred dollars.' " Bagley, acting as middleman in the negotiations, said, "I would go back and talk to the governor, almost always with Ed Meese standing there, but that wasn't a requirement. The governor would comment, and we would come out with twelve hundred dollars."

The Democrats insisted on cost-of-living increases for recipients. "The Democrats were demanding it, and so was I," said Bagley. "He obviously knew the issue and he realized there hadn't been a cost-of-living increase for ten years." Speaking of the children depending on welfare, Bagley said, "We told him those kids don't have constituents. He agreed. It was the most liberal provision of the welfare bill I know of."

Reagan participated in all of the first week's discussions, along with Moretti. Then, after the outlines of an agreement were reached, both men left the remaining five weeks of talks to subordinates, returning at crucial moments.

In the end Reagan gave up what he wanted most: a permanent ceiling placed on annual welfare appropriations. He also failed to write into the law tighter controls on those who would qualify for welfare, although he used administrative regulations to cut down the rolls. He got a pilot "work-or-else" program to force able, employable welfare recipients to find jobs. More money was given to district attorneys to pursue absent parents and make them support their children. In a move welcomed by Democrats, money was set aside for family-planning programs.

Reagan administration officials considered the program a great success. Administrative changes made even before passage of the law decreased welfare rolls by 161,000. By June 30, 1973, they said, the welfare rolls had dropped by 352,184. A state social welfare department report said welfare spending was $1 billion less than if welfare rolls had continued to grow.

Critics pointed out that national economic forces may well have been as effective as the Reagan program in reducing the welfare roles. In a 1980 article in the *Washington Monthly,* Barbara E. Joe, who had served in the state social welfare department under the Democrats before Reagan's governorship, concluded: "Demographics, not legislation, were controlling the change in California's welfare system . . . all across the country, falling birth rates (and generally falling unemployment) caused the number of Aid to Families with Dependent Children to decline after the program reached its peak in 1972."

But for those studying Reagan's performance as governor for clues to how he would serve as President, figures were not the whole story. What was most important was that Reagan was able to marshal enough political power to change the rules of debate on welfare in California. It was true that he compromised in the end. But the resulting laws and regulations began to change the idea of welfare back to temporary aid for the most needy, reversing the philosophy that had dominated state government for many years. It was a political victory, a philosophical change for the state and an indication that Reagan, rather than being a mere compromiser, had become an effective negotiator in tough legislative confrontations.

The California welfare program has major social implications for a nation moving into a technologically oriented economy in which prosperity will be determined by industry's ability to build a better computer than the Japanese or Europeans. In the thirties, forties and fifties, welfare for the truly needy made good sense. Industry, after recovering from the Depression, needed many unskilled workers. The untrained could find work in shipyards, steel mills, tire companies and auto plants. But today there are fewer jobs of that nature, and those that exist—in construction, restaurants, the garment industry and hotels—are being filled in increasing numbers by immigrants who work for the minimum wage or less. Welfare was supposed to be a temporary aid until a job came along. But what if there are no jobs for the unskilled? In the past, aid for the truly needy was an attractive political slogan. But in a troubled and complex economy it is a limited and simplistic solution for many whose real need is to find a job that provides at least minimum support for their families.

12

DISSENT ON CAMPUS: A SPECIAL TARGET

From the beginning of his political career, Ronald Reagan was hostile to the University of California and the rest of the state's vast system of public universities and colleges. The special target of his 1966 campaign was the University of California's Berkeley campus, the oldest of the schools and the one with the longest tradition of academic excellence and liberal political dissent. His speeches about "the mess at Berkeley" were always enthusiastically received because part of the resentment of middle-class Californians toward government was prompted by the demonstrations at Berkeley. In the middle and late sixties, the political activity and the long-haired bearded life style at Berkeley had made the university and all of higher education an object of public distrust. No longer were Californians enthusiastic about paying big taxes for public education. Hidden away in the hearts of parents was the fear that their own children might one day go away to college, grow beards and march against authority.

The intensity of the clash between Reagan and the higher-education system was due to the suspicion with which he viewed campuses that had been promoted by previous administrations. For decades, California governors had been defenders and protectors of a system that had been considered the greatest achievement of state government. They reflected what were then the views of the state's citizens, who saw the faculties and campuses as a source of pride and a rare resource.

Almost a hundred two-year community colleges offered a free education to any high school graduate who wanted it—technical training in printing, drafting, restaurant management and other trades, as well as academic courses for those who planned to transfer to four-year colleges. The nineteen state universities, open to anyone who finished in the upper third in high school, provided a four-year education and most graduate degrees. And finally there was the University of California for the upper 12.5 percent of California's high school graduates—nine campuses famous for diversity, high academic standards, graduate schools and accomplished faculties. In his book *The Pacific States of America,* Neal R. Pearce reflects the pride most Californians felt for these schools during the forties, fifties and early sixties: "Many things Californian evoke superlatives; no institution merits more than the University of California. Despite its many tribulations, UC remains the most successful institution of higher education that the United States, and perhaps the world, has ever known. . . . The benefit that has accrued to California's people through their fantastic investment in UC is almost beyond estimation. Without the university's distinction in agricultural research, the physical sciences, technology and water conservation, California would be, as an economic entity, a weak shadow of what it is today."

But in 1964, public attitudes were changed by a small but vocal student group, Berkeley's Free Speech Movement and the first of the sixties student protests. The immediate cause of the trouble was the Berkeley administration's sudden refusal to allow use of the sidewalk in front of the campus' Sather Gate. Until then, the plaza in front of the gate had served as a forum for any speaker, no matter how radical the message. But on September 30, 1964, five students attempting to collect money and gain support for an off-campus political group were threatened with discipline for breaking a new rule forbidding political activity in front of Sather Gate. A day later some two thousand students surrounded a police car to prevent it from taking away another young man who defied the rules by operating a Congress of Racial Equality table on the spot. The days of demonstrations had begun.

There were deep, underlying causes for the protests. The 1960s student generation had many socially conscious activists. Students who had spent the summer in the South with the civil rights movement returned to Berkeley in the fall semester of 1964 convinced of the virtue of direct action, to further political and social causes on the campuses and in the community outside. Some of them also resented the fact that much of the university's research was devoted to developing nuclear arms and increasing profits for the state's big businesses, such as agriculture. There was also longstanding resentment against the cold bureaucracy of the big university system.

During this difficult period in the university's history, its president was Clark Kerr. Kerr had also been a special target of Reagan's during his governorship campaign.

Completely opposite Reagan in appearance, style, interests and philosophy, Kerr had been the university's president since 1958 and presided over the school during its greatest growth. Before that, he had been a professor and later chancellor at Berkeley. Far-right elements had always considered Berkeley a sanctuary for the left, and both as chancellor and faculty member Kerr had fought their assaults. In 1952, as a professor, he led a fight against a loyalty oath. As president, he gave an honorary degree to a Berkeley professor of psychology, Edward C. Tolman, who had resigned years before after refusing to sign the oath.

Reagan and Kerr met for the first time after the 1968 election at a dinner party given by H. R. Haldeman, then a UC regent and later President Nixon's chief aide who was eventually convicted as an architect of the Watergate cover-up. The meeting added to Kerr's impression of the governor's hostile attitude. "He barely greeted me," Kerr said of his meeting with Reagan. One of the university regents rose to make a toast to Reagan: "to the man who will bring a big breath of fresh air into the university." Reagan accepted the toast and replied in measured words that he hoped that faculty members would now teach their students to respect the morality of the community. Kerr, a Quaker, later said he thought to himself that youngsters should be taught a morality higher than that of the community.

Soon a couple of events occurred that should have convinced Kerr that his future had already been decided. In late November, regents' chairman Theodore Meyer "advised me to look for another position." In December another regent urged him to quit. The regent, a Republican once active in state politics, told Kerr that "[my] days were numbered, that it would be better if I resigned than be fired. He said that since I had served with Brown, it would be better if I resigned while Brown was governor and not embarrass the new governor. He did not say he was speaking on behalf of Reagan, but he was quite concerned that Reagan not be embarrassed and the new governor have a clean slate." According to Kerr, the regent concluded the conversation by saying, "I don't expect you will make a fight of it because I know how devoted you are to the university."

Later that day Kerr approached the regent and resumed the conversation. He asked what purpose his resignation would serve the university. The regent replied that his fellow members of the board "would be friends again." And the regent added, "We wouldn't have any trouble in Sacramento." Kerr replied, "We will have trouble regardless of who is president." Kerr also told him that the university might have difficulty finding a replacement. "We don't expect any trouble in getting your replacement," the regent said.

The University of California board of regents, while outwardly designed to be free of politics, is actually sensitive to election results. Sixteen of the regents are appointed by the governor for sixteen-year terms. Theoretically, there will always be a group of regents who were appointed by previous governors—thus preventing the incumbent chief executive from exercising absolute control. But the board also has eight ex-officio members, including the governor—members who are regents only because of other offices they hold. They are the lieutenant governor, often a member of the governor's party; the president of the state board of agriculture, a gubernatorial appointee; the president of the alumni association; the superintendent of public instruction; the university president; and, at the time, the president of the Mechanics Institute. Most of these ex-officio regents opposed Kerr. They, along with some of the sixteen-year-term regents, provided a substantial anti-Kerr majority on the board.

Just after Reagan's inaugural something happened that pushed Kerr closer to dismissal. On January 3, 1967, Reagan's finance director, Gordon Smith, informed university and state college officials that the new administration was proposing to cut higher education budgets by 10 percent and to ask for tuition. Kerr opposed the cuts and was thrust in the middle of the fight. University and state college officials leaked to the press details of what Smith had told them, and protests were staged on college campuses. Reagan insisted that he had not decided on any budget cuts, that Smith had just talked about tentative plans. It was a confusing time, one that cast considerable doubt on the credibility of the Reagan administration. "A lot of tentative things have been proposed in an effort to balance the budget and get the state out of the mess Governor Brown left it in, but there has been no final decision on anything, including tuition," said Lyn Nofziger. Reagan's language was more colorful. "It is like Chicken Little running around saying the sky is falling in," he said of those who were protesting his financial plans. "They have invented a boogeyman." He reiterated that no final decision had been made. But the concern of the university and colleges was well founded. Within weeks, Reagan presented a budget that imposed 10 percent cuts and asked for tuition.

The uproar that resulted surprised the young administration, and Reagan blamed Kerr for much of his trouble. On January 12 Kerr went to Sacramento to confer with the governor and a group of regents, and after the meetings regents Meyer, Haldeman and Philip Boyd returned to the governor's office for another discussion, from which Kerr was excluded.

Kerr was particularly concerned because he had an appointment with Reagan and Lieutenant Governor Robert Finch the following Monday. But when he repeatedly asked Meyer "if there was anything I should know before I talked to the governor," Meyer replied, "The governor will tell you."

Kerr now sought a reprieve from the dismissal he saw was imminent. He sent an emissary, the university's vice president, Charles Wellman, to regents Meyer and Boyd to offer a compromise. He would resign, effective June 1968, giving the regents more time to find a replacement. This would have allowed Kerr to remain president through the university's centennial year, something he wanted to do very much. More important, it would have avoided a dangerous precedent, appointment of a new president with the election of a new governor. Wellman returned and reported that it looked "like the situation was without solution."

But on Monday, Reagan and Finch canceled the meeting. Kerr went to Sacramento anyway, for this was the evening of the university's annual reception for legislators. At the event Kerr found himself in the position of a doomed man appealing to judge after judge and being coldly ignored. Assemblyman William Bagley, one of the president's few supporters, urged Kerr to make a public statement that he wanted to get along with the governor. Kerr agreed, imagining this could iron out some immediate sources of contention between him and Reagan.

After discussing the idea of a public statement, Bagley and Kerr sought out Meyer. The assemblyman repeated his suggestion, but Meyer put his head down and shook it, refusing once more to help Kerr.

At the reception, legislators were happily drinking and eating from the Sutter Club's ample table. Kerr almost desperately began looking for Reagan's assistants in the crowded room. First he saw Nofziger. "I told him there had been no effort on my part to have any conflict with the new administration," Kerr said. "He just listened." Then Kerr talked to Battaglia and two other Reagan assistants, Dirk Eldredge and Jack Lindsay. They listened, but did not say a word either. They asked no questions. "So I went home."

On Friday, Reagan, as the new governor and president of the board of regents, would attend his first meeting at the statewide university administration building across the street from the Berkeley campus. Kerr would also be there, acting as an executive officer who presents proposals to board members for a decision. Before the Friday session began, Kerr tried once again to clarify his status. He went into another room with chairman Meyer and Mrs. Dorothy Chandler, the vice chairman, and told them that if a decision had been made to let him go, action should be taken now instead of waiting another month. He explained it would be impossible for him as a lame-duck president to represent the university in budget negotiations with Reagan. Meyer and Mrs. Chandler, in turn, asked him to resign. He refused.

In asking for the board to take action immediately, Kerr said later, "If I was asking for anything, it was quick execution." This was a crucial point in the dispute between Reagan and Kerr. The governor insisted that Kerr, in talking to Meyer and Mrs. Chandler, precipitated the vote on his job and was responsible for his own dismissal. (In fact, when he arrived at the Los Angeles airport after the meeting and reporters asked him about the firing, the governor appeared surprised at their questions.)

After their conversation on Friday, Kerr, Meyer and Mrs. Chandler joined the other regents, including Reagan. But at twelve-thirty, Meyer asked Kerr to wait outside. With Kerr gone, the regents began a long discussion of him. Finally, Alan Grant president of the state board of agriculture, made the necessary motion for Kerr's dismissal.

Someone pointed out that it would be injudicious for Grant, a Reagan appointee attending his first meeting, to strike the deathblow. The motion was made by Laurence Kennedy, Jr., one of Brown's appointees. The vote was 14 to 8 against Kerr.

Meyer and Mrs. Chandler left the room and talked once more to Kerr. They again gave him the option of resigning. "I've fought a lot of tough battles for you," Kerr replied. "This is one you'll have to fight for yourself. On this matter, I am not open to persuasion." The university staff was called into the regents' room to hear the news, and Kerr followed. But he had to endure the humiliation of being refused admittance by a woman at the door. "I told her that unless the chairman personally barred me, I was going in," he said. Kerr briefly thanked the staff and the regents for their cooperation in the past, and then he remembered something. There were still some matters he had not presented to the regents for their approval, and the idea of leaving the business unfinished offended his orderly mind. "The only thing I could think of was that I had all those items on the agenda," he said. He asked for permission to remain on the job until the meeting was completed. Permission was granted and, recalled Kerr, "we went through the agenda—and I got everything completed."

Kerr was calm when he talked to newsmen afterward. "I have had a feeling of being in the middle of the Perils of Pauline," he said. "Pauline always got saved—until today." He criticized the regents for yielding to "political winds in the state," and added, "This is not done in the good universities in the nation and it is even out of fashion in the mediocre and poor ones." He did not show his emotions, but he was hurt. He left his office in the statewide university building immediately after the meeting ended and did not return— not even a few days later when his staff wanted to give him a present.

Reagan continued to deny any responsibility except to cast his vote as a single member of the board. "Who said I was responsible?" he asked. "It was the board's decision. It was Kerr, himself, who made the proposition that he wanted it settled one way or another." But four days after Kerr's firing, Reagan admitted at a news conference that he had discussed the resignation with some of the regents in advance of the meeting and implied to them that he thought Kerr had outlived his usefulness. "The regents had come to me and told me . . . they had believed that a majority of the board felt that he should resign and that they were considering asking him to resign," said Reagan. "They did not know whether it was the same number of regents that would vote to take any stronger action. I told them what my own feeling was with regard to the possible need for a change, but that I would not initiate such a procedure, and certainly did not feel that in my first meeting as a regent this was something that was properly on the agenda." He said he let the regents know his opinion of Kerr. "I believe the people of this state had lost confidence in the university, and I believe that the long embroilment —it just happens that sometimes people involved in that kind of controversy have outlived their usefulness, whether rightly or wrongly, and I just call to your attention that I so voted." But despite his own feelings against Kerr, and the meetings he had with the anti-Kerr regents, he maintained that "no one had any intention of bringing this up at this time or at that meeting."

Like Reagan, chairman Meyer told conflicting stories about Kerr's dismissal. The day of the firing, he indicated to newsmen that "certain regents"—not Kerr—initiated the vote. Asked if Reagan had conveyed to him a wish to be rid of Kerr prior to the afternoon meeting, Meyer replied, "Well, the governor had discussed the subject with me and others. I think he should be the one to say what he said to me and to anyone else." On Monday, Meyer issued another statement, which contradicted what he had said on Friday and supported Reagan's contention that Kerr had himself touched off the dismissal by seeking a vote of confidence.

The campuses did not become quiet after Kerr's firing. Instead, student protests took a new direction, and the nation's political turmoil enveloped the campuses. Protests against the Vietnam war and demands for black and Hispanic studies were combined with the existing student political consciousness and resentment against the impersonal bureaucracy of the system. The unrest that had begun at Berkeley spread to other places. Soon police, wearing helmets and carrying clubs, became part of the campus scene.

Berkeley was the leader in the violence and frequency of its demonstrations, the most famous of which occurred in 1969 when three thousand national guardsmen were called out by Reagan against students who wanted to turn a plot of unused university property into a "People's Park." As three thousand students were protesting police action in clearing the area and enclosing it with a steel mesh fence, a National Guard helicopter sprayed tear gas and nausea gas on them. When the protest continued, sheriff's deputies opened fire on the demonstrators with shotguns loaded with birdshot and buckshot. James Rector, twenty-five, was fatally wounded; another man was blinded by a shotgun blast; a policeman was stabbed; and sixty-three people were treated for other injuries. Berkeley was declared in a state of emergency by Reagan from February 5 through June 2, 1969.

There were also riots on the urban campus of San Francisco State College and on the oceanside UC Santa Barbara campus, previously known as a surfer's haven. On the idyllic campus of UC Santa Cruz, located in a redwood forest, students blocked a bus carrying Reagan to a UC regents meeting. Reagan's rhetoric during this time was even tougher than it had been during his campaign. After the Santa Barbara violence, which brought national guardsmen and Los Angeles County sheriff's deputies to the area, Reagan said, "If it's a bloodbath, let it be now," an inflammatory statement he later said was a figure of speech.

During this period the governor and his staff kept a close watch on the demonstrations and those who participated. His inquiry into the political state of mind on college campuses was one more illustration of how much both government and public attitudes had changed toward higher education. When, for example, demonstrations occurred in Berkeley in October 1968 over whether academic credit should be given for lectures by Eldridge Cleaver, the Black Panther party's minister of information who had written *Soul on Ice* while in Soledad Prison, Reagan was kept personally informed by telegrams from John Oswald, the university's vice president. Immediately after students had entered the Berkeley administration building to stage a sit-in, Oswald wired Reagan a report on the situation: "At 7 P.M., university police secured the doors to Sproul Hall. There were 150 students inside at that time, including several who swept up the debris from the sit-in. A discussion and votes by the 150 led to the decision to go peacefully when arrested, rather than resisting. In addition, as the night wore on, those inside counseled those outside Sproul Hall to be restrained in their actions." But police response was to take no chances. A total of two hundred and twenty officers went into the building, arresting the fewer than a hundred students who were left inside. The following day, protests continued, and about a hundred students moved into Moses Hall, administrative center of the College of Letters and Science. Police cleared the hall by arresting seventy-six students.

During these tense times, daily reports were sent to the governor's office. When campus protests were occurring over the Cambodian invasion, Ed Hickey, in charge of Reagan's security, gave the following report to Alex Sheriffs, Reagan's education adviser, on May 4, 1970:

San Jose State: A rally is scheduled at 12:30. SDS [Students for a Democratic Society] is the prime mover. There will probably be an attempt to take over Tower Hall or the Administration Building. Three half gallon jugs with wicks were found hidden on campus this morning. San Jose Police Department expects a confrontation.

University of California, Berkeley: The campus is quiet. An illegal rally is scheduled for noon. Sponsors and speakers are unknown.

University of California, San Diego: It is understood takeover of Urey Hall will last until 1700 hours. [Chancellor William] McGill has suspended one student for 10 days, another for 14 days. The fourth floor of Urey Hall contains $2 million of computer equipment. Some malicious mischief has occurred on the fourth floor but computer has not been damaged. Bonner Hall [across the street] has been evacuated because of a bomb threat.

Interestingly, the report included two private schools, Stanford University and the Claremont Colleges. Of Stanford, Hickey reported: "A student strike is underway. The entrance to all main buildings are blocked. All teaching functions have stopped." Claremont was more peaceful: "Twenty anti-ROTC protesters sitting in at the registration office. No problems. A demonstration is scheduled at the post office at 1330."

Anonymous tipsters provided information. On May 19, 1969, a person whose name was later blanked out on the administration's memo on the incident called Sheriffs with a report that implied that the UC Santa Cruz administration had not done enough to stop a demonstration: "At 6:30 or so this morning, the Santa Cruz administration building was taken over by students. They have chained the door shut. As of quarter to ten, no one had told them they shouldn't be doing this. Chancellor Dean McHenry was having a meeting with the provost to see what to do next."

Later in the morning the informant called again: "McHenry met with the provost, asked the provost to identify the students involved. The provost refused to do so. As of a half hour ago [about 2:30 P.M.] no one had yet told the students what they were doing was naughty."

The governor also tried to find support on the campuses. The administration observed approvingly as Dr. Sidney Hook of New York City, a leading academic of the student and faculty left, visited several California campuses, speaking on behalf of the University Center for Rational Alternatives, which he organized as a force against violent protest.

Some California academics willingly showed their support for the governor. For example, in October 1969, twenty-one faculty members, believing too many of their colleagues supported the demonstrations on California campuses, came to Sacramento to talk to Reagan. For two hours he listened to the complaints of the professors, who shared his belief that the faculties were dominated by radicals. The meeting was described by Sheriffs in a memorandum that is a revealing glimpse into the administration's attitude toward political dissent in that year of turmoil, when it seemed as if the great system of higher education that California had built was coming apart:

. . . One faculty member stated, and the others nodded, "We are cowed. We can't even express our own opinion in the classroom."

A number believe that tenure was the key to our problems, that for a number of years the faculty has been recruiting its own kind and that we suffer now is academic freedom without the balance of responsibility or objectivity. One ex-administrator present suggested that it would be necessary to have a central campus committee to function as watchdog on hiring and on grading. It was revealed at San Francisco State a study of grading showed it often to be dishonest and unscrupulous. We were told of one department that allowed all of the students to grade themselves—"in the name of democracy."

The selection of top administrators on the basis of their popularity with the faculty itself produces administrators who are merely spokesmen for the faculty. One member of the group said, "Every time I think of campus problems, I think of a large and complex ship without a captain, responding only to the machinations of the crew." It was stated by one that most private institutions select their administrators from the private sector, primarily from business. The Ph.D. syndrome for administration was described as a public education phenomena.

As we listened to these academics, we wondered more and more how many more there were like them on their campuses. To gain an impression, the governor asked each to estimate for his campus. The results were as follows:

San Francisco State College: Two-thirds of the faculty okay. "We're not outnumbered if we make a real effort."

California State College, Dominguez Hills: Responsible faculty are in a distinct minority by a ratio of two to one.

San Diego State College: Majority are all right, but the [academic] Senate has been captured.

Sacramento State College: The majority would support responsibility if it had leadership.

California State Polytechnic College, San Luis Obispo: A very large majority of responsible faculty.

San Fernando Valley State College: A highly organized political leftist faculty leadership but a majority of the faculty would not be radical in a secret ballot.

Long Beach State College: Physical sciences, eighty percent responsible; social sciences, sixty percent not.

Sacramento City College: . . . If the radicals are in charge, tenure is the only protection for the responsible.

San Diego City College: Only five or six radical faculty members on the campus.

U.C. Berkeley: Radicals are definitely in the majority but there are more good guys than one might think.

U.C. Davis: Radicals definitely a minority.

U.C. San Diego: The faculty power groups are radical-liberal but a majority under leadership would be responsible.

U.C.L.A.: Eighty percent would be all right, but become confused on issues and, unless they get a chance to think about it, may vote against their best interests.

In their rather lengthy presentation of the above—for faculty members by nature and habit deliver lectures—these points came out a number of times:

1) It is not practical to hope to organize moderates. The faculty personality does not prepare him for fighting. He will retreat.

2) Therefore, good administrators are a must.

3) With each passing month, through inbreeding and through involvement of normal students in radical affairs, the situation gets ever more bleak.

4) Tenure is a two edged sword—it does protect the good guys from the bad.

5) On most campuses, there are verbal and militant leftists, a few moderates with voice, and "mush" in the middle . . .

Sheriffs concluded that the situation was becoming "bleak" with "normal" students getting involved with radicals. But he felt the meeting with Reagan was a "shot in the arm" for faculty members the administration considered moderate.

Students as well as faculty were brought to the governor's office. As Sheriffs recalled, "We'd say to Chico State, for example, 'Send twenty to forty students, a random sample or at least a variety of points of view, to come up and chew the fat so we can understand something about what students are thinking, real students, and they can understand our point of view.' "

But, as an October 10 memorandum from Sheriffs indicated, not all the meetings were a success. Sheriffs said he felt an hour-and-a-half meeting had not gone as well as a previous session with faculty members. "The format of the meeting was quite different from that of the faculty group," Sheriffs wrote. "In the latter, the governor listened quietly for almost 45 minutes before entering actively into the conversation. Also, again, the faculty was clearly wishing reassurance from the governor that he would not desert them, whereas with the students, three or four of whom were aggressively liberal . . . the governor was pulled into defending himself against stereotypes. I think next time we should lean more on the format that we followed for the faculty and let the good students themselves defend us if need be." Sheriffs complained of "ringers that somehow got in our group" and concluded that "the crying need on the campus, with only one part of the faculty speaking, and with radical control of student government and student press, is for the ability to hear from all sides of the question, or better, the truth about matters concerning them."

Sheriffs' use of the term "radical control" shows that the Reagan administration's interest in the campuses went beyond eliminating violent demonstrations. The governor was also concerned about the content of political thought on campuses. And in his speeches, in office memorandums and in the kind of information his office collected, he showed over and over again his hostility and opposition to radical or liberal political thought by faculty or by students.

Another indication that the administration considered such ideas dangerous can be seen in the testimony by Herbert E. Ellingwood, Reagan's legal affairs secretary, before the permanent subcommittee on investigations of the Senate Government Operations Committee in July 1969. Ellingwood's testimony dealt with Berkeley, which he said "typifies what is happening on many of our California campuses, and, in fact, many campuses throughout the nation." He said Berkeley "has become the vanguard of student disorder. There is substantial reason to believe that the rampant, current philosophy of student revolt has been developed, tested and subcontracted from Berkeley to other institutions around the country." But it wasn't only disorder that Ellingwood objected to. He also objected to the liberal causes the Berkeley students were advocating. For example, he criticized as "detrimental to the fabric of the surrounding community" activities such as demonstrating against discriminatory hiring practices in local businesses and protesting the Vietnam war. He also disapproved of activities of the Welfare Rights Organization, which was encouraging potential welfare recipients to take advantage of provisions of the state welfare law.

Nobody would argue that a governor shouldn't be informed about developments on tumultuous campuses. He is, after all, the official who must decide whether to send the National Guard onto a campus. But Reagan went further than keeping track of demonstrations. He was interested in what went on in the classrooms. He wanted to know how the faculty was divided between "radical-liberals" and "good guys." Fortunately, the Reagan administration's investigations of politics on campuses had little effect. In California, local police departments undertake most of the law enforcement, and a state justice department investigative unit is deliberately kept small because of the state's traditional bias against employing a large police apparatus. In Reagan's governorship, both Meese and Ellingwood, former deputy district attorneys, obtained information from their own contacts in law enforcement. More information was available from a state justice department computer linkup between local police agencies and the state. Even so, information gathering capacity was limited and crude.

But the amount and quality of information is not as important as the fact that it was gathered at all. By inquiring into the political beliefs on campus, especially those that differed from his, Reagan weakened academic freedom. More than that, he displayed an unsettling fear of political dissent. His behavior raised a question of how he would treat political dissent in a national time of crisis when, as President, he can give the command to unleash the huge investigative powers of the FBI and other federal agencies.

By the end of 1970 the campuses had quieted in California and the rest of the nation. Both sides were exhausted from years of combat. In the 1970 election, Republican candidates who campaigned against campus disorder found their fiery speeches ignored by voters more worried about a recession that had overtaken the nation in the fall. By January, Reagan's interest had shifted to reducing the welfare rolls.

The effects of that tumultuous period on the state's education system have been debated for years, and there are no certain conclusions. Developments in educational policy were overshadowed by news of unrest on campuses and Reagan's reaction to it. A big increase in state scholarships, for example, went all but unnoticed. But some results were certain. Tuition was imposed for the public universities for the first time in state history. By the end of Reagan's administration, UC and the State University and College System were being granted about 90 percent of their operating budget requests, compared to the 96 percent or more they had received in the previous administration. That increased the student-faculty ratio and reduced money available for maintaining buildings, starting new programs and improving libraries. In fact, in 1972 Reagan's finance department proposed that UC sell its rare-book collections to provide money for the state treasury.

The anticipated exodus of professors did not materialize, mainly because of a national shortage of academic jobs. Still, a few prominent faculty members left, driven away by the political climate or a shortage of research funds. But as William Trombley, the respected Los Angeles *Times* reporter who covered higher education during this period, pointed out, figures do not tell the entire story. In 1973, with the Reagan administration drawing to a close, Trombley drew from his experience in covering education to write an eloquent summary of Reagan's effect on his main target, the University of California. "The Reagan years ended," Trombley wrote, "with the sense—intangible, hard to prove but unyielding—that a great university, the greatest this country has put together with public funds, is slipping down to the level of mere adequacy. The end result of the tight budgets, the denigration of professors, the suspicion of motive and purpose is a university less than it was and much less than it might have been."

13

REAGAN AND THE TAX REVOLT

In the eight years of his governorship, Ronald Reagan and the legislature overtaxed Californians as no government had ever done in the state's history. Reagan's tax increase of 1967 was the highest state tax increase in the nation's history. It came to $844 million the first year and $1.01 billion the second. Other large tax increases were enacted in 1971 and 1972, only slightly tempered by minimal relief to property owners and other taxpayers. As Robert Kuttner put it in his book *Revolt of the Haves:* "During the Reagan years, the combination of a conservative governor and a liberal legislature led to an odd compromise. Government stopped churning out new social programs, but the state taxing structure became even more steeply progressive . . . When Ronald Reagan left office in January, 1975, he bestowed on his successor a growing state surplus and highly elastic revenue machine that Sacramento veterans said was sufficient to prevent the need for any tax increase through the rest of the century." The phenomenon was deeply troubling to ultraconservatives in his administration. "This administration proclaims that it has made savings through reform measures and government efficiencies," Lewis K. Uhler, a hard-line conservative aide warned in a memorandum. "However, these claimed successes have not manifested themselves in the form of direct tax relief. What the taxpayer needs now is tangible, dramatic evidence of the success of our reform effort and the fact that somebody in government really cares about the tax burden he bears."

When it came to taxes, Reagan, for most of his governorship, was a study in frustration. He was given to colorful lectures on the evils of high taxes and then, time after time, he was persuaded to accept them by assistants and legislators who had more facts and overwhelmed him with their arguments. It showed how Reagan's reluctance to go into detail and insistence on staying far above the battle led to policies that were opposite to what he sought. This was particularly true in the case of his most startling reversal, his acceptance of withholding of state income taxes.

In a nation where most wage earners have their taxes withheld and welcome the convenience, it was difficult to understand Reagan's objections. They were philosophical. He argued that workers should be fully aware of the taxes they were paying; that workers would too readily accept high state taxes if they paid in relatively painless installments through withholding. Repeatedly he said "My feet are in concrete" on the issue. He was one of the few people in the capitol who felt that way. Civil servants in the state finance department had long favored withholding. The old system, under which income taxes were paid twice a year, resulted in tremendous cash-flow problems for the state. In addition, budget analysts said too many Californians were able to evade taxes because there was no withholding at the source. Both Democratic and liberal Republican legislators accepted these arguments. Democrats had another reason for advocating withholding. By bringing in more money, it would make additional funds available for new social programs.

Reagan refused to include withholding as part of his first tax-increase package in 1967. But the campaign for it was renewed the following March, just when people were beginning to compute tax bills that reflected the highest combined state and local tax rates in the country. At that point Reagan's trusted adviser Gordon Luce, who was business and transportation secretary, told him of growing support for withholding. "There were those firms and employes who want withholding because it seems easier to pay their taxes," he reported. As an alternative, Luce proposed a voluntary withholding plan in which employers would set up bank accounts in employees' names and deduct future tax payments from paychecks "somewhat like a Christmas club." That sounded good to Reagan, who later proposed the idea.

In a cabinet meeting that month, Reagan listened while his advisers talked about withholding. Caspar Weinberger, then the finance director and later President Reagan's Defense Secretary, shared the governor's opposition. He told the cabinet that legislators were preparing to make their case for withholding as a forthcoming legislative committee hearing. "I would like to see it on the ballot," said Reagan, "not through legislation. And frankly I would say 'You are fools.' If we had withholding, there would be no squawking [over taxes] now. Withholding is strictly for the benefit of the government, not the people. Sugar-coating something that is painful. In opposing it, we thought it is the will of the people. Now I say let the people make the choice."

Two days later, at another cabinet meeting, Weinberger discussed legislative Republicans who were torn between their loyalty to the governor and what many of them considered convincing arguments for withholding. "I want you to know now that on withholding, I will tell the Republicans that I won't unduly influence them," Reagan said. "All they have to do is walk over my dead body. With my feet in concrete."

Reagan repeatedly objected to a provision of withholding that would greatly increase revenue in the first year. The increase came from the fact that taxpayers would actually be paying two years' taxes in one year. Withholding would begin in July, and then, a few months later, taxpayers would have to send the state a check for the preceding year's taxes. Reagan said one of the double payments should be canceled or "forgiven." "It really is amazing how many who advocate withholding will retreat if you mention forgiveness," Reagan told the cabinet. "I don't agree," replied the state controller, Houston I. Flournoy, a moderate Republican who favored withholding. Weinberger sided with Reagan. "Some still cool off if you mention forgiveness," he said. "Especially those who want to use the windfall [for state spending] without giving any consideration for next year [fiscal problems]." A month later Reagan initialed his approval on a cabinet memo from Weinberger to oppose withholding in the legislative session.

By October 1969, however, a Field Poll showed that 53.5 percent of those surveyed favored withholding. In addition, Reagan was being criticized in newspaper editorials for being too stubborn. Most important, the slow method of twice-a-year tax collections threatened to hobble state operations. In the past the state had borrowed from various state funds, such as pensions, to meet its bills until the income-tax collections came in. But the finance department was now forecasting that in two years, increased state spending would make that impossible.

At this crucial point Reagan was being even more strongly urged to reconcile with the legislature. He was up for re-election in 1970 and did not want to run as an obstructionist. He appointed Verne Orr to replace Weinberger, who had resigned to join the Nixon Administration. The new finance director, who believed in reconciliation, had learned to be a salesman in his many years as an automobile dealer. Orr's appointment had been inspired by Holmes Tuttle, the kitchen-cabinet member especially close to Reagan and a major auto dealer who knew Orr through the business. Tuttle had first succeeded in urging Reagan to appoint Orr director of motor vehicles. Orr had made a good impression on both Reagan and the legislature, and was highly regarded for his ability to smooth over hard feelings caused by the combative Weinberger.

"My nature is to get along with people," said Orr. Some evenings he would drop in the office of Assemblyman Bagley, the chairman of the revenue and taxation committee, for drinks. "I'd try not to be stuffy," he said. "I'd say what did you bullshitters talk about today, and we just tossed it around a little bit."

Orr quickly accepted the opinion of civil servants who maintained that withholding was needed for the state to pay its bills. "My staff said to me you have got to tell Governor Reagan that we cannot continue more than two years without withholding," he said. He knew it would be difficult to persuade the governor. "I was only five or seven days into the darn job," he said, "and here was a deep-felt conviction of Ronald Reagan's. You don't move in easily and upset those."

First he went to Meese, by then the main access to Reagan and the man who controlled the flow of information to the governor and into cabinet meetings. He asked for time to make a major presentation to the cabinet on withholding. Then he drew up charts on butcher paper, explaining in diagram form how, as a result of slow income-tax collection, the state ran out of money at the end of each fiscal year. He also explained that the higher income-tax rates which had been approved early in the administration had increased popular demand for withholding from taxpayers, who wanted a less painful method of paying. Another argument was that withholding would provide $150 million a year in additional revenue that could be used as aid to local government so that property taxes could be cut.

With Reagan and the rest of the cabinet listening, Orr made his presentation. After he finished, Houston Flournoy backed him up. Reagan, who had obviously been impressed by the charts, looked silent at Orr for a few moments. Then he spoke, wondering why no one had told him the bad news before and added, "You mean, it's like the emperor's clothes." Orr said yes, and there was another long silence. "Finally Reagan said, 'Well, I'll have to give it some thought.' So he thought about it for a month, roughly, and then he announced he would reluctantly support withholding." Or as Reagan put it when he made his announcement, "That sound you hear is the concrete cracking around my feet."

While the decision was popular among officials and politicians in Sacramento, it did little to help Reagan with a growing and potentially more serious political problem. The famous California property-tax revolt was beginning, partially caused by the tax policies of the Reagan administration and his failure to make major reductions in property taxes that were becoming unjust.

Property taxes were rising. A 1963 reform law, designed to prevent county assessors from favoring business, had the unforseen effect of raising property taxes on homes. A booming population was rapidly expanding the suburbs. Farmlands and vacant lots were turned into shopping centers and tracts, raising the value of adjoining land. Long-time residents, many of them retired, formed homeowner groups to protest the increased taxes. In Los Angeles, these groups joined the United Organization of Taxpayers, headed by a man regarded by established politicians and the press as just another right-wing crank, Howard Jarvis. "We did know that the American dream of home ownership for everyone was being sabotaged by exploding property taxes," Jarvis later said in his autobiography *I'm Mad As Hell,* written after he became famous.

A property-tax limit sponsored by L.A. county assessor Philip Watson had appeared on the state ballot in 1968 and had lost 2 to 1, but the initiative and the strength of its campaign had frightened Reagan and the legislature so much that they had finally gotten together for a moderate property-tax-reduction bill. When a similar measure was placed on the 1972 ballot, Reagan's aides, in a confidential memo, warned him that public attention was focusing on his failure to cut taxes. The main concerns of the public and the news media, according to the memo writers, were: "When will you present your [tax] proposal to the legislature and what will it contain? Will the public really get what was promised? Will you compromise with the legislature on something less than what you promised?"

The last question was the most important, since Reagan had been doing just that sort of compromising. The question was being raised by new forces that were gaining strength in the administration. These were more conservative advocates of tax reductions who felt that the compromises that had seemed so politically attractive in 1970 were now hurting the governor. One such advocate was Lewis Uhler. He was a former John Birch Society member and had joined the administration as head of the Office of Economic Opportunity, which supervised anti-poverty programs. In that job, he conducted a long campaign against the California Rural Legal Assistance, a federally financed legal-aid group which had filed several lawsuits on behalf of the rural poor against the Reagan administration's cutbacks of social programs. Uhler made other attacks on the poverty programs he was supposed to supervise. In the ideological spectrum of a conservative administration he was at the far right, opposed and disliked by moderates such as Orr. Yet through Meese, who had brought him into the administration, Uhler had considerable influence. The two had attended UC's Boalt Hall law school together and each year Meese, Uhler and their wives joined other Boalt classmates for a reunion.

Uhler was unhappy with the way the administration was going. "I think there was some recognition that the process was . . . leading to a rate of growth that was higher than we really wanted," he later remembered. More than that, he said, there was a feeling that "in the sixth year of an administration, you get into a prosaic business as usual, mundane posture. If the remaining years of the administration were to be utilized to gain much ground for responsible policies, you have to move aggressively, set goals and objectives, set a time frame and move with it."

The intensity of Uhler's feelings was shown in a memorandum he wrote in 1972. In dramatic language, he said it should be

the administration's policy to seize the initiative wherever possible and to aggressively sell the principles and programs of the administration.

The image which we desire to project with regard to this administration is best described as bold, glamorous, exciting, dynamic, fearless, honest, competent, involved and action oriented.

Not happy with the way the administration's case was being presented, Uhler proposed a media control center as part of

a complete public relations effort. . . . It is absolutely essential that we constantly monitor all the media on a 24 hour basis and feed monitoring results through a media control center. Through this means we can determine daily progress with respect to the administration as a whole and any individual programs in which we are engaged through a process of media quantification, i.e. amount of air or screen time or newspaper space times a factor for the coverage of that media times the intensity, pro and con, of the presentation. [When coverage was unfavorable, Uhler had] a suggested operating principle—discipline the media. A number of the media find they can "bomb" the administration with relative impunity. Furthermore, those who directly criticize the administration are often treated better than those who are very friendly. We should adopt a policy of "playing with our friends," that is, identifying those who are consistently friendly and give them a first opportunity at the news and greater access to our department and agency newsmakers. Those who go out of their way to hurt the administration, and especially those who lie, ought to be disciplined by simply denying them access to the news. Their managing editors would soon get the message.

In April 1972 Uhler drafted a memorandum in which he argued that the only way to limit government spending was to write a limit on taxes into the constitution. In vivid language, he argued against the idea of compromise with legislators. Lawmakers, he said, were so influenced by constituents' demands for schools, swimming pools, roads and other services that they were incapable of cutting taxes. "I am absolutely convinced that legislators, if left to their own devices, will, in short order, put an end to the Republic in the name of improving it unless we, the people, take aggressive action, change the environment in which they operate, change the rules of the game."

The argument that the administration needed a new approach caught on. Reagan and his cabinet went up to the foothills east of Sacramento and spent two days in a motel thinking up ways to make a strong finish in his final two years. They decided to set up task forces to create new programs in three areas: tax reduction, reform of local government, and law enforcement. When Uhler was given charge of the tax-reduction task force, it was victory for the conservatives who had watched for years while tax policy was shaped by those more to the center.

Looking back on it, Uhler's foes in the administration now play down his importance, referring to him as an "unmanned missile." But the fact that he was given responsibility for tax reduction was a sign that Reagan and Meese had bought Uhler's much more conservative approach.

What happened next was crucial to the development of Reagan as a presidential candidate and President. Uhler provided Reagan with the arguments and information he needed to support his instinctive disapproval of the state's high taxes. Previously, Reagan had not especially liked what was going on, but he did not know how to stop it. But now Uhler went far outside the capitol for his tax-reduction task force, recruiting scholars who would later form the academic brain trust of Reagan's presidential campaigns and his presidency. Flying to Chicago, he recruited Milton Friedman, the Nobel Prize–winning economist and leading academic proponent of putting limits on taxes, government spending and the supply of money. Uhler also went to a center of conservative political and economic thought, Stanford University's Hoover Institution on War, Revolution and Peace, where he enlisted Martin Anderson, W. Glenn Campbell and Dan Troop Smith.

Each of these men questioned the assumptions of those who had been shaping tax policy. Campbell complained of too much government regulation and high taxation. Anderson, who once was a special assistant to President Nixon, later became Reagan's chief adviser on domestic policy in the 1976 and 1980 campaigns and then in the White House. He was the leading advocate of reductions in welfare spending, a critic of government social programs who wrote in 1980: "The war on poverty has been won, except for a few mopping-up operations." Smith, who had been a tax-policy deputy in the U.S. Treasury Department, was critical of the progressive income tax, which was taking increasingly large amounts of money from taxpayers simply because inflation was causing their income to rise. "This built-in tax increase . . . permits the government to finance through increased taxes government expenditures without having to vote higher taxes," he wrote. "The situation is bad from all standpoints except for those who want to conceal the increasing burden of expanding government." He also wrote critically of the way the progressive income tax is used "for the avowed purpose of redistributing income and wealth."

The task force concluded that "the only way revenues flowing to government can be controlled with certainty is to impose external constraints on the amount of money which government had available to spend. This can be accomplished only through placing a limitation on the taxes which government may impose." Uhler and his team of academics recommended that a ceiling on state taxes be written into the state constitution. That would require a vote of the people.

In December, Uhler gave Reagan a memorandum arguing for the plan. Reagan brought it with him when he and Nancy went to Arizona to visit her parents at Christmas. When he returned, he told Uhler that he liked the proposal. Reagan decided to go ahead with a special election on the tax limit. It was scheduled for November 1973, and the limit plan would be the only issue on the ballot.

The decision thrust Reagan into the most manipulative form of California politics, the initiative campaign in which proposed laws, called propositions, are placed on a ballot. Conceived by the early-twentieth-century reformers as a way of allowing the people to make their own laws, the initiative had been perverted by California's highly merchandised politics. Often business interests would use the initiative to try to write protections for their industries into law. At other times, conservationists or election-law reformers would mount campaigns to limit development or business participation in politics. Millions were spent on the campaigns by advertising specialists who used imaginative methods to reduce complex issues to simple slogans for billboards and television commercials. "Keep California Green" was the theme for one such campaign. Thinking it was a conservation measure, Californians approved it. All the initiative did, however, was give a tax break to private golf clubs. In that type of contest, victory often went to those who struck the latest and lowest blow. Such politics were beyond the experience of Reagan and his aides, who were used to campaigning for governor in easy and relatively gentlemanly contests against weak opponents.

A sufficient number of signatures were gathered by Reagan supporters to qualify the measure for the election. Reagan himself even circulated a petition for forty minutes in his Pacific Palisades neighborhood. "This is the most startling thing that ever happened to me," said Mrs. Virginia Ferguson when she opened her door and found Reagan, felt-tipped pen in hand.

Reagan had more money to spend than his opponents. His opponents were paralyzed by an inability to agree on strategy, but Reagan's old foe, Robert Moretti, effectively campaigned against the tax-limit proposition, Proposition 1, making it a partisan issue and appealing to Democrats to vote against it. Watergate gave his message even more partisan appeal. On October 2, slightly more than a month from the election, campaign executive Terry Chambers wrote to his county coordinators: "The opposition is winning 'the battle of the news media' through the big-lie technique. They are scaring the undecided and uneducated vote into their own camp." Chambers, complaining that money wasn't allocated properly, told Michael Deaver that he was "sick and tired" of not having enough pencils, typewriters and paper. "I like champagne but so far I only have a beer budget," he said.

But even if these minor organizational problems had been overcome, there was a major flaw, the complexity of the language of the initiative, which was a laborious 5,700 words long. Uhler and another attorney, Anthony Kennedy, had used intricate language to make sure that the proposition would take effect without legislative and court interference. At the end, the complexity became an issue in itself, and an embarrassment to Reagan. On October 26, less than two weeks before the election, Reagan was interviewed by newsman George Reading on television station KTVU in Oakland.

"Do you think the average voter really understands the language of this proposition?" asked Reading.

"No, he shouldn't try. I don't either," Reagan replied.

In Los Angeles, Harry Lerner, a hard old veteran of California initiative campaigns, had been waiting for such a misstep. Lerner had been hired to work against the Reagan initiative by the firm of Whitaker and Baxter, which was running the anti-Reagan campaign. Lerner and Whitaker and Baxter, the first of the campaign merchandising firms, had won many initiative campaigns with devastating last-minute advertisements, and Reagan's remark gave them their opening. A few days before the election, advertisements appeared in newspapers declaring, "When A Proposition's Chief Sponsor Doesn't Understand It, It's Time For The Rest Of Us To Vote No On Proposition No. 1."

Reagan, trying to rescue his campaign, played a personal role in fighting back. When a reporter called his campaign headquarters for clarification of his remarks on television, Reagan returned the call himself and said, "I was being facetious." All he had intended to say was that while the precise legal language of the proposition was difficult to understand, the concept was simple. He said he had meant that "you can understand Proposition 1, and it isn't all that complicated. What is complicated is, of course, in this day and age, the legalese that must be employed in legislative matters, in bills and in amendments and so forth to prevent misunderstandings in future challenges in lawsuits or whatever may occur. If anything I was making a pitch for the people not to get confused by this legal language but to go to the meat of the issue and understand what it really does, which is not very complicated."

The explanation did no good. On election day the proposition lost 66 percent to 44 percent. Reagan's attempt to rectify his tax policy had failed.

What remained on the books was a tax law far more confiscatory than Reagan wanted. His inattentiveness to detail and his penchant for going along with the most persuasive of his subordinates had led him down the wrong path, a path of high taxes contrary to his beliefs. The size of Reagan's tax increases is often cited as a sign of political strength and as evidence that he is not as conservative as he represents himself in his speeches. But tax policy was evidence of weakness rather than strength. He accepted liberal ideas not only because they were politically expedient but because he lacked the intellectual resources to oppose them. Only when Uhler and the other conservatives counterattacked and provided him with strong arguments was he able to assert his conservative ideas.

In the years after his governorship, Reagan reinforced his conservative economic views with visits to the Hoover Institution at Stanford. The economic policies he advocated during the presidential campaign and the economic team he brought with him to Washington reflected the influence of the economic conservatives. Like preceding Administrations, they were confronted by the two insolubles of the economy: inflation and stagnant economic growth. The solutions were huge spending cuts and tax reductions. Compromises would be grudging, the mistakes of California not repeated. Reagan's political career has often been marked by battles for his mind between opposing forces. In the case of economic policies, the conservatives won.

14

REAGAN AND THE VANISHING LAND

As governor, Ronald Reagan was confronted with some of the most perplexing environmental questions of the day—the location of nuclear power plants, air and water pollution, and the need to preserve mountains, farmlands and beaches from the undisciplined population growth that has always been California's special curse. Much to the surprise of his critics, he left office with an environmental record that greatly strengthened the government's hand. Two state agencies had been created to control waste and air pollution and to take responsibility for determining nuclear power plant sites. In the case of the latter agency Reagan, in signing the legislation that created it, took away control over power plant siting from the business-dominated public utilities commission. A Redwood National Park—its ultimate size far larger than Reagan had originally favored—was created with his assent. Highway engineers were refused permission to build a new freeway across the Sierra Nevada, the tall granite mountain chain that stretches for more than four hundred miles along the state's eastern border. Defying two powerful interests, Southern California's development-oriented businesses and the state's farming industry, Reagan stopped construction of a high dam that would have flooded a beautiful Northern California valley and displaced Indians who had lived there many years. He supported bond issues, approved by the voters, to buy more park land and improve water-purification facilities.

The record seems to contradict the rhetoric of a man who has ridiculed government environmental controls and minimized the dangers of pollution. It was, after all, Reagan who once commented on the idea of preserving more California redwood trees: "The economic needs of the lumber industry should be considered. A tree is a tree—how many more do you need to look at?" Noting that there were already 115,000 acres of redwoods then being preserved in state parks in California, he said, "If this 115,000 acres were stretched in a line and a road run through the middle, one could drive for two hundred miles and see nothing but redwoods on both sides . . . we have made adequate provisions for redwoods." And it was Reagan, campaigning for president in 1980, who said of smog, "I have flown twice over Mount St. Helens on our West Coast. I'm not a scientist and I don't know the figures, but I have a suspicion that that one little mountain out there in the last several months has probably released more sulfur dioxide into the atmosphere of the world than has been released in the last ten years of automobile driving or things of that kind that people are so concerned about." (However, the facts refute this. The Environmental Protection Agency has estimated that sulfur-dioxide emissions in the nation total 81,000 tons a day, while sulfur-dioxide emissions from the Mount St. Helens volcano ranged from 500 to 2,000 tons a day.)

Reagan's environmental record differed from the tone of his speeches because, in the day-to-day working of government, he followed the advice of a subordinate who was an environmentalist; he was pushed by a legislature concerned about preserving California's resources; and he was sensitive to the political power of the environmental movement, which was at its peak during his governorship.

When Reagan became governor, it was clear that California's natural beauty was disappearing rapidly. Around the Los Angeles basin, mountains untouched by bulldozers rose above the smog and there were still bighorn sheep roaming wild in the Angeles National Forest. In the Sierra Nevada is Lake Tahoe, the largest mountain lake in the country. Its bright-blue water spans twenty-two miles against a backdrop of wooded mountains. Swimmers could still see the sandy bottom in many places, but murky signs of pollution were increasing. The lake was surrounded by tall garish hotels which destroyed the landscape and produced sewage, and casinos, bill-boards, pizza parlors and neon signs cluttered the south shore of the lake.

Like Tahoe, California had retained its beauty but decay was setting in. There were almost 10 million vehicles crowding the highways, each spewing noxious waste into the air. Man had used landfill to reduce the size of San Francisco Bay from almost 700 square miles to about 400, in the process destroying the natural shoreline habitat of fish and wild birds. "California is a unique bright land, and somehow or other we must keep her so," warned California Tomorrow, a private conservation organization. It asked: "How polluted can a bright land become and still be bright?"

There was growing awareness of the danger. The California-based Sierra Club, along with newer environmental groups, was sounding the warning. Homeowners, seeing their subdivisions surrounded by newer subdivisions and shopping centers, demanded controls on development. Ecology suddenly became a popular movement. Environmentalist lawmakers, who had traditionally taken a beating from business interests, gained influence in the legislature. By 1970, at the end of Reagan's first term, the whole nation was celebrating Earth Day, confirming the political power of the ecology movement.

Thus Reagan's approval of stricter state controls was a smart political decision. But there was another, more important reason for his behavior. It is a clear example of the Reagan method of governing: delegating great authority to his department heads, remaining aloof from bureaucratic struggles and then accepting the recommendation of the person in charge. Under the Reagan system, success goes to the strong. Reagan, smiling and unscathed by combat, confirms the victory by adopting the winner's policy. In the case of the environment, the winner was the secretary of the state resources agency, a man dedicated to the preservation of the state's environment, Norman B. (Ike) Livermore.

Livermore is a fourth-generation Californian and a Republican. His brother was Republican county chairman in San Francisco and had played a key role in bringing moderate Republicans into Reagan's campaign for governor. After a lifetime in the lumber industry, Livermore had resigned as treasurer of the Pacific Lumber Company to head the resources agency. On the surface, his appointment seemed to be a surrender to the loggers. But Livermore was also a member of the Sierra Club. He had grown up in the Sierra Nevada and had led mule trains along its rugged trails. "I've spent a thousand nights in the Sierra," he said. "Being up there gives one a chance to be by himself away from the telephones, and the camaraderie around the campfire is one of the greatest things of all." But he also admired man-made works and respected private industry. He liked to visit Jedediah Smith Redwood State Park, for on one side are the "primeval, almost religiously inspiring coast redwoods. And on the left is a sawmill. They're both necessary." He conceded: "I am a living contradiction."

Even before Reagan became governor, one of the state's most important environmental battlegrounds had been the North Coast, the cold, foggy counties two hundred miles above San Francisco. Here was the northern home of the last great stands of the redwood, the tallest tree known to man. Some of them had been growing since before the birth of Christ. Once they had covered much of the coast of California, reaching from what is now the Oregon border down through San Francisco to below Monterey and Big Sur. Since redwood is a durable, all-purpose building material of consistently high value, most of them were gone before Reagan took office. The giant trees still covered the mountains of the North Coast, however, sometimes reaching unbroken from the sea to the mountain peaks. But except for 50,000 North Coast acres in state parks, the redwoods were falling to the logging companies at the rate of a billion board feet a year.

Lumber made a one-industry economy. People there approached the land with the nineteenth-century outlook that resources were limitless and were placed on earth to be exploited. Local government, the newspapers, radio and television all reflected the viewpoint of the big lumber companies that controlled the economy. The North Coast rejected the idea that the redwoods were a national treasure. To the people there, the trees meant payrolls, money to keep the economy running. The strength of this influence was apparent when the Eureka League of Women Voters warned that a proposed $30 million paper-pulp mill would cause air pollution and pour potentially poisonous waste water into the bay. City councilmen scoffed. "If there's anything that's discouraging, it's the little old lady in tennis shoes crying," said one advocate of the project. ". . . they are going to bring in thirty million dollars here; we should be thankful to them."

For years conservationists had advocated that the federal government buy the redwood groves from the lumber companies and create a Redwood National Park. The lumber companies, of course, opposed the idea. They had a counterproposal: turn the existing state parks over to the federal government for a Redwood National Park. But conservationists objected on the grounds that the lumber-company proposal would not increase the size of the redwood park land. Reagan's famous campaign remark of "a tree is a tree" seemed to put him on the side of the lumber companies. But campaign rhetoric took a back seat to the realities of the way the Reagan administration worked. As head of the state resources agency, Livermore opposed the lumber companies' plan to turn the state parks over to the federal government. Livermore's main opponent on the issue was the North Coast's congressman, Republican Don Clausen. At the outset, Reagan supported Clausen. But Livermore repeatedly made the point to him "that it was nothing more than donating the state parks to the federal government." He also said he believed a majority of the voters favored a bigger park. In those early months of the administration, Livermore recalled, the park issue had a low priority. But Livermore persisted, negotiating personally with Clausen and with the state's senior senator, Thomas H. Kuchel, a Republican, who favored an intermediate-sized park of 64,000 acres.

In the next two years Livermore estimates he presented at least twenty-five cabinet issue memos on the park. Progress was slow. At first Reagan resisted. One day, when Livermore made still another park presentation, "The governor said, 'Ike, you're going to raise my adrenaline.'" Finally Livermore put together a plan for a 53,000-acre park, big enough to satisfy Kuchel and the Sierra Club but with enough protection for the lumber companies to gain Reagan's approval. Today the park is there, an odd-shaped hybrid of state and federal holdings, fulfilling the goal of protecting more redwoods than before Reagan's term in office.

A second environmental challenge came in 1968, in the same North Coast area in lightly populated Round Valley, south of the redwood forests. This one was more complex, for it involved a water project backed by the state's biggest economic interests. Running through Round Valley was the Middle Fork of the Eel River, one of five Northern California rivers that had escaped the dam builders, and which still ran unobstructed, or wild, through the mountains and forests of a portion of California that looks much as it did thousands of years ago.

A hundred years ago, people were not concerned about protecting wild rivers. All rivers ran free. But men built dams to prevent floods, to store water for irrigation and to create hydroelectric power. By the 1960s, most of the nation's great rivers were shackled by dams and reservoirs, and concern was expressed that one day children would never have the chance to see a river running free.

But many business interests regarded these wild rivers an archaic remnant of a rural past. The industrial firms, financial institutions, large property owners, agricultural businesses and construction firms that influenced water-development policy in Sacramento and in powerful committees of Congress felt they needed more water for expansion of their holdings, water that could only come from the few rivers that had not already been dammed. In a state where the climatic conditions range from drought to downpour, it had been the practice to capture water behind big dams and send it through aqueducts to the dry south. Imported water had brought population growth and prosperity to the semi-arid plain of Southern California. It brought varied agriculture to the Central Valley. All recent governors had accepted the economic arguments for the growth of the water system, none more enthusiastically than Reagan's predecessor, Governor Brown, the leading advocate of the state dams and aqueducts which carry water from north to south.

In 1968 Reagan's director of water resources, William Gianelli, was prepared to go ahead with the damming of the North Coast wild rivers. Gianelli, a Democrat who had served in the state department of water resources under Brown, believed in the water project and its expansion. The Reagan administration had appointed Gianelli despite his party registration to appease some of the state's most influential water-project advocates. Lou Cannon put it this way in his book *Ronnie and Jesse,* a study of Reagan and his long-time Democratic rival, Jesse Unruh: "The governor's advisers, though willing to go outside the government apparatus for a corporations director . . . were unwilling to play citizen politician with the state's water resources policy, which ironically was the policy most in need of re-examination."

Although Gianelli was technically under Livermore, it did not work that way at first. In the previous administration, the water resources director had held all the power, since he was actually in charge of building the water project. The engineers and contractors worked for him. Meanwhile, the resources secretary was a figurehead. Livermore quickly moved to take command, supported by the finance director, Caspar Weinberger, and Reagan's executive secretary, William Clark.

Livermore's control was consolidated in the fierce bureaucratic struggle over the Round Valley project. He defeated the powerful economic interests which favored the Dos Rios dam by marshaling the political power of the environmental movement and by shrewd understanding of Reagan's cabinet system of government. Gianelli had economic clout behind him, but under Reagan's chain-of-command governorship, Livermore had access to Reagan to argue that the dam was too costly and not really needed, and that Round Valley would be destroyed for nothing. Gianelli's path to the governor was blocked by Livermore. The fight was waged within the administration, hidden for the most part behind Reagan's geniality and the image of unity he promoted. Reagan, in fact, was uninvolved most of the time. This is demonstrated in a progress report to the cabinet written by Livermore during an early stage of the fight: "I have not recently brought the matter to the cabinet's attention nor have I discussed it except very briefly with the governor to keep him generally aware of the matter."

In the beginning, Gianelli seemed assured of victory. There was no reason to believe that years of routine approval of such projects would be reversed. At the end of 1968 Gianelli wrote to Livermore: "We moved ahead with our agreement with the U.S. Army Corps of Engineers looking toward corps financing and construction of Dos Rios reservoir [and dam]." For 1969, he said, the department would try for "early authorization of federal construction of the Dos Rios project."

Livermore had some allies: sportsmen concerned about steelhead in the river, the Round Valley Indians, other residents of the area, and those who believed in wild rivers. But as Cannon points out: "Construction of the Dos Rios super dam . . . seemed a foregone conclusion. The U.S. Army is accustomed to Indian opposition and conservationists and small farmers have rarely stopped the corps." Moreover, for years the Army Engineers had been accustomed to enthusiastic cooperation from California water officials. But opponents proved effective. Richard Wilson, a Round Valley cattle rancher and a friend of Livermore's, put together an organization to fight the dam. Livermore said he received three thousand letters on Dos Rios, most of them against the project.

Finally Livermore gave notice of his opposition in an interview with a reporter. The pressure on him grew intense. The big agricultural firms favoring the dam had the support of Reagan's agriculture secretary, Earl Coke. Southern California business interests pressed their case through the Los Angeles County chamber of commerce. "Finally," Livermore said, "I passed the word that if he [Reagan] approved it, I'd resign."

Livermore took his case to the cabinet. He listed the arguments for the dam, and then presented the arguments against it, concluding with the one that seemed to have the most effect on Reagan, the fact that the Indians would be forced from homes that had been guaranteed by a federal treaty. In another meeting, pro-dam forces made a final personal appeal to Reagan. "I was nervous as a coot," Livermore remembers of the meeting.

In the end, Reagan told the engineers to study other sites for the dam. "There are very serious questions in my own mind about protecting Round Valley," he said. "It is a place of great beauty. Another concern I have is for the community of Covelo and for the future of the Round Valley Indians who have inhabited the valley for centuries." Livermore said he believed the plight of the Indians was the clinching argument for Reagan. It was another example of how Reagan—often harsh and unsympathetic when speaking in the abstract—is moved by the misfortunes of individuals.

Another water-project issue on which Livermore persuaded Reagan to go against major economic interests was a proposal to build a dam on the Middle Fork of the Feather River, another of California's wild rivers. So rugged was its canyon that few fishermen or hikers ever found their way to the river. But good fishermen could take an easy limit of big rainbow trout from the stream. The departments of Interior and Agriculture listed the river as one of seventy-three streams in the nation which should be part of a system of wild rivers protected from dams.

The river was in jeopardy when Reagan took office. An irrigation district controlled by rice growers wanted to dam it. The project would have allowed the district to sell hydroelectric power to the Pacific Gas and Electric Company, and it would have provided free water for the growers. Under Governor Brown's administration, the state water commission had approved the project, as had another state agency, the water rights board. Only the courts or the Federal

Power Commission could stop it. Reagan's own legislative aides expected him to side with both the farmers and the utility company. But the chain of command prevailed, and once again he followed the advice of the man he had placed in charge of resources. Reagan allowed state agencies to fight the project in the courts, and he supported adoption of a legislative resolution asking the Federal Power Commission to refuse to license the project. Eventually the river was saved when it was made part of the nation's wild-river system.

Following Livermore's advice, Reagan made some other surprising environmental appointments. He retained Governor Brown's director of fish and game, Walter Shannon, who had alienated the lumber industry with his criticisms of their logging practices. Reagan had been under heavy pressure to appoint someone more friendly to private business. And for parks director Reagan hired one of the most imaginative parks experts in the nation, William Penn Mott, Jr. In Oakland, the drab city across the Bay from San Francisco, Mott had built an imaginative Children's Fairyland when he was parks director there, persuading local businesses and clubs to pay for replicas of scenes from fairy tales. Not wanting any open space to go to waste, he even had flowers planted on boulevard dividers. Building parks, said Mott, is like building a church: "You've got to have faith."

Not everyone approved of Reagan's environmental policies, especially his determination to give city and county governments, which are strongly influenced by local business, the power to control construction. An example of this was his handling of the controversy over Lake Tahoe. About three hundred miles east of San Francisco and six thousand feet above sea level, the lake, with its forests of pine and fir coming down to the water, had once been hard to reach. But the transcontinental highways across the Sierra Nevada were improved after World War II, and people found their way to the lake. Hotels, motels and subdivisions were built on meadows and hillsides. Creeks became clogged with dirt and refuse from construction. This, along with sewage seeping from cesspools and inadequate treatment plants, began to pollute the lake. Neither the state governments of California and Nevada nor the five counties surrounding the area would act to curb the construction that was ruining the lake. What was needed was a regional government to enforce controls on sewage disposal and development.

Tahoe resembled the North Coast area in that it was a one-industry area. The industry was the gambling and vacation business, summer and winter. Like the businessmen of the North Coast, residents were willing to sacrifice long-term values—preservation of the lake's beauty—for short-term gain. They did not believe that the lake was in immediate danger of pollution, despite the testimony of scientists from the state department of public health and the United States Health Service.

Early in 1967 Reagan and his family drove up to Tahoe for an inspection and a visit with Paul Laxalt, then governor of Nevada and now a senator who is Reagan's friend and close political adviser. After the visit Reagan said conservationists had exaggerated when they warned it would be too late to save the lake if action was not taken that summer. In fact, he was so little concerned with the threat of pollution that—in the interest of economy—he, at one point, tried to delay a $2 million loan to a Tahoe sewer district for a sewage-disposal system. Later he agreed to lend the money. But when the federal government threatened to act if local and state apathy continued, the state was pushed into moving. After doubts and delays, a bill was passed setting up a regional planning agency for the Tahoe basin. It had Reagan's support. Local government, however, was given a majority of votes on the agency's board. The fate of the lake was still in question. Those who were concerned about its preservation doubted the willingness of local people to curb development, since they had never shown any inclination to do so before. It seemed to many conservationists that the lake was still in the hands of those who were spoiling it.

Putting local government in charge of environmental planning was a consistent Reagan policy. His 1972 environmental report stated that "state government should intercede in local matters only where necessary." It also declared that "the protection of environmental resources of statewide significance is principally a local government responsibility." That philosophical outlook continued in later years. When Western business interests and politicians organized the sagebrush rebellion in the late 1970s to promote state and private takeover of millions of acres of federal lands west of the Rocky Mountains, Reagan supported it. After he was elected President, Reagan sent a telegram to a meeting of the sagebrush rebels: "I renew my pledge to work toward a sagebrush solution . . . to insure that the states have an equitable share of public land and their natural resources." That statement concerned environmentalists who believed that the states, if given the land, would open it up to uncontrolled development by loggers, ranchers and the oil and coal interests wanting to tap the vast Western resources.

In his years as governor, Reagan was pushed by an aggressive and persuasive subordinate, an environmentally conscious legislature and political realities into approving programs that differed from his own personal philosophy of little government control. But by the time he became President, the political situation had changed. The environmentalists who had promoted Earth Day were out of style in an energy-short, economically troubled nation more concerned with jobs and the price of fuel. Powerful unions were siding with industry for a relaxation of environmental controls. The Western states' solid 1980 vote for Reagan gave them more influence to push the sagebrush rebellion. State control over resource-rich land was politically popular in a part of the country that was at the heart of Reagan's political support. There is no doubt Reagan left California with more safeguards for its beauty than were there when he took office. But his appointment of James Watt of Denver, a leader of the sagebrush rebellion, as Secretary of the Interior cast doubt on whether he would take the same course when it came to the immeasurably greater resources of the nation.

15

REAGAN AND
THE LAW

In the fall of 1978 Ronald Reagan performed a political act that was
highly unusual for a man given to law-and-order political speeches
that verge on the inflammatory. John Briggs, a right-wing state
senator, was winning great support for another of those voter-
initiated proposed amendments to the state constitution that dominate California's political life. The proposal would have removed
homosexual teachers from classrooms. The anti-gay movement was
at its height. Voter initiatives against gays had been approved in St.
Paul, Minnesota; Eugene, Oregon; Wichita, Kansas; and in Dade
County, Florida, where Anita Bryant, the singer, led a nationally
publicized campaign against the homosexual community. The anti-
gay movement was hoping for victory in California, which would
have been its most important success. But to the surprise of many,
Reagan came out against the proposal and dealt the anti-gay cause
a serious blow.

The story of Reagan's timely assistance to the gay community
illustrates two important facets of his character. One was an in-
grained respect for the law that led him to oppose an initiative that
clearly violated civil liberties. He was also concerned about the plight

of the individual and the fact that the proposal could have damaged the personal and professional lives of many teachers.

Long before Reagan entered the campaign, opponents of the Briggs initiative knew his support was necessary for victory. They understood that the only way to win was to obtain conservative support. In this way, the campaign against the Briggs initiative would seem more than just a gay movement. Instead, the campaign would be more broadly based, composed of non-gays as well as gays, and people of all views, including those in the mainstream of power and influence. In a state such as California, without traditional political structure, the only way to win the support of unorganized voters is to obtain endorsements from well-known public figures who symbolize something to the population. These endorsements, publicized on television, radio and in newspaper advertisements, are the modern California equivalent to the old political boss getting out the vote for his candidates and causes. In this particular campaign, there were two public figures who would be most valuable to opponents of the Briggs proposal. They were John Wayne, the politically conservative actor whose roles had made him a symbol of rugged American individualism and Western manhood, and Reagan, the nation's leading conservative politician, a symbol of law and order and support-your-local-police politics.

Of the two, Reagan, by then a major contender for the 1980 presidential nomination, was the best choice. But members of the anti-Briggs campaign were not sure at first that they could get his public endorsement. It would be bad for him politically, since the conservatives who were the heart of his support for the presidency were also the strongest supporters of the Briggs initiative.

His record as governor gave gays little encouragement. Reagan had advocated many policies opposed by civil libertarians, among them the death penalty and the weakening of the rights of accused criminals. He appointed judges who believed in "judicial restraint," code words which meant they would refrain from limiting police power in the manner of the U.S. Supreme Court under Chief Justice Earl Warren. He felt the police should have fewer restrictions in making arrests. "I once played a sheriff who thought he could do the job without a gun," Reagan once told a national conference of sheriffs. "I was dead in twenty-seven minutes of a thirty-minute show. You may still have your guns, but there are those who've done

everything but tie your hands and take your guns. It is time for
society to give those on the firing line the weapons needed in the fight
against crime." He rejected the idea that poverty and other of society's ills are responsible for crime. "Let us have an end to the idea
that society is responsible for each and every wrongdoer," he said.
"We must return to the belief in every individual being responsible
for his conduct and his misdeeds with punishment immediate and
certain." He talked as though society were besieged by criminals.
"Man's determination to live under the protection of the law has
pushed back the jungle down through the centuries," he said. "But
the jungle is always there and somehow it seems much closer than
we have known it in the years preceding."

But Reagan's feelings about the law are more complicated than his
speeches indicate, and these beliefs are important to his character
and crucial in assessing what he brings to the presidency. Despite the
fiery speeches, in practice he is a humane man, with great respect for
the law and its institutions. Perhaps because he is not burdened with
much legal education or with experience in courtrooms, he ap-
proaches the law with the innocence of one whose views were shaped
by schoolboy history lessons about great judges such as John Marshall and Oliver Wendell Holmes. The intent of the Briggs initiative
clearly ran contrary to that tradition. It would have unleashed school
boards on witch hunts, with public hearings against any teachers
suspected of "advocating, soliciting, imposing, or promoting" private homosexual acts. And these hearings—which would have the
power to ruin lives—would operate without the court's protections.

Thus the outlook was not entirely bleak for the campaign against
the Briggs initiative as its leaders began attempting to set up a
meeting with Reagan. The most perceptive of the initiative opponents knew they had other advantages in pressing their case with
Reagan: Reagan and his wife had spent many years in the film
business, where gays are an important force; colleagues and, no
doubt, friends from those days were gay. Gay leaders also knew that
gays had been involved in one of the most traumatic experiences of
Reagan's governorship. Two staff members had been accused by
other aides in 1967 of homosexuality. Reagan, believing the accusa-
tion, fired the staff members. But when assistants leaked the story to
reporters, the governor firmly denied their published reports. He was
attacked in newspapers around the country for being untruthful,

which did not help him in his 1968 campaign for the Republican presidential nomination. What his critics did not understand was that his denials protected the identity of the two. "If there is a credibility gap, and I'm responsible, it is because I refuse to participate in trying to destroy human beings with no factual evidence, and I'm not going to do that, and if that means there is a credibility gap, so be it," he said. "There is a credibility gap."

The gays who were to meet with Reagan decided to center their arguments on one aspect of the issue—that the initiative would violate civil liberties. Before the meeting they were asked by Reagan's aides to send the governor and Meese an analysis of the initiative. They prepared the analysis in binders, containing legal opinions, newspaper clippings and other material. The approach worked. When Reagan met with the delegation he was, one of the campaigners recalled, "appalled by the unfairness of the procedures [proposed by the initiative]. That was what he asked questions about." Reagan adviser Lyn Nofziger said Reagan "thought it was a badly drawn bill and a lot of people could get hurt. Present laws were sufficient."

After a lengthy discussion between him and his staff, Reagan publicly opposed the initiative in September, but he used a low-keyed approach in issuing a statement. Word went out in a newsletter Nofziger sent to members of the Citizens for the Republic, Reagan's political organization. When the anti-Briggs campaigners heard about it, they called newspapers and television and radio stations. Reagan's statement was just what the beleaguered campaign had hoped for: "I don't approve of teaching a so-called gay life style in our schools but there is already adequate legal machinery to deal with such problems if and when they arise." Noting the threat of public hearings by school boards, he asked: "What if an overwrought youngster disappointed by bad grades imagined it was the teacher's fault and struck out by accusing the teacher of advocating homosexuality? Innocent lives could be ruined."

The quotation was used in newspaper, radio and television advertisements. One of them carried pictures of Reagan and Governor Jerry Brown. The ad said: "At least they agree on one thing."

The Reagan endorsement had a devastating effect on the Briggs campaign. The Los Angeles *Times* poll showed that by November 1, a few days before the election, it was losing, 62 percent to 29 percent with 9 percent undecided. "I could see no other reason for it going that way except for the Reagan endorsement," said I. A. Lewis, director of the poll. "I was stunned to see it going the way it was going." Briggs, aware of the damage, sourly commented, "I can't believe the Hollywood crowd has gotten him to take that kind of position . . . I am personally more concerned with the safety and education of children than I am concerned about pandering to the homosexual community so that I might pick up a few dollars for my campaign or pick up that vote out there [from homosexuals]."

The charge that Reagan was unconcerned about children and was making the endorsement for political reasons was a serious mistake on Briggs's part, especially since Reagan did not particularly like him. Reagan increased his opposition, speaking out more publicly. During this period he was writing a column that appeared in newspapers around the country, including many in California. He used the column for a last, strategically timed attack on the Briggs measure. In a column that appeared the week before the election, he wrote about two propositions on the November California ballot: one was Proposition 5, which limited smoking in public places, and the other was the Briggs measure, Proposition 6. Concerning the latter, he said: "Whatever else it is, homosexuality is not a contagious disease like the measles. Prevailing scientific opinion is that in individuals, sexuality is determined at an early age and that a child's teachers do not really influence him." He concluded with a ringing warning: "Will California rewrite that old line, 'As California goes, so goes the nation?' Here's one heterosexual non-smoker who, where Propositions Five and Six are concerned, hopes the answer is 'no.' " His hope was realized. The measure lost, 58 percent to 42 percent.

Briggs was enraged. "That one single endorsement—Ronald Reagan's—turned the polls around," he said. In a notably incorrect prediction, Briggs added, "For Ronald Reagan to march to the drums of the homosexuals has irrevocably damaged him nationally."

Reagan's respect for the law and legal institutions, which swayed his decision on the Briggs initiative, was even more evident in his manner of selecting judges. He appointed judges with care, leaning on the recommendation of other judges and lawyers. He promoted many judges from lower courts to appellate courts, believing strongly in judicial experience. He placed great faith in the recommendations of the state bar, the lawyer-run organization which regulates and disciplines the legal profession. His judges were expectedly conservative and Republican. Most were white males. But after he left office, both Republicans and Democrats praised the quality of Reagan's judicial appointments.

As he did in other areas, Reagan left the details and the early decision making in these appointments to subordinates. He rarely questioned the recommendations of the local screening committees, dominated by judges and prominent attorneys. The process produced good judges, but because of his inattentiveness to detail it also produced some judges not to his liking. California Supreme Court Chief Justice Donald Wright shocked and angered Reagan by writing the majority opinion overturning the death penalty, which Reagan supported. Reagan said the decision "makes a mockery of the constitutional process . . ." As a result of the decision, Wright was called "Reagan's Earl Warren" by those who remembered President Eisenhower's shock at finding out how his Chief Justice felt on the issues. Although Reagan was furious, Wright, who has since retired, did much to maintain the high standards of the state supreme court, and the fact that he got the job was a tribute to Reagan's system of appointments.

Wright had come to the notice of the Reagan administration because he was part of the appointment process in the early years. As a member of a Los Angeles County screening committee, he was serving with Reagan's friend and personal lawyer, William French Smith. Names came to the committee from the governor's office, where politically knowledgeable appointments secretaries had screened them. It was in the governor's office that political decisions were made resulting in mostly Republican judges. The local committees, such as the one Wright and Smith served on, would make further inquiries. "As it turned out," Wright said, "another judge and I did all the work, and the reason for this is easy to understand. Being the presiding judge of the Los Angeles court, I could call up any judge in the country or any lawyer and ask a question, 'Tell me what you know about Joe Smith as a lawyer in the San Fernando Valley or Long Beach,' and they'd give me their frank answer."

(In California there are trial courts—municipal and superior courts—and the appellate courts, including the state supreme court. The governor makes all appointments. Municipal and superior court appointments do not have to be confirmed, but a commission on judicial appointments confirms all appellate court nominations.)

Wright's work on the committee brought him in contact not only with the influential Smith, but with legal and political aides on Reagan's staff. Soon it got him a promotion to an appellate court, and then Smith and Reagan staff members Ned Hutchinson and Herbert Ellingwood asked him to be chief justice of the state supreme court. "We met in Mr. Smith's offices because he apparently felt there would be 'spies' in the [appellate court] building who might well say, 'Why in the world are these people calling on Justice Wright?' " Wright's reaction was, "You don't mean me? You must be crazy." Years later, when he recalled that day and Reagan's anger at his death-penalty decision, Wright added, "I guess later on they thought they were.

"Up to that time [of the supreme court appointment] I had seen Governor Reagan twice in my life. Once I was on a committee of three judges who called on him in Sacramento to see whether or not he was going to sign a bill which would create additional judgeships in Los Angeles County . . . We finally got in to see him around five o'clock in the evening and he was very very tired. We presented our position; we were told to do it very quickly. He said, 'Well, that sounds fair to me. I will not veto the bill.' . . . That interview with him probably lasted ten minutes."

After Wright joined the court majority in overruling the death penalty, Reagan tried to make the best of the situation and told reporters, "Well, he wasn't against the death penalty when I appointed him. He was questioned at great length for a number of hours about his views, and on the basis of his expressed philosophy, he was appointed." Reagan said that Wright had specifically told him he favored capital punishment. But Wright said neither Reagan nor any of his associates, including Smith, had asked him for his philosophy on any issues. "Nobody ever did," he said. He had flown to Sacramento for a visit with Reagan after being asked to take the job. "We had a very short conversation," Wright said. "He was very pleasant. We did not go into anything about my personal judicial philosophy or anything of that type. Primarily, he wanted to know if I would accept the job. I can remember at the end, as I left, I laughingly said, 'Well, you know, Governor, there is one thing I neglected to ask—what does the job pay?' He laughed and said, 'If you had asked me that first, I wouldn't have appointed you.' "

The next time Wright saw Reagan again, in Sacramento, was the day the governor announced his appointment. "When my wife and I arrived in Sacramento that morning, the governor was very busy on other matters," said Wright. "So his secretary said, 'Why don't you and Mrs. Wright walk out in the garden around the capitol and then come on back [later] when we will meet with the press. So I really didn't see the governor at all until the very moment when we walked into the room [with the press]." A few minutes before, a secretary had handed Wright a small card that contained the substance of Reagan's announcement, praising Wright as a man "committed to the principle of justicial restraint . . ." The governor also reiterated his belief that the legislature, not the courts, should decide whether the death penalty should be retained. Wright read the statement. The assistant asked Wright if he agreed with them. "I said, 'Yes, I agree in general with them,' but there are several items in there that I don't agree with." Then he said, 'But you have no objection to the governor making those statements?' And I said, 'I don't think it's my business to object.' "

Years later Wright was asked how Reagan got the idea he was for capital punishment. Wright thought it had come from an answer he had given on a somewhat different issue. "One of the newsmen asked me about the death penalty and I said, 'Well, it is the law of this land, and if a case came before us I would be compelled to follow the law as it now stands.' "

Wright's appointment had been the logical result of a system of governing that delegated much authority. In this case the authority was given over to advisory committees dominated by judges and attorneys and tilted heavily in favor of those with previous judicial experience. Wright was well thought of in the Los Angeles legal community. He had started at the bottom of the judicial ladder, in the municipal court. He and other judges appointed by Reagan tell much the same story, of being recommended by legal colleagues and then getting the jobs after interviews notable for an absence of searching questions about judicial philosophy.

Appeals Judge James Hastings recalls answering twenty questions on a form which the administration gave to judicial candidates. They dealt mostly with education and background in legal practices. He talked with Meese; legal affairs secretary Herb Ellingwood; Hutchinson, the appointments secretary; and others, but it was "an introductory kind of meeting . . . they were not in any way telling me how to be a judge . . ." Justice Hugh A. Evans remembers "probing, revealing questions" from Meese, Ellingwood and Hutchinson, seemingly intended to provide a sense of his views on judicial restraint. Justice Edwin Beach said, "I may have been considered firm in my attitude toward criminal law and sentencing," but when Meese, Ellingwood and, briefly, Reagan interviewed him, "There was no particular emphasis on political or philosophical points of view."

According to his supporters, Reagan's attitude toward judicial appointments showed a respect for the principle of an independent judiciary, which is at the heart of the Constitution. They also regarded it as an answer to concern expressed by President Carter's supporters in the 1980 campaign that Reagan would pack the court with right-wing ideologues. That fear was heightened by a plank in the 1980 Republican platform which declared: "We will work for the appointment of judges . . . who respect traditional family values and the sanctity of human life." The plank was placed there at the insistence of right-to-life anti-abortionists, one of the Moral Majority groups politically important to Reagan.

In addition to being respectful of the institutions of the law, Reagan often moved in enlightened directions when the law was presented to him in terms of the plight of the individual. Besides initiating the policy of conjugal visits in California prisons, he supported seventy-two-hour furloughs for inmates soon to be paroled. Going along with the thinking of national prison reformers, he endorsed construction of new prisons near population centers, where families could more easily visit prisoners. Commenting on Reagan's belief that young offenders should be kept out of "college of crime" state prisons with hardened criminals, the Los Angeles *Times* said his "views on penology are among the most enlightened in the nation."

And although he supported capital punishment, one of his most troubled moments as governor was the 1967 execution of Aaron Mitchell, a black who had killed a white policeman during a robbery —the only man to be executed during Reagan's governorship. The crime had broad political and social implications, and the prospect of the execution prompted demonstrators to gather outside Reagan's house in Sacramento the night before Mitchell was to die. They thought the governor, in refusing to commute the sentence, was carrying out the wishes of his middle-class white constituency and that the execution was a symbol of bigger changes that were on the way. The demonstrators were correct. Social policy was changing that year, and there was to be a tougher attitude toward crime.

General aid to black slums had been slowed. Reagan was attempting to repeal or modify the open-housing law to calm white fears of blacks moving into their neighborhoods. He was hinting that welfare fraud was a widespread offense.

Moreover, Reagan had made capital punishment a political issue in his first gubernatorial campaign, charging that there had been no executions in four years because Governor Edmund Brown opposed the death penalty. He was mistaken. Most of the executions had been postponed because of court decisions, although Brown had granted clemency in some cases. Brown had also refused clemency at times, and some executions had taken place while he was governor. But Reagan was convincing when he told audiences that executions had been put off for so long that there was a need for an "urban renewal project on death row." In fact, condemned men had overflowed San Quentin's capacity, and the state prison system had been forced to add more cells.

In office, Reagan repeatedly made it clear he would use the death penalty. Early in his term, he met with officials of the American Civil Liberties Union of Southern California to discuss the issue, and the session provided a rare view of the intensity of his feelings. The men were escorted into the governor's big meeting room rather than his private office. At the outset Reagan said he was familiar with the capital-punishment issue and had, in fact, debated it when he was in school. One member of the group said he was concerned by some of Reagan's campaign statements indicating that he would rely on the courts' verdicts in death-penalty cases rather than use the governor's discretion to grant clemency. Reagan replied that the statement was wrong, that he would overrule the courts if the facts warranted it. Then the conversation turned to a general discussion of the death penalty. To counter the arguments of civil libertarians, who opposed the death penalty, Reagan related the details of a particularly macabre case and then asked his visitors how they would have dealt with the killers in that case if there were no death penalty. One of those at the meeting recalls listening in surprised silence while the governor graphically described the crime, which involved the sexual mutilation of the male victim.

Governor Brown had turned down Aaron Mitchell's appeal for clemency the year before, but the state supreme court had accepted another appeal and ordered a new trial. At this trial Mitchell was sentenced to death again, and once more he asked the governor for clemency. Reagan's adviser on capital-punishment cases was Meese, whose outlook was much like that of a policeman. As a young deputy district attorney he had helped direct the police during the Free Speech Movement demonstrations of 1964, when they arrested protesting UC Berkeley students. He was, in the words of an associate, "a man who has no doubts about solid virtues of American life, who is convinced there is a right and a wrong."

On Tuesday, April 11, 1967, Reagan looked at the case one last time, leaned across his desk to Meese and said, "I think it will be my decision not to intervene." Later that day Reagan, more solemn than usual, explained his reason to reporters. "In this particular instance the man, the father of two children, who was killed was a policeman. I think that if we are going to ask men to engage in an occupation in which they protect us at the risk of their life, we of society have an obligation to them to let them know that society will do whatever it can to minimize the danger of their occupations. I think any policeman is entitled to that. There are no bands playing or flags flying when he shoots it out with a criminal on our behalf."

Meese attended to the details of carrying out Reagan's decision. He telephoned Mitchell's attorneys and Lawrence Wilson, the warden at San Quentin. Later he returned to the governor's office. It was a moment he would long remember. Reagan was upset, talking earnestly to Nofziger. He had agreed earlier to fly south to Anaheim for a civic ceremony and throw out the first baseball for the opening of the California Angels' new stadium. Now, with the condemned man awaiting death, he didn't want to leave Sacramento. But assistants told him that appearing at the new stadium was part of his responsibility as governor, and finally Reagan said, "All right, you tell them I'll go down." He ordered his chartered jet to stand by to return him to Sacramento as soon as the ceremony was finished. Meese said, "I'll meet you at the airport." Reagan replied, "Don't inconvenience yourself. If there's anything new, come out."

Reagan returned home from the baseball stadium before ten o'clock. He had an assistant telephone to the capitol, where Meese was waiting in his office to find out about Mitchell's condition because that afternoon Mitchell had slashed his wrist. Although the wound was not serious, the suicide attempt did dramatize the agony of the condemned man and had made the whole execution process seem more brutal. Meese had talked to Warden Wilson and was able to report that all was under control.

As usual, Reagan went to bed early that night, facing for the first time the pre-execution ordeal so dreaded by his predecessors. On such a night in 1960, Governor Brown had sat alone in his study and pondered the case of Caryl Chessman, awaiting death for committing sex crimes against his kidnap victims. Brown's advisers told him to let Chessman die. His conscience insisted that he spare the man. Brown compromised and gave Chessman a reprieve until the legislature could vote on abolition of the death penalty. When the legislature refused to end capital punishment, Chessman was executed. In later years Brown often talked about the awful burden he carried that night.

Reagan later told a close friend about his emotions the night before Mitchell was to die. He had gotten up and thought about Mitchell. Outside, the marchers still paced back and forth in front of his house. He glanced down at them and asked himself if there was anything more he could have done in the case or if there were any facts he had not considered. Alone with his conscience, he concluded he had done all he could and he returned to bed. "There is no question about it," he said later, "this is one of the worst features of the job. But it must also be just as bad for the judges involved, for the jurors, for all the others who have had to participate in this. It is not an easy task to be the last resort and have to deny clemency."

When morning arrived, the gas chamber was ready. Fifty-eight witnesses, many of them reporters, waited in the beige room that adjoined the "smoke house," as prisoners called the chamber. They heard Mitchell groaning and screaming in his prison cell, twelve feet away. At 10:01 A.M., three guards escorted him into the chamber. He was limp and still groaning. "I'm Jesus Christ," he shouted—words that Warden Wilson said Mitchell often used. "He was quite religiously oriented," Wilson said. Straps were placed around Mitchell's arms, chest, abdomen and legs. One guard patted him on the knee twice as if to reassure him. His head slumped down and then he looked up at the witnesses. At 10:04, potassium cyanide tablets were dumped into a vat of acid. Mitchell's chest was racked by spasms; his head bent forward; he exhaled as if he had a dry cough, and then his body slumped forward against the straps. At 10:16 Mitchell was pronounced dead, and Warden Wilson notified Meese by telephone.

Reagan had been waiting in his office. At 10 A.M. he had buzzed Meese on the intercom and asked if there was any word. At 10:18 Meese walked down the hall to Reagan's office and said the execution had been completed. For a few minutes, neither man said anything. Then some of the tension disappeared and they chatted casually. Before Meese left the office, Reagan once again remarked, "This is about the toughest decision anyone will ever have to make."

The Aaron Mitchell case showed how Reagan was troubled when the death penalty was no longer an abstraction, or a subject of a flamboyant campaign speech. His speeches on capitol punishment, like so much of his rhetoric, had been unyielding. But when he had to face the life-and-death issue, alone with his conscience, the issue became more complicated. He could no longer take the death penalty as lightly as he did when addressing conservatives at a Republican meeting. That was clear later in his administration when he was confronted with the case of another killer, Calvin Thomas, who had thrown a fire bomb into the home of a woman friend and killed her baby. The prosecutor had asked Reagan to refuse clemency, but Meese looked over Thomas' record of epilepsy and brain damage and told Reagan, "I think this is one where you might want to consider clemency." Reagan replied, "I've been thinking that too." He spared Thomas' life.

As President, Reagan's view of the law, particularly as it will be expressed in his power to nominate Justices of the Supreme Court, will affect the nation for many years. Five of the nine Justices are more than seventy years of age. Particularly after his support of the right-to-life plank in his party's platform, his critics expressed concern he would insist on strict ideological tests for his appointees. But Reagan's record as governor, and his subsequent statements and actions, do not support such fears. During his 1980 campaign he said he would follow the same general approach in appointing judges that he used in California. And he said that while he wanted judges sympathetic to his conservative philosophy, he would not base his appointments on their views on a single issue, such as abortion. "You look for a certain compatibility, broad compatibility, with your own philosophy," he told Wallace Turner of the New York *Times.* "This would be what I look for in judges."

It is true, however, that he will be working under different rules. Senators have a major voice in appointing most federal judges. Traditionally, regional and political considerations have been important in appointments to the Supreme Court. But Reagan's views will be a strong factor. In 1978 he ignored the Moral Majority and helped the gay community defeat an initiative that would have done irreparable harm to their movement and to the cause of civil liberties. As governor he took great care in appointing judges. He supported a prison-system director, Ray Procunier, who was considered a national innovator in prison reform. He agonized over the death penalty when he was the one who had to let a man die. He was, in short, a humane and concerned man who respected the law and the independence of the judiciary, qualities that he brought to his presidency.

16

THE
PRESIDENT

As 1980 ended, the Californians began to settle into Washington, just as they had in Sacramento fourteen years before. Ronald Reagan had been elected President and now the scouting expedition—the transition team—was clearing the way for his inauguration on January 20, 1981. Many Sacramento veterans were scattered around federal office buildings and in the transition team headquarters in a poorly maintained government-owned building with dirty walls, torn carpets and two elevators constantly jammed with job seekers. Their presence in the dismal building showed that in taking over his awesome new responsibilities, Reagan would lean on those who had helped him when he first stepped into the role of governing and leading people.

All the newcomers were filled with a deep sense of wonder at being there. At this early stage even Meese sounded as if he were an unsophisticated tourist. One evening he interrupted an interview with a reporter to take a call from William Webster, the former federal judge who directed the FBI. When Webster offered to come to the transition office for a conference, Meese quickly refused. "No, Judge, I'll go down there," he said. With some enthusiasm, he added, "I've never been in the new FBI Building." In another part of Washington, Robert Carleson, Reagan's old welfare cutter, was at the Health and Human Services Department, preparing a report that would point out where reductions might be made. He borrowed a cigarette from an assistant and commented that he had not smoked all day. "I've been sitting in meetings with the Surgeon General the last two or three days and I feel funny about smoking there," he said in a voice that reflected surprise at finding himself in the company of the Surgeon General. After Reagan gave his first televised speech as President, Michael Deaver complimented him, and then added, "Sometimes I have to pinch myself to see if this is real." Reagan smiled. "So do I," he said.

Their awe was understandable. In the past few years it had often seemed that Reagan's road to Washington was blocked, first by Richard Nixon and then by Reagan's age. But the advisers who most believed in the inevitability of the Reagan presidency understood that other forces were at work. Years of political and social turmoil —the civil rights revolution, the Vietnam war, Watergate and a crushing inflation—had left the nation troubled and adrift. Reagan had waited through those years, his bids for leadership rejected, his ambitions subjected to ridicule by journalists and politicians who refused to take him seriously. His frustrated assistants would occasionally compare Reagan to Winston Churchill in the 1930s, ignored, ridiculed and, only as a last resort, summoned to the leadership of a collapsing nation.

But there was something about that dream that wouldn't die. It was evident on a sunny but chilly morning in December 1972 in Scottsdale, Arizona, when I interviewed Reagan at a Republican governors conference. He sat in the sunshine by the swimming pool and talked in a most relaxed and confident way about how he intended to continue to be a power in national politics when his term as governor ended at the beginning of January 1975. "I know you can't unload," he said. "Once you've taken this on, there is no way in the world you can put it aside and say, 'I don't care anymore.' There are a number of things that can be done. For years I was on the mashed-potato circuit [giving speeches]. As a matter of fact, at one point I was told by professionals in the field that I was second only to the President of the United States in demand as a speaker. Now, this was prior to the governorship, and I feel so strongly that there is such political and economic mythology in this country that that may be the direction I'll take. Maybe I'll hit the road again and try to preach the word." In the story that I wrote for my paper at that time I emphasized that his plan was an excellent way to begin a campaign for the 1976 Republican presidential nomination, for it would allow him to speak out on national issues, keep his name before the public and make speeches for scores of Republican candidates who would become indebted to him. Later, at a party, Michael Deaver asked if he could see a carbon of the story after it had been sent to the newspaper. I gave it to him and he brought it over to Reagan and Mrs. Reagan. When he returned the story to me, he said they were pleased by my interpretation.

Their pleasure reflected the fact that preliminary plans were being made for a presidential race in 1976, though at the time prospects did not seem bright. With the overwhelming defeat of George McGovern in the 1972 election, Nixon appeared to have greater power over the government and the Republican party than ever. His Vice President, Spiro T. Agnew, had won a reputation for inflammatory rhetoric that surpassed Reagan's, and he was trying to lock up the conservative Western, Southwestern and Southern support that was a Reagan source of power in national politics. Agnew's resignation in disgrace was months away, as was the full political impact of the Watergate scandal that would drive Nixon from office. Nevertheless, Robert Walker, a Reagan staff member who was an experienced political manager, had been assigned to explore the prospects of a Reagan presidential campaign. According to Donald Livingston, a top Reagan assistant at the time, organization and planning meetings were held, and by 1974 "we felt he was going to run for President." In May of that year a meeting was held attended by Nofziger; Staunton Evans, the conservative columnist; John Sears, who would be the campaign manager; Richard Wirthlin, the pollster; and a few others. "Wirthlin's polls said we had a shot at it," said Nofziger. "We all said 'Go for it.' " By then, Nofziger said, Reagan had "ninety percent made up his mind to do it."

When Reagan left office in January 1975, Deaver and another former administration aide, Peter Hannaford, had set up an organization that allowed Reagan to earn a living while he ran for President. He became a radio commentator, taping five-minute broadcasts that were syndicated around the country. He wrote a newspaper column and made speeches to business and political groups, charging between $2,500 and $5,000 for each appearance. The demand for his services was so great that the radio programs and the speeches brought Reagan a substantial income and allowed Deaver and Hannaford to arrange the expensive logistics of a national campaign. Even though Reagan was out of office, Deaver and Hannaford made sure he still traveled like a governor. His appearances were carefully scheduled. Advance arrangements ensured that a hotel room and a car with a driver would await him at airports. Even a security force was provided.

The plan worked. Instead of slipping into the obscurity of being an ex-governor, Reagan remained a formidable presence on the national political scene. Each day, throughout the country, his voice was heard on the radio, denouncing welfare, demanding a restoration of traditional moral values, and showing at every opportunity that he did not think much of American policies under the man who had become President, Gerald Ford. The program was particularly popular in areas he was counting on for convention delegates, the South, Southwest and parts of the Midwest. In Iowa, where the first delegates would be selected in 1976, he was heard every day by thousands of motorists driving home in the late afternoon traffic on WHO, the same powerful, clear-channel station that had carried his re-creations of Chicago Cubs baseball games many years before.

On November 20, 1975, Reagan entered the presidential race. Despite losses in early primary elections, he almost took the nomination away from President Ford. But in the end, it didn't work—not even a desperate attempt to win Northeastern moderate support by enlisting Senator Richard Schweiker of Pennsylvania as his running mate. That plan, like so much of what happened during Reagan's governorship, was conceived by his assistants. Reagan hardly knew Schweiker, whose beliefs were more liberal than his.

But the political power of Ford as resident of the White House— the President's power to bestow appointments, federal grants and favors—stopped the Reagan drive at 1,070 delegates, 70 votes short of the 1,140 needed for the nomination. "Stay in there," Reagan told campaign workers afterward. "Don't give up your ideals, don't compromise." Those who were in the room when he spoke to California delegates in Kansas City that day remembered tears in his eyes when he said, "Look, it's just one battle, and it's going to be a long war, and it's going on as long as we will wage it . . . Nancy and I are not going back and sit on a rocking chair and say, 'That's all for us.' "

Journalists, forgetting that Reagan usually meant what he said, wrote sad farewells to him that day. But it was premature, for that year of 1976 brought the election of Jimmy Carter, and his failure to deal with the country's problems in a way that satisfied voters. It was this, and political frustration, that put Reagan in the White House four years later.

American politics had shifted to the right in a way that benefited Reagan. It was not a simple shift to conservatism. The change was subtle and contradictory in a way that puzzled analysts. Public opinion polls showed growing support for major government social programs. Since the Depression, the nation had been firmly committed to government's role as the protector of the unfortunate. For example, in 1964, 64 percent of those polled by the Survey Research Center of the University of Michigan favored the government helping Americans obtain low-cost health care. In 1978, a CBS News/ New York *Times* poll showed the number had grown to 85 percent. And despite continued reports of grumbling about welfare costs, a 1974 Gallup poll found that 66 percent opposed reducing health and welfare programs. There had also been a liberal shift in attitudes toward the way Americans conducted their private lives. A 1969 Gallup poll found that 15 percent of the population favored legalized abortions for married women who simply did not want more children. That figure had risen to 40 percent in a survey taken nine years later.

On the surface, those attitudes were obstacles to Reagan's winning the presidency. But other, more powerful forces were obviously at work in the country. While approving many government services, Americans had also become mistrustful of government, particularly Americans in the white middle class who had been among the beneficiaries of the New Deal. In their minds, the Roosevelt successors had gone too far. In 1964 Lyndon Johnson, in a final burst of New Deal generosity, gave America the Great Society, pushing programs to help the poor to new limits. But outside Washington, events were sharply changing public attitudes. The civil rights movement, with massive civil disobedience, moved into the North, accompanied by demonstrations for desegregated neighborhoods and schools. The mid-sixties produced new and complex changes in opinions. Feelings were contradictory. Public opinion polls found Americans were becoming less prejudiced and favored a more equalitarian society. But at the same time they were unhappy about the Democratic Administration's strenuous civil rights efforts. As Everett Carll Ladd, Jr., and Seymour Martin Lipset observed, they objected "not to the directions but to the pace of the change."

By the fall of 1966, the Gallup poll reported that 52 percent of those surveyed felt that the Johnson Administration was pushing racial integration too fast, a large increase over the 32 percent who shared that feeling in June 1963. Other traumatic events were occurring—the black urban riots, beginning with Harlem in 1964 and Watts in 1965; the Vietnam war with its military failure abroad and demonstrations at home; finally, there was Watergate. All the events contributed to a startling growth in distrust of government. In 1966, 41 percent of those surveyed by the Harris poll had expressed considerable confidence in the presidency and the rest of the executive branch. By 1979, it was just 17 percent.

At the same time, the middle class was becoming more prosperous, leaving the cities for homes in the suburbs. Two- and three-car families were the norm. White middle-class suburban sanctuaries became filled with families who were afraid of losing what they had worked so hard to attain. The unrest threatened them, as did social programs directed toward minorities asking for even more help. The inflation of the late 1970s was the final evidence that government was not only taking too much of what middle-class families had but adding to their misery by overspending and mismanaging the economy.

The beginning of this change of attitude coincided with Reagan's entrance into politics and contributed to his success. The issues provoking the discontent were emotional ones, and Reagan spoke about them with special intensity and effect. He was not a regional bigot, as George Wallace seemed to be. Nor did he appear to be an uncompromising, warlike ideologue as Barry Goldwater seemed during his presidential campaign of 1964. Rather, Reagan was just another put-upon taxpayer from the suburbs. His complaints, illustrated by stories of government waste and incompetency, were simply more articulate accounts of the same complaints heard at a supermarket or a meeting of a neighborhood improvement association.

Reagan's election as governor, regarded at the time as another sign of California's eccentricity, was actually the first evidence of this historic political change. California was the first suburban state—the place where the subdivisions grew biggest and fastest after World War II. The state's rich and diverse economy provided more opportunities than other areas for families to move upward. But although it gave them so much economically, California also produced new threats—hippies in the Haight-Ashbury section in San Francisco, demonstrations at Berkeley, riots in Watts. Reagan entered politics at that moment of history. And he brought with him the final important ingredient of the new political structure, the televised campaign which made it possible to reach a mobile, suburban population. Campaigning in a state without party structure, he used television to speak to the newly discontented, whose main source of information was becoming the TV set. No precinct captains existed to guide their votes. Family political traditions became less important to those who had left their old neighborhoods. Although the majority of California voters were registered Democrats, their party registration did not mean as much as the message they heard from Reagan on television.

By the late seventies much of the rest of the country had emulated California. Suburbs dominated the cities. Party loyalty had weakened, even in old bastions of Democratic boss rule such as Chicago. Inflation solidified voters' lack of confidence in government. That, along with unemployment, shattered the faith of some of the most loyal to the old Democratic coalition: the Roman Catholic, ethnic union members who saw the closing of the old plants where they worked in the Northeast and Midwest.

By 1978 it was apparent to Reagan and his advisers that events were on their side. The year before, Lyn Nofziger, using $1 million left over from the 1976 presidential campaign, had set up an organization known as Citizens for the Republic. The goal, he said, was to take over the Republican party. Reagan raised money for the organization by giving paid speeches. He also returned to his radio broadcasts and his newspaper column, which he had dropped during the presidential campaign. Periodically, strategy meetings would be held by Nofziger, Meese, Deaver, Sears, pollster Wirthlin and a few others. By late 1979, Wirthlin's polls showed Carter's vulnerability. Throughout the country, even in Democratic strongholds, voters were turning on him. One day, Nofziger said, the advisers met with Reagan at his house in Pacific Palisades. "He said, 'Fellas, what should I do?' Everyone in the room said, 'Let's go.' "

After a slow start in the Iowa caucuses, Reagan defeated George Bush in New Hampshire, and the way to the nomination was clear. The path to the White House was also unobstructed. Lack of faith in the presidency as an institution weakened the political value of Carter's incumbency, no matter how many federal projects he awarded to populous cities. Inflation was worse than ever, and the white-middle-class feeling that government was giving too much help to poor minorities—first evident in years before—grew, to Carter's detriment. In the summer of 1980, public opinion polls showed Reagan picking up much more support than Carter among working-class whites who had hostile attitudes toward government programs for poor blacks. Worse yet for Carter, the blacks who had helped him win the presidency in 1976 did not show the same enthusiasm in a year when unemployment hurt them badly. Finally, national anger at the continued captivity of the American hostages in Iran destroyed whatever hopes Carter may have had. In the end, Carter carried only six states and the District of Columbia.

Within days the Californians began moving East. Meese quickly became the most visible and powerful, but shared responsibility with James Baker III, the chief of staff. Baker, a Texan, had directed Bush's unsuccessful presidential campaign and became part of the Reagan team after the nominating convention. Soon Reagan joined them in Washington. His inauguration came at a moment of great national joy—on the day the hostages were freed.

His speech was a homage to the working men and women who had elected him, an attempt to build a new political coalition of the middle class and wealthy. There was an echo in the speech of his "Forgotten American," the suburbanite he has spoken of for many years who has been ignored amid what he considered the better organized efforts of the poor. "We hear much of special-interest groups," he said. "Well, our concern must be for a special-interest group that has been long neglected. It knows no sectional boundaries or ethnic or racial divisions and it crosses party lines. It is made up of men and women who raise our food, patrol our streets, man our mines and factories, teach our children, keep our homes and heal us when we're sick. Professionals, industrialists, shopkeepers, cabbies and truck drivers. They are, in short, 'we the people.' This breed called Americans."

As President, Reagan quickly moved beyond the words of that patriotic, simplistic address. As he had promised in his speeches, and as he had done in California, he sought to change the direction of government. He filled his Administration with like-minded men. The conservative quality of his assistants was assured by the informal "kitchen cabinet," which supervised major appointments. First Smith was the key figure, as chairman of the transition appointments team. When he became Attorney General, the job was taken over by

Reagan's old friend William A. Wilson. Adopting the policies of conservative economic advisers, Reagan immediately proposed an income-tax cut that was designed to revive the economy by increasing spendable private income. He proposed discarding or limiting social programs he considered failures. In short, he turned the nation onto a new course, one much more sympathetic to the corporations that control much of American life. With his words Reagan intended to revive the national spirit, and with his policies he would let the corporations revive the economy. There were hard times ahead. Special-interest groups protested an Administration that so clearly wanted to change the nation's direction. In one of those terrible events that too often determine the course of history, a young man shot him. But Reagan survived the attempted assassination with remarkable strength, humor and luck, and went on to the difficult and complex job he faced. If he failed, the cabbies and teachers he praised in his inaugural would turn against him. The time for simple answers had ended.

INDEX

About the Author

BILL BOYARSKY was born in Berkeley, California, and graduated from the University of California at Berkeley in 1956. Boyarsky's journalism career began with the Oakland *Tribune,* and in 1960 he joined the Associated Press covering California politics. Since 1970 Boyarsky has worked as a political reporter for the Los Angeles *Times,* including a two-year stint in its Washington bureau. A veteran of three presidential campaigns, Boyarsky has known Ronald Reagan since 1965, following his political career from the start. Out of this experience he wrote *The Rise of Ronald Reagan,* published in 1968.

Currently City/County Bureau Chief for the *Times,* Bill Boyarsky lives in Los Angeles with his wife Nancy, with whom he co-authored *Backroom Politics.*